"I've read the manuscript at least five times. The tale that Chuck weaves around Shannon—the sharks, the history of South Africa, how teenage boys minds work (raised three myself, and he is spot on)—is masterful. I've read many manuscripts over the years, and of all of them, this book is the one that truly deserves to be in every library and on the *NY Times Best Seller List*."

> *Dr. Marie Levine*
> *Executive Director*
> *Shark Research Institute*
> *Princeton, NJ*

"Trauma has a way of shouting so loudly that it often overshadows the bigger picture's beauty and complexity. Knowing Shannon, the person, is to know an incredible human whose company and conversation are warm, inviting, and always inspiring. Without diminishing the traumatic moment of Shannon's shark attack, *Child of the Wild Coast* is a refreshing, honest, and contextual look into the origins and development of Shannon's faith story. It calls to each of us to live out our lives with genuine integrity and in pursuit of our Creator's purpose."

> *Roy Harley*
> *International Director*
> *Christian Surfers International*

CHILD OF THE WILD COAST

The story of Shannon Ainslie,
dual great white shark attack survivor

Charles E. Allen III

RIVER BIRCH PRESS

Daphne, Alabama

ISBN 978-1-956365-19-1 (print)
ISBN 978-1-956365-20-7 (e-book)

River Birch Press
P.O. Box 868, Daphne, AL 36526

Dedicated to my parents,

Dr. Charles E. Allen Jr. and Elsie L. Allen,

whose love and support gave me

the roots to grow and the wings to fly

Contents

Acknowledgments

I want to extend my deep appreciation to Shannon Ainslie for opening his life to me in over forty lengthy Skype interviews and in countless e-mail, Skype, Facebook, and Zoom exchanges. I met him in person, in Louisville, in 2017. He has become a great friend over the years and swears he's going to teach me to surf and take me to Nahoon Reef. Some friend!

I also want to thank Shannon's family, more than 100 of Shannon's friends, fellow surfers, and countrymen, and others working in the surfing, marine, and news reporting communities who spent time with me in one or more interviews—either by Skype, e-mail, Zoom or other means—or who assisted me by performing local research, providing background information, granting text, image, and video licenses, and permitting the derivative use of materials. My deep appreciation goes to Shannon's siblings, Brandon Ainslie and Candice Annesley, who did some heavy lifting for me in South Africa.

I especially want to recognize Shaun Ridgard who gave me such a poignant interview concerning the Carter-Corby attack in 1994. Shaun passed away from cancer on December 13, 2018, leaving a wife and three children behind. He was a good Christian who helped others in their faith.

Finally, I want to single out The Shark Research Institute, the East London *Daily Dispatch*/Arena Holdings, and Screenocean/Reuters for their extensive assistance with research, data, and video sources.

Without the kindness of so many people, this book would not have been possible.

Foreword

Given the level of public fascination with sharks in the post-*Jaws* era, the fame thrust upon fifteen-year-old Shannon Ainslie on July 17, 2000 comes as no surprise. An expert surfer, the lean, curly-haired South African was not necessarily the *greatest* board rider in history, but he may have been the *luckiest*...so lucky that his ordeal in the cold, dark waters of infamous Nahoon Reef—an ordeal caught on video—remains a worldwide media sensation.

Shannon finds no serendipity in his survival that day. He believes that God protected him when a one-ton great white struck him at combat speed on the crest of a wave. He believes that God protected him again, seconds later, when he found himself face-to-face with white death deep in the water. He believes that God answered his prayer for help, bringing him safely to shore on a strange and solitary white wave that seemed to rise from nowhere in a calm sea.

This is the story of a young man who regards himself not as the luckiest but as the most *blessed* of surfers. It is the story of the sport he loves, the terrifying shark encounters of his friends, and the beautiful, if troubled, land he calls home. It is the story of a young man who grew up on rural farms during the traumatic post-apartheid era, learned to surf early in his tempestuous teens, survived surfing's greatest perils, and emerged from his trials with a deep and abiding faith.

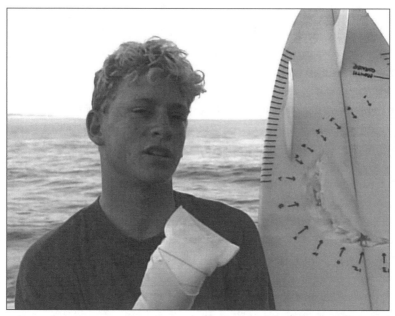

And I have loved thee, ocean! And my joy
Of youthful sports was on thy breast to be
Borne, like thy bubbles, onward: from a boy
I wanton'd with thy breakers—they to me
Were a delight; and if the freshening sea
Made them a terror—'twas a pleasing fear,
For I was as it were a child of thee...

—Lord George Gordon Byron
The Dark, Blue Sea

1
VICTORIA BAY

Wedged in the rocky palisades of South Africa's Wild Coast, Victoria Bay has the unlikely look of a Tahitian paradise. Triangular in shape and 300 meters wide at the mouth, the bay's verdant shores converge inland at a tiny and secluded beach. The western shore—the right side as you look out to sea—is heavily forested and ascends with a moderate pitch from behind a row of bungalows. The eastern shore strikes a more ominous pose, its stony ramparts rising precipitously from giant boulders at water's edge.

The easterly ocean current requires surfers to enter the water from a rocky point on the bay's western cusp. From there, the waves carry young athletes inland and away from the dangerous eastern rim. Most of the time, they do.

On a sunny August morning in 2007, twenty-three-year-old Shannon Ainslie pulled into the car park behind the little beach. He had made the two-hour drive from his home in Jeffreys Bay to watch his teenage surfing students in a competition. Events were scheduled for under-12 and under-20 boys and under-16 and under-20 girls. The morning heats started at 9 a.m. and proceeded uneventfully. Over the next two hours, however, the ocean took on a darker mood. Storms beyond the horizon were pushing an unexpected surge into the bay. Slowly, almost subtly, some waves began reaching four meters, more than twice the height of the kids.

Sensing the rising danger, officials hastily canceled the event, and packs of teens barefooted their way back from the point, boards under their arms. But a few, including a lanky blond fifteen-year-old named Remi Petersen, noticed his coach carrying a surfboard toward the point. For Shannon Ainslie, the "macking" (surfer slang for powerful) waves represented challenge and opportunity. He loved big waves. He longed for them. He trained for them.

The fruits of Shannon's training were manifest. His 5-foot 9-inch frame was robust and powerful. Two-a-day swim practices, water polo practices, surf team practices, lifesaving training, surfer's marathons, river mile swims, professional surf coaching, and over 14,000 hours of free surfing had de-

1

veloped his legs, arms, and upper body to fullback proportions. Constant sunshine had bleached his sea of blond curls to a light yellow hue. He was fearless in big water, and he could hold his breath longer than a sea turtle, the latter skill courtesy of agonizing breath training sessions back home in J-Bay. Every day, he would paddle at a lifesaver's pace from Albatross to Inner Point and back, a round-trip of two kilometers. In constant anaerobic debt, he would stop every thirty seconds, plunge beneath his board, and swim around furiously until his lungs screamed.

For several hours, Shannon shared the menacing waves of Victoria Bay with five or six experienced riders including Remi who had returned to the water with him. Ten years later, Shannon would brag of Remi, "He's one of the wildest, craziest surfers on the planet...maybe even worse than me!" Remi, who is often seen wearing a bodacious top hat and a huge smile, describes himself as "sometimes a bit overboard in public but as loyal a friend as there is." Everyone who knows him agrees.

"I went back in," Remi notes, "because I was the last one out there, and I was worried that something might happen to Shannon, and he wouldn't make it back out of the water."

Something did happen. The waves reached storm height, and the two young men—coach and student—found themselves marooned amid watery monsters the size of two-story houses.

The power of such water is difficult to explain, but some basic math might help. The front or back profile of a typical surfer is one square meter in area. Each meter of wave height looming above a surfer, therefore, contains one cubic meter of water—1,000 kilograms or 2,200 pounds of it. Get locked in by a breaking six-meter wave, and six tons of seawater—the weight of three mid-sized SUVs—smash you into the seabed and roll you like a mouse in a washing machine. The impact is attenuated over a few seconds, yes, but it is still Borg-like. Resistance is futile.

Shannon avoided this fate in the early going. He caught a well-formed six-meter wave and soaked it for a quad-burning run of more than 200 meters. Exhilarated by the ride, he turned and headed back out. Twenty meters into his paddle, though, he found himself in the dangerous impact zone—the place where the waves break. Just then, a mountainous swell formed ahead of him. The game was afoot—the boy versus the sea—and the sea was playing for keeps.

Paddling with every fiber of his being, Shannon tried to clear the zone in time and crest the top of the surging dome, but his board was too small and the water began breaking along more of the wave-front than usual. Like an unexpected tyrannosaur rising from behind a hedgerow, an eight-meter wall of dark green fury went vertical in front of him.

Desperate, but in control, Shannon stopped paddling so he could slow his heart rate and take one last deep breath. Then he leaped from his board, diving headlong into the base of the wave just as the towering mass collapsed on top of him. The impact blasted his surfboard to particles and wrenched his leg rope so hard that it nearly dislocated his hip. The wave's astonishing pressure held him on the seabed for a brief eternity, his body pitching and rolling for fifteen seconds in a violent, loud, and airless universe. Finally, the trailing edge of the wave cycle began lifting him with its powerful suction. Gasping for air at the surface, he surveyed the damage. Only a quarter of his surfboard remained. The rest had vanished in the chaos.

The small fragment connected to his leg rope was too small for flotation. Worse, it was acting as a sea anchor, dragging him back into the impact zone. Quickly, he released the tether, leaving him effectively naked in a deep and violent sea. Wetsuits offer no buoyancy. He had no surfboard. He had no lifejacket. He had only his strength, his wits, and his faith.

The wave that claimed his board was just the opening act. Six more waves overtook him in rapid succession. As each watery behemoth arrived, Shannon plunged deep into its cold heart, tumbled beneath it, and struggled to the surface for increasingly desperate gulps of air. The exhaustion following one such encounter would drown an average man, even a fit one. His only hope was a moderate wave, a wave he could body surf toward shore, but the sea denied him that simple mercy. Instead, the sea pulled a new weapon from its quiver. Shannon was caught in a powerful rip current.

Notoriously lethal, a rip is produced when opposing currents collide near shore and return to the sea in powerful outflows. The rip that carried Shannon was the product of huge amounts of water piling up inside the sharply tapered bay. The rip was dragging him hundreds of meters away from the sheltered beach and toward the boulders on the bay's rugged eastern cusp. There, the waves were discharging their furious energy on the rocks and sending giant plumes of spray high onto the cliff face.

Recognizing his grave peril, Shannon sought help from Remi who tried to ride out the onslaught somewhere beyond the break, further out to sea:

When I saw that I had only a quarter of a board left, I got worried. I yelled and whistled for Remi who was somewhere beyond the impact zone, but the ocean's roar was too loud for him to hear, and when I saw him get out of the water, I knew that I was all alone. I tried not to worry and panic. I had trained for this, so, in my mind, I thought this was a good opportunity to see if my training would work out for me. I also thought it would be a good opportunity for others to see how courage and strength can save your life.

The roaring and thunderous sounds of the waves under the water were so loud and intimidating. I had a lot of thoughts racing through my mind at one stage...thoughts about how other people don't make it in these conditions and how I could be one of those people. I thought it would be a super lame way to die, but I managed to control my thoughts and my fears of drowning and began to think of ways to get out of the situation.

I tried to swim across the rip current but the whole bay had turned into a giant rip current, so that didn't work! When my plans to get out of the current didn't work, I knew that I was in real trouble. I looked to the east side of the bay where I was heading and thought of going with the rip current and letting the giant waves wash me onto the cliff where I could try to climb to safety. To get to the cliff, I saw that I had to swim past huge boulders which would be seriously dangerous for me. If I got stuck in between them, the waves would smash me against the rocks. Even if I managed to reach the cliff, I'm not a rock climber, and the seven- and eight-meter waves crashing against the cliff were running twenty meters up its face. If I headed toward that area, I knew my chances of surviving and not breaking a bone or getting a concussion were probably one percent.

My last-resort idea was to let the current take me out past the big waves and then swim up the coast to the next bay where I might be able to reach shore through a beach break. That idea triggered many fears. If I went out there, I would be one kilometer out to sea where there are more sharks, and I didn't want to get attacked by a shark again! If I went out there, I also knew that I would have to swim two to four kilometers through huge ocean swells to reach the next beach, and that would have taken forever. I didn't know if I would have the strength and energy to stay out at sea for a few hours, much less overnight. I didn't know if someone would try to rescue me, and if they did, whether they would be able to find me. I didn't even know if anyone would care if one surfer drowned. It was also wintertime, and I knew that a night in the cold sea would lead to certain hypothermia. Still, an open ocean swim to the next beach seemed like the best option.

Back on shore, surf contest officials and parents of young contestants noticed Shannon's plight. They called the National Sea Rescue Institute and tried in vain to throw a board to him. Others gathered on the eastern cliffs and tried to direct him to safety, but Shannon could not understand their frantic gestures. Fatigue was taking its toll. His peril was extreme, but he managed to keep his greatest enemy at bay:

I knew if I started panicking, I would drown. I tried to stay focused and remember all the times I had trained at home for big waves and had trained to hold my breath. Every time I got held under the water, I struggled holding my breath, but I remained calm. But I was getting very close to the cliff.

Before I made up my mind to let the current take me out to sea and away from the crashing waves, though, I decided to pray. I hadn't prayed yet, and I remember wondering why I had not done it. So, I asked God to help me out of this situation. Then, just as I was praying, a thought suddenly came to mind. Instead of diving seaward into the heart of each wave, I could dive shoreward into the water ahead of the waves. I could try to body surf the waves underwater and beneath the rip current. So, I tried it. The impacts were terrific, but slowly it began to work. I started making slight progress toward the beach.

Taking each watery blast in the back as he swam, Shannon finally reached white water, the frothy chop shoreward of the impact zone. Then he rode smaller waves toward the less-battered boulders inside the bay's eastern cusp. Even there, he was slammed against the rocks as he tried to gain purchase. Using his last ounce of energy, he hoisted himself onto the giant stones.

Overcome by the most profound exhaustion of his life, he could not gain his feet. He lay on his back, his chest heaving and his face and hands blue-white with cold. His body began shaking as his adrenaline rush subsided. For 30 minutes, he had gone toe-to-toe with Poseidon, a nasty and unforgiving foe with millions of notches in his trident. But Poseidon had lost his prey this day. Shannon Ainslie, the survivor of a world-famous shark attack at age 15 and three other shark encounters, had cheated the sea yet again.

"Remi!" Shannon gasped as his student raced to his side. "Didn't you hear me screaming for your help?"

He had not...a fact that haunts Remi to this day. "I remember feeling really bad and almost scared knowing he could have drowned because I hadn't been paying attention," he says. "Now, I am always on the lookout for my mates in the water when there is surf of consequence."

But Remi need not be haunted. The violence of the sea had rendered communication and visual awareness completely impossible.

Shannon felt blessed to be alive. As he stood there, trembling and spent, on the cold, wet boulders of Victoria Bay, he felt he had one last obligation to fulfill. With sea spray pelting his uplifted face and his tightly-closed eyes, he uttered a humble "Thank you."

Had he listened closely at that moment, the exploding breakers might have beaten out a reply.

"You're welcome," a Voice might have whispered in the driving mist. "Glad I could help you again."

It was not the first time that Shannon Ainslie had needed help from his Higher Power to reach the safety of dry land.

It would not be the last.

2

THE COST OF FREEDOM

Shannon Russell Ainslie was born at Frère Hospital in East London on September 21, 1984—as it happens, the fourth annual International Day of Peace. The second child of Shane and Michelle, the boy was two years younger than firstborn, Brandon. The family moved to Cape Town soon after Shannon's arrival, and life was good.

Shane held a franchise for the sale of confectionery products in the country's Eastern and Western Cape provinces. He sold and distributed butter biscuits, popcorn, homemade chips, and roasted peanuts out of distribution centers in Cape Town, Port Elizabeth, and East London. Shane purchased his products in wholesale lots costing R10,000 (10,000 South African Rand or roughly $4,000 at prevailing exchange rates). The lots were shipped directly to Shane's employees at the distribution centers. He hired staff at each center to take phone orders and deliver products to businesses and homes. Customers were billed for prior deliveries upon delivery of new orders, a practice that encouraged repeat business. The confectionery business was lucrative, and the Ainslies had a lovely house and car.

With the birth of his sister, Candice (née Ainslie, now Annesley[1]), in 1987, three-year-old Shannon became the dreaded "middle child," caught squarely between the eldest and the cutest. This status would become troublesome as Brandon and Candice achieved national prominence in swimming. More troublesome, however, was the status of his homeland.

International opposition to apartheid had grown throughout the 1970s. During that time, the United Nations encouraged the world community to divest its business interests in South Africa until white minority rule, white-only suffrage, legally mandated segregation, and violent suppression of black militants and reformers ended. These divestment efforts reached their apex in the late 1980s. By then, the United States, the United Kingdom, and twenty-three other nations had imposed severe trade sanctions on the apartheid government of Prime Minister P. W. Botha. By the time Candice was born, a nation that had boasted the world's second-fastest-growing economy in the 1960s, behind only Japan, had become the world's weakest. Companies closed. Inflation skyrocketed. Jobs disappeared. A nationwide state of emergency was declared due to militant anti-apartheid resistance by black Africans led by the African National Party (ANC). The government of P. W. Botha fought back with curfews, bans, executions, torture, censorship, over 30,000 detentions, and violent raids in which black children were shot like game. The government even developed nuclear weapons. Whites, comprising just 14 percent of the population, felt beset on all sides by communists and black militants, but many of them recognized the horrors of the apartheid regime as well.

Taking power in 1989, Prime Minister F. W. de Klerk quickly realized that apartheid's days were numbered and that white South Africans would have to adjust to a new and uncertain future. When Nelson Mandela was released from prison in 1990 after twenty-seven years' confinement for anti-apartheid resistance, the dismantling of apartheid continued apace—a process that required four years and culminated in elections on April 27, 1994. For the first time, black South Africans were granted suffrage. The ANC won, and Mandela became president. To this day, April 27 is celebrated as Freedom Day, the date when South African blacks shed the yoke of white oppression.

The pressure on white South Africans was profound. Despite Mandela's assurances to the contrary, fears abounded that blacks would confiscate white property, money, and jobs and drive whites out of the country or even kill them. Similar white repression had occurred in other African nations, often with devastating consequences for white and black citizens alike. The most frightening example was right next door—Zimbabwe.

In the late 1990s, Zimbabwe's president, Robert Mugabe, launched an unconstitutional program of mandatory land redistribution, taking land from white landowners—many of British heritage—and redistributing the land to blacks. Roving bands of black army veterans were allowed to confiscate highly-productive farms, driving white landowners from their property and killing those who tried to stay. Whites fled the country. Once a major food-exporting nation, Zimbabwe soon depended on international aid to feed its citizens. Inflation rose from an annual rate of 32 percent in 1998 to an astounding high of 89.7 sextillion percent as measured by Prof. Steve H. Hanke of the Johns Hopkins University, on November 14, 2008![2]

The country resorted to printing 100 trillion dollar notes, and prices doubled every 24.7 hours.[3] Average life expectancy from birth in Zimbabwe plummeted to just 44.65 years by the year 2000.[4] In 2010, Zimbabwe received a Human Development Index rating of 0.140 from the United Nations, placing it 169th among the 169 nations evaluated—dead last.[5]

Since the end of apartheid, the fears of white South Africans have been magnified by militant minorities. Julius Malema, the ANC's Youth League leader, challenged President Jacob Zuma to nationalize the mining industry in South Africa, a confiscatory act frightfully similar to Mugabe's land redistribution program in Zimbabwe. Rumors abounded that there were camps in Mozambique where South African blacks were being trained to kill whites using, among other weapons, traditional machetes called pangas.

In South Africa, black and "coloured"[6] citizens outnumber whites by nearly ten to one,[7] so the fears of South African whites were certainly understandable during the early 1990s when apartheid was being dismantled and uncertainties about black majority rule were growing. Fears of repression by the black majority arose just as worldwide trade sanctions against the pro-apartheid government were producing their most dire effects in South Africa—massive business closings and a vanishing economy. Jobs became scarce, and countless jobs were lost. With unemployment skyrocketing, the loss of a job could be devastating.

In 1991, Shane's cash flow began mysteriously dwindling. Unable to supervise all three of his distribution centers at once, he was unaware that he had been taking delivery of lots bearing only half of the product he had been paying for...until he began checking the arriving lots himself. By then, however, he lacked sufficient funds to pay an attorney to sue the franchisor. Unable to keep up with his mortgage and bills, he lost his house and his car.

With jobs all but unavailable, Shane, Michelle, and their three children moved in with Michelle's mother Lynn Duminiet, in Cape Town. Tensions arose in the marriage and for a brief while, the couple separated. Understandably, Shane fell into a state of depression. "I was down and out, negative, depressed, and even suicidal, but did not try," he laments. "So at job interviews, I was giving all the wrong signals." And during this trying time for the family, Shannon was a sensitive seven-year-old.

Unable to find adequate work in Cape Town, Shane finally convinced

Michelle to move to East London, a city of 480,000 in South Africa's Eastern Cape Province. In December 1991, the family moved in with Shane's mother, Elaine Ainslie, at 22 Albany Street in the North Central district, just north of downtown. Shane started looking for work in January and landed a job in the East London harbor off-loading ships of grain destined for food-starved Zimbabwe. The lading work was supposed to be temporary, but he stayed with the job longer than expected. Meanwhile, Shannon started Sub B, or second grade, at Hudson Park Primary School.

Shannon had no way of knowing it at the time, but his family's move to East London had brought him to the very frontier of the Wild Coast, a rocky and untamed shoreline that begins at Jeffreys Bay just to the west of East London and extends 250 kilometers east to Port St. Johns. The shore is marked by steep palisades, reefs, wide arching beaches, and a tiny cove that harbors the most dangerous water in the world. In the rugged country above the Wild Coast are the black villages of rural Transkei. Home to the country's native Xhosa population, Transkei is afflicted with grinding poverty, rampant crime, and the ravages of AIDS. During the 18th and 19th centuries, Transkei served as a border region, a hilly buffer separating British colonists from indigenous black populations.[8] To this day, the athletic teams representing the eastern half of the Eastern Cape Province call themselves "Border" teams.

3
A Sporting Life

During his spectacular career, American swimmer Matt Biondi managed to win eleven Olympic medals, eight of them gold. His very first swim competition, however, was an unqualified disaster. Only five years old, the boy false-started, climbed out of the pool, and returned dripping wet to the block. Eager to atone, he false-started again, resulting in disqualification. But the race wasn't the only thing he lost. His Speedo came off on the second dive as well.[9]

Shannon Ainslie's introduction to aquatic sports was equally exasperating, if not quite as embarrassing.

First Try

In March 1992, Shannon's dad obtained a used surfboard from his teenaged nephew, Russell Annesley. Shane spent R100 (100 Rand, or about $40) repairing dings and replacing fins. Then, he drove his two sons to Orient Beach, a tiny city strand at the mouth of the East London harbor. A longboarder, Shane wanted to share the joys of surfing with them. The boys, though, were quite young—Brandon nine years old and Shannon seven.

Brandon went in first. He spent thirty minutes trying in vain to pop up on the board in the white water just inside the break. He finally came ashore in frustration. Shannon took to the water next, but he had almost no chance of controlling the board. He was the smallest kid in his entire second grade at school—standing barely 3-feet 4-inches tall and weighing forty pounds soaking wet. Still, he grabbed the board and raced aggressively into the sea. Nothing went right. He had no wetsuit, and he was worried about sharks. Small waves grabbed the surfboard and whacked the tow-headed youth black and blue. Finally, he stormed ashore and threw the board down. "I can't do this," he barked crossly, stalking off in a huff.

"Shannon can get cheeky," Shane confirms. "He complained that it was too cold and that he wanted to lie down and tan, but then, a few minutes later, he asked if he could go swimming saying, 'It's only cold when I surf.'"

Each day for nearly two weeks, Shane took his boys to Orient Beach or to wide, dune-backed Nahoon Beach in the hope that his sons would hear the call of Duke Kahanamoku. "I'm not big on my kids watching television," Shane says with wisdom sadly lacking in most homes today. "I wanted them into sports where they could vent their energy and aggression."

Surfing just didn't click with the boys. They were too young. The refurbished surfboard spent most of the time in a closet.

Like Matt Biondi's first race as a swimmer, Shannon's frustrating introduction to aquatics was only a temporary setback. The spindly youth would soon embark on an aquatic career of finger-pruning proportions.

Entering Standard 1 (third grade) at Hudson Park Primary School, Shannon joined the school's swim team. In fourth grade, he began swimming for Harlequins Aquatic Club in East London. When he arrived at Hudson Park High School as an eighth-grader, he joined the swim team there too. Because of his diminutive size, however, Shannon could never achieve the competitive speeds of his siblings.

With the constant support and encouragement of their father, Candice and Brandon achieved national rankings as swimmers in high school. Both reached the senior national division, the level from which Olympic swimmers are selected. A backstroke and butterfly specialist, Candice was ranked fourth and fifth in the 200- and 100-meter backstrokes, respectively, and Brandon achieved a ranking of second in a butterfly event.

Shane believed in a "three S" philosophy—school, Sunday school, and sports. He encouraged hard work in school and pushed his kids athletically. He spent a lot of time taking Brandon and Candice to swimming competitions. But his time with them meant less time with Shannon, and the middle child craved his father's attention. Like many young males, he languished in the misguided belief that athletic success was necessary to earn a father's pride. So, he found other ways to succeed.

On February 13, 1995, the tiny ten-year-old entered the Surfer's Marathon, an 18-kilometer foot race along the beaches from Yellow Sands to Nahoon Beach. The race drew 1,200 runners. Despite being on the shy side of four feet tall, the boy not only won his age division, but he was also the youngest person in the race! A photographer captured the little blond kid leaping from a raft after crossing the Nahoon River mouth, the photo caption reading, "They start 'em young!"

In sixth grade, Shannon joined the Nippers, a youth lifesaving club. In beach-oriented nations like Australia and South Africa, lifesavers, as they are known, are revered. They save thousands of lives each year and maintain their prodigious physical skills with constant training and lifesaver competitions.

With the Nippers, Shannon participated in competitive ocean swims, run-swim-run races, Malibu board races, and last but not least, beach flag races. And, oh, how he loved beach flags.

The physical aspects of beach flags were made to order for the aggressive youth. In each contest, Speedo-clad boys lie on their stomachs in the sand facing away from a finish line twenty-five or thirty meters behind them. At the starter's signal, the boys jump up, turn, and sprint to the finish where they try to retrieve a "flag," usually a short segment of hose stuck in the sand.

Like musical chairs, each race features one less flag than the number of competitors in the race. The runner without a flag is eliminated, and a new race ensues. Pushing, shoving, undercutting, and grappling are rules of the day, and full-out body blocks take place near the flags, complete with sand burns, bruises, and occasional spots of blood. Noses, mouths, ears, eyes, and Speedos fill with sand and fights are not unheard of. In the final race, two boys, exhausted from their preceding heats, lunge for one remaining segment of hose. On that last dive for glory, two sweaty bodies, red with sand abrasion, collide in a cloud of exploding silicon, churning legs, and grinding shoulders. Shannon lacked the physical size and speed to win regularly, but he loved the physicality of the game, and no one beat him for lack of effort.

In 1996, Shannon decided to give the Buffalo River Mile a shot. He was twelve and still smaller than many ten-year-olds, but he was a competitive little cuss. He hated losing, and he feared no one.

The event was held on November 11 and had an illustrious history, once drawing top competitors from around the world including South African swimming champion, Jonty Skinner. A former world-record holder in both the 50- and 100-meter freestyles, Skinner won the event several times, once with Shane in the water. "I swam in the 1969 race when I was fourteen," Shane recalls. "Jonty Skinner won...and I came in last!"

On the day of the race, Shannon's aunt, Sandra Leigh Quirk (nee Ainslie), dropped the boy off at the Buffalo River Harbor near downtown. From the start, the event was beset by shark concerns. "People were talking about sharks because great whites had been seen in the harbor recently," Shannon reflects. "I was nervous about sharks that day." Still, he managed to win the entire under-16 division, beating kids who were three years older—a significant achievement given the differences in physical maturity at those ages.

Shannon modestly claims that his victory was hollow. "All of the best swimmers were at a major swimming gala in Bloemfontein, and I didn't get to share the victory with my dad because he had taken Brandon and Candice to the gala. But I got another chance the next month!"

On December 14, the Nahoon River Mile rolled around—an annual summer event. The race took place on a hot, sunny Saturday morning just off the ramp at Princess Alice Drive in the community of Nahoon Beach. Hundreds of swimmers, family members, and friends gathered for the 9 a.m. start. The atmosphere was festive. Families brought chairs, blankets, cameras, and binoculars and gobbled down hot dogs, boerewors (farmer's sausages), and rolls. Shane was happy to be there for Shannon this time, though all three of his kids were participating. All the best swimmers were there too—a true test.

Despite his youth, fourteen-year-old Brandon was the favorite in the open division. Candice was expected to do well among the under-14 girls. Shannon was not expected to place. His division, the under-14 boys, was teeming with skilled swimmers from local schools and swim clubs—guys who regularly bested him in pool races. His most daunting opponent was Mark Randall. A month shy of his eleventh birthday, Randall was a tall, exceptional swimmer who was destined to become a four-time All-American at the University of Alabama and win the 2010 South African national championship in the 400-meter freestyle.

The Nahoon River flows south along the eastern edge of the city and shallows up in sandbars at the back of the beach before flowing in small channels to the sea. The competition started and finished on the inner edge of one of the sand bars. The turnaround point was a buoy half a mile upriver.

At the starter's signal, hundreds of competitors—men, women, boys, and girls of all ages—raced en masse across the sand, bumping, shoving, and splashing their way through knee-deep water until they reached swimmable depth. Most of the best swimmers in each division had prime starting positions at the front. Shannon started in the back and got knocked around a bit in the heavy traffic:

> When I got to deeper water, I was quite far behind, and I was not swimming very well. After a quarter-mile, though, I established a good rhythm. As I approached the half-mile buoy, I got a good view of my competitors. They had just made the turn and appeared to be struggling. But I got a surprise when I rounded the buoy. Several of the better swimmers were still behind me! A top-fifteen finish was in range, I thought, so I kept picking up my pace and got through the pain into a sort of swimmer's high. Entering the final quarter-mile, though, I wasn't sure how well I was doing.
>
> About 400 meters from the finish, I noticed I was overtaking one or two of the better swimmers in the race, and I felt proud of myself. This gave me a surge of motivation and energy to swim even faster, which made me more tired but not too tired. I felt fit and strong! At the very end, as I was passing still more guys, I realized I was doing well. There were still a few guys in front of me, so when I got to the end, I wasn't thinking about winning.
>
> The last fifty meters were very shallow, so we had to run in knee-deep water. When I got to that section, I turned around and saw one of the guys in my division who was a very good swimmer and thought, 'If I'm ahead of him, I must be doing very well.' I out-sprinted him by about three or four meters to the finish line. There was a man there who was sorting us out by division according to the numbers on our shoulders. When he grabbed my arm and pulled me into the under-14 line, he said, "You're first!"
>
> I was so happy and surprised. I had this big smile on my face and when the other guys in the under-14 division came in behind me, I felt kind of bad because they were the real swimmers. They congratulated me, and I them. I felt super because my brother and sister always did so well in swimming, and I never used to thrive in swimming as they did. When I won this race, I thought I might be a good swimmer, and I knew I wasn't bad after all.

Shane was thrilled. "Shannon came out of the water just ahead of Randall," he recalls, "and he got a burst of adrenaline...just gave it everything he had, his short legs churning like pistons. When the catcher told him he was first, he threw his hands up and was so excited and happy."

Brandon won both the open and under-18 divisions, and Candice finished top three in her division. But Shannon was the happiest. He not only won the under-14 division, he won the under-16 prize as well! Brandon was eligible for the under-16 award too, but a pair of awards apiece seemed appropriate.

Shannon receiving trophy and R300 check after winning Buffalo River Mile in 1996. (Courtesy of Shane Annesley)

Today, the only local mile swim competition is the Merrifield Mile, which is held at an inland reservoir behind the Wriggleswade Dam. The reason is probably sharks. The Nahoon River Mile, it seems, had been riskier than it seemed. On November 9, 2006, a canoeist on the Nahoon River grabbed the tail of a 1.5-meter bull shark and suffered lacerations on his arm.[10] Bull sharks, or Zambezis as they are called in South Africa, are regarded by most experts as more dangerous to humans than great whites, and unlike other sharks, are often found in freshwater rivers far from the sea.

Earning a Father's Pride

Shannon's next test of athletic mettle came in a swimming pool but not one with roped lanes. He took up a sport more suited to his physical nature—water polo. He loved the endurance and aggression required by the sport, and when he joined the Hudson Park water polo team, he prospered. He made up for his diminutive size with heart. He swam fast, fouled often, and never backed down.

In 1998, an important day arrived—selections for the Border Water Polo Team, the team that would represent the region in national under-14 competitions. Team aspirants gathered at the Joan Harrison swimming pool in East London. Shannon, the smallest boy in the pool, had little hope of making the team, but he wanted to qualify with every fiber of his being:

> I was thirteen years old and in grade eight. I was very small and had never excelled in swimming or other sports like my brother and sister. You have to be really fit, strong, and fast to make a provincial team, and when you make the team, you are looked up to and honored. Before high school, I was kind of a loser because I was angry and aggressive and had no friends. When I got to high school, everything changed. I joined the surfing and water polo teams. All of the coolest and most popular guys and girls were surfers and water polo players, so I made new cool friends and that made me feel cool and popular—important when you are an impressionable teen.
>
> I never thought I had it in me to make the Border team, though, and I remember the day of the trials very clearly. Schools from all over the Eastern Cape sent players to try out. We had various physical tests to perform, like running, and then they divided everyone into eight or ten teams and began grading players during matches. Eventually, they got it down to teams of thirteen boys each, the Probables and the Possibles. I was on the Pos-

sibles. After that match, I thought that more of the guys on the Probables would make the Border team. They were bigger, stronger, and better than my teammates.

I remember playing so hard and swimming so fast that day. I thought this was the one chance I had to prove myself and make the cut! I was physically spent at the end of the day, but that was part of the test, and I pushed through to the very end. I outswam most of the guys on the other team and was so proud of myself because, although I was the smallest guy there, I was the fastest. Still, I thought it would be just another disappointment for me.

Displaying every rib in his scrawny body, the pale youth crawled out of the pool in which he had given his last measure of energy. Wrapping himself in a towel, the waterlogged thirteen-year-old sat with the other competitors and waited for the judges' selections.

As Shane watched from the stands, the head judge read from a list. Only thirteen boys would hear their names. A hush came over the venue, and Shannon's head remained bowed as the names were issued...five names...ten names...it was nearly over. Then he heard two magical words.

"Shannon Ainslie."

The boy sat upright, looked skyward with his chlorine-reddened eyes tightly closed, and pumped a fist discreetly next to his face. He ran to Shane afterward, his voice quavering with emotion and his eyes glistening. Shane's eyes moistened too. For young Shannon, it was the kind of moment he had only dreamed about—walking out of an arena with his father after making a provincial team. He has so wanted to make him proud. Shane, of course, had always been proud of his middle child, but now the middle child knew he had earned it.

Second Try

On Saturday, April 11, 1998, the day before Easter, Shane had to work. As was his habit on weekends, he dropped the boys off at Nahoon Beach at 7 a.m. and made a point of leaving that unused surfboard with them... the one Russell Annesley had given them. Shane clung to the hope that his boys, left to their own devices, would give surfing one more try. Shane understood that physical challenges, sibling rivalry, and testosterone are powerful combinations in young males. Besides, his boys were thirteen and fifteen years old now. They were bigger. And on that Easter weekend in 1998, Shane's plan bore spectacular fruit.

That autumn day (April is autumn in South Africa) was hot and sunny, and the beach was a bit crowded. Eventually, the brothers tired of swimming and began fooling around with the board. As usual, the experience proved frustrating, but with no father to impress, acceptance of failure was easier somehow. Soon, failed attempts led to marginal attempts. Then, for both boys, marginal attempts led to moments of pure epiphany.

We're all familiar with these moments. I recall the exact date, time, and place of my first successful parallel turn in snow skiing—the kind of turn a beginner must master before negotiating steep terrain. It occurred at 10:30 a.m. on December 30, 1979, just below an access road that crosses the Silver Hollow run at Park City Resort in Utah. Leaning downhill as I picked up speed (that's the counterintuitive part) and then carving through that turn created a moment of enlightenment that was unlike anything I have ever experienced. Instantly, I was flying down mile-long intermediates. The next day I was skiing expert terrain. I was hooked for life.

And so it was with Shannon. First, he had to learn to stand on the board as it drifted in the white chop shoreward of the wave break. The task is tricky. Surfboards are not stable at slow speeds; they want to roll. With much effort, though, he got the hang of it. Then he moved further out and tried to catch a wave. Fall after fall ensued, but he kept trying. Finally, his moment of epiphany arrived. He caught a left-handed wave, one that breaks from left to right as seen from shore. This was not ideal for the right-handed youth, but he was too new at surfing to appreciate the disadvantage.

As a wave approached, he paddled hard toward shore and rose with the swell. At just the right instant, he popped up. Suddenly, he found himself on the face of a wave, racing to his left. Almost immediately, he started to fall—his usual fate—but he caught himself! He rode a few more seconds and nearly fell again, but he caught himself a second time! Four times he nearly splashed; four times he recovered. He rode the wave for a good ten or twelve seconds.

You could have heard him from Cape Town. The little kid laughed, yelled, and pounded the water with excitement. Then he spotted a beautiful girl, perhaps nineteen or twenty years old, in the water nearby.

"Did you see my wave?!?" the world's newest surfer inquired.

"She looked at me like I was weird," he remembers, "but I was too happy to care. I wished my father could have been there to see it."

The Ainslie brothers became surfing fools in short order, their joy in the sport trumping any lingering fear of sharks. Shane was thrilled. He took the boys on dozens of surfing tours and spent hundreds of hours making videos of his sons as they tackled breaks all along the Wild Coast. Soon, Shannon joined the Hudson Park High School surfing team and tried to cram Wednesday surfing team practices between his Hudson Park and Harlequin's swim practices.

If you sense that Shannon was spending a lot of time in the water, you'd be correct. Entering tenth grade, he was dedicating twenty-seven hours a week to organized aquatic sports practices, and that does not include evening swim meets, evening water polo matches, and free surfing in the remaining daylight hours.

"Sometimes, there were quintuple practices!" he laughs. "I would have Harlequins swim practice at 6 a.m., school swimming or water polo practice at 2 p.m., school surfing practice at 4 p.m., Harlequins again at 5 p.m., and then maybe a swimming gala or water polo match that evening! On those days, I would be in the water for about seven hours!"

Add to this schedule his weekend lifesaving training, his mile swim competitions, and his endless hours of free surfing, and you start to wonder if you should check him for gills. He was once asked, jokingly, if he had noticed any strange flaps forming on the sides of his rib cage. "Yes!" he laughed. "Surfers do get odd rib cages that start to stick out after a bit!"

Given enough free time, surfers would never leave their beloved waves. On his 17th birthday, Shannon and Brandon surfed for four hours in the morning, downed a breakfast of bananas and bread, surfed another four hours, ate sarmies (sandwiches) for lunch, and then surfed another four hours! Shannon's arms were so noodled by day's end that he couldn't even paddle to shore. He just drifted in like a pile of seaweed.

Schedule relief came in tenth grade when Shannon was promoted to first-team wing on his school's water polo team. The sport requires endurance, aggressiveness, and physicality—qualities he had developed from thousands of hours of combat with the ocean. He felt he needed to quit both swim teams so he could dedicate himself to his water polo team, his surfing team, and, of course, his free surfing:

> I got so tired of the swimming practices every morning and every afternoon. I hated swimming so much. It's boring. You just swim up and down the pool the whole time. There's no point to it. That's why I quit. But being physically tired from water polo or surfing was a good feeling, and especially from surfing. I would only get tired after being in the water for a very long time, like five hours or more.

Shannon was a strong swimmer, mind you. By the time he gave up competitive swimming at age fifteen, he could finish a fifty meter freestyle race in less than twenty-eight seconds and a fifty-meter butterfly in less than twenty-nine. He was just better at endurance events like water polo and mile swims, and he preferred surfing over all of it.

Opportunities to surf were plentiful. The Wild Coast teems with excellent breaks—places called Queensberry, Yellow Sands, Glengarriff, and Bonza Bay. But the best break of all—a world-class point break—was right in Shannon's backyard.

4

NAHOON REEF

From the air, Nahoon Reef looks like a shark's tooth. Located on the southeast side of East London, the triangular field of black stones juts seaward from the foot of a fifty meter high bluff. The reef vanishes completely at high tide, but, when the water is out, a 200-meter jetty of slippery stones pierce the cold waters of the Indian Ocean.

Surfers call Nahoon (pronounced nah-HOON) a "point break"—a partly submerged promontory over which a current flows, pushing wave cycles upward into epic lines. Nahoon Reef is a world-class point break with powerful right-handed waves that reach lengths of 200 meters on a normal day and up to 500 meters on a good day.

A key to understanding Nahoon Reef is the assessment of its bottom. The reef is a bed of rocks, and so is the seafloor on either side of it. Shannon's friend Alistair Cokayne learned this the hard way. "The water there is

Nahoon Reef (in background). Shannon's attack occurred beyond dark wave at left. (Courtesy of Brandon Ainslie)

only two or three meters deep," he warns. "Get caught inside, and Nahoon can slam you right into the rounded boulders on the bottom."

In 1976 and 1978, the reef played host to the Gunston 500, a world championship qualifying event. South Africa's surfing prodigy and 1977 ISP[11] world surfing champion, Shaun Tomson, won both competitions as part of his ridiculously impressive run of six consecutive Gunston 500 victories from 1973 to 1978. South Africa's national surfing championships are held at Nahoon on occasion. South African Open and Junior Billabong events are held there too.

To reach the reef, you drive southeast from town along Nahoon Reef Road, a sand-swept lane that passes by the East London Golf Course and its lofty view of the ocean. After descending through scrub and dunes, you arrive at a narrow car park that stretches ninety meters to your left. Like a shelf carved into the side of a hill, the little lot is bounded at the back and on both ends by steep bluffs. All thirty-three parking spaces face the sea.

From the car park, you enjoy an elevated view of the sea. Arrayed below you are vast beds of rounded black rocks, many of the stones partially submerged in tidal pools. Glancing left, your view is blocked by Nahoon Corner, a rocky promontory with a staircase that leads to wide, popular Nahoon Beach just beyond. Looking right, your view of East London is obscured by the cliff that backs up the reef. As you look out to sea, the ocean swell arrives from the right, beyond the reef, and breaks around its tip, driving those long right-handed lines toward the car park.

Behind you, surfers wax boards by their cars and strip naked under towels, some discreetly…some not so much. They pull on tight wetsuits as a hedge against hypothermia and carry their boards to the reef end of the car park where they pass through a narrow gap between a massive boulder and the cliff wall. The boulder, fully two-and-a-half meters high, stands sentry over the upper end of a sixty-meter-long concrete slipway referred to as the "pipe" or "surfer walk." Built for the 1976 Gunston 500, it's a bent line of bulky five-meter-long concrete blocks laid end to end—essentially a thick stone sidewalk that offers safe passage to the water's edge over treacherous beds of slimy, urchin-infested rocks. The pathway is mostly submerged at high tide. At low water, however, it extends to rock-strewn shallows where surfers drop their boards in the water and paddle out along the left side of the reef.

Walking down the slipway, you can smell salt spray, a gift of the waves breaking over the reef's submerged shallows. In summer, you can catch an occasional waft from the city sewage works 500 meters to the west. But in winter, you might notice an acrid smell, a marine smell. From late May until early August, sardines make their annual run eastward from Cape Town to Durban, and seagulls hover over the waves and pools in search of fish dinners. The fishy smell and the hovering gulls, however, augur the presence of something else…something hidden and ominous. Great white sharks are also partial to sardines and follow the migrating schools up the coast.

As a young teen, Shannon Ainslie didn't need fish smells or diving sea-gulls to appreciate the danger at Nahoon Reef. "We'd see sharks every other day in June and July during the sardine run," he recalls. "You'd see a fin for a few seconds, and then everyone would race for shore. Then the lifeguard over at Nahoon Beach would raise the shark flags."

Surfers traditionally abhor strangers on their breaks, a phenomenon known as "localism," but this is rarely an issue at Nahoon where visitors are better tolerated…mostly because people are more concerned about sharks. The risk of getting snaked off a wave by a rude out-of-towner pales in comparison to the risk of becoming a hot lunch. *Surf-Forecast* publishes this re-dundant and not entirely humorous warning about Nahoon: "Take care of sharks, urchins, rips, rocks, and sharks."[12]

Nahoon's unique risk can be summarized rather easily. Sardines run up the coast in winter. Great whites follow the sardines in winter. Nahoon's best surfing occurs in winter. So, whether you're a 130-pound, curly-haired surfer looking for a good ride or a 2,000 pound, 15-foot great white shark looking for a good meal, Nahoon Reef is where desire meets opportunity.

About Risk

You always hear that you're more likely to be killed by lightning than by a shark, and statistically, that's entirely true. Over a recent 25-year period, the death toll from sharks in South Africa was less than one per year.[13] But for those who challenge the waters of the Wild Coast, the risk of shark at-tack seems far worse than the risk of a lightning strike.

Ask English surfer Ian Peter Brittan who dropped his board into the steely-cold waters of Nahoon Reef while on a world tour. Ian's haunting impressions, from his *Bali living Blog*, are shared here with his kind permission:[14]

One of man's greatest fears is being attacked, ripped apart and eaten by a wild animal. It's a primal terror, residing deep in our psyche from the days when we were far more exposed to predators. These days we rarely come into contact with ferocious carnivores living, as we do, in the relative safety of modern society. Surfers, however, find themselves paddling around on the edge of the ocean where wildlife is abundant and in some parts of the world, rife with sharks.

Should you surf South Africa for two months, all along its rugged coast, you'll become acquainted with that psychological fear, all day every day. The locals say, amongst other things, that you'll never see the shark that gets you as it will hit you from below, behind, and from out of the depths. They'll also tell you that, if you spot a fin get out of the water. It makes sense, but it also poses a conundrum: if I see a shark fin then I've got time to get back to shore. But if I don't see anything in the water, life is still far from being ok. The conclusion would be that it's almost better to see a shark than not, and that's the insane situation you're left with.

It's a truly hideous experience. If you think about it too much, you'll end up sitting there, bracing yourself for an almighty impact. Any second now and you're going to get hit at 60 miles an hour by a Mack truck, lifted out of the water and ragged by a thrashing beast. And you won't see it coming. The soldier on the battlefield never hears the shot that kills him.

Whereas other sea creatures can employ evasive tactics, surfers can only paddle at about 5 miles an hour in any one direction, leaving them effectively stranded. In other words, you're a sitting duck...a lure begging to be hit. Ironically though, despite it putting the fear of God into you, the immobility of a surfer has actually saved many a life as sharks are used to their prey making a run for it. The apparent heroism or disdain for the threat of a Great White will cause the shark to think twice before attacking an object that is ignoring him. This is the cause of many a bump before a bite, as Whitey tries to resolve his confusion, giving the surfer time to get to land and clean the crap from his wetsuit.

Ultimately, the attack doesn't happen then. Even so, it's hard, almost impossible, to relax and go with the flow while this menacing threat is potentially lurking below you. South Africans, socially conditioned to this danger, will tell you not to worry about it. But if you're some wildlife virgin from England, with no experience of man-eating sharks, you can't help but freak out. I thought that after South Africa I'd be ready and willing to surf any region of the world where dangerous sharks were in abundance, accustomed as I'd be to their presence and threat. But the reverse is true. Never again would I be willing to go through that gut-churning experience of waiting helplessly to see if something was hungry enough and in the mood for a bit of dumb English tourist.

The laws of probability state that there's almost no chance you'll get taken. But I challenge you to tell me what you think of chance when you're surfing some famously shark infested spot with a recent and impressive record of attack fatalities. Ask yourself how irrational you're being as panic fights to take control of your mind and throw you into disarray. You're more likely to be hit by a bus than attacked by a shark, they famously say. Oh, yeah? Paddle out at Nahoon Reef and tell me what you think of statistics. Go on...

5

TOO YOUNG TO DIE

If you accept Ian's challenge and decide to paddle out at Nahoon Reef, you'll have to walk down that slipway to reach the water's edge. Near the top, just after you pass that big boulder, you might notice a granite plaque just off the left side of the path. Heavily eroded by salt air and wind, but still readable, the plaque memorializes seven Nahoon surfers who have lost their lives. The plaque creates an impression that is, oddly, both deceptive and accurate at the same time. Only two of the seven deaths occurred in the water. And of those, only one was the result of a shark attack.

Steven Theron, a well-known boxer for the Border (Eastern Cape Province) team, drowned in the surf there in 1982. The shark-related fatality occurred on July 9, 1994, when twenty-two-year-old Bruce Corby lost his right leg and forty-eight hours later, his life to a great white. The other five died due to disease, fire, and homicide. If you aren't aware of these facts before seeing the plaque, you might conclude that sharks are a huge risk at the reef.

But you would be correct. Nahoon area swimmers and surfers have fallen victim to twenty-three shark attacks since 1961.[15] Of those attacks, two proved fatal, not one. Bruce Corby's name appears on the plaque. The other name is conspicuous by its absence...lost, it seems, in the mists of time.

We can clear those mists, here, with the generous help of the East London *Daily Dispatch*.[16] In the 1970s, the newspaper took a courageous and leading role in exposing the atrocities of the apartheid regime including the beating death of Steve Biko in prison in 1977. The paper's editor, Donald Woods, who had befriended Biko, made a dramatic escape from South Africa on January 1, 1978, with evidence of Biko's murder—an event heralded in the movie *Cry Freedom* (1987) featuring Denzel Washington as Biko and Kevin Kline as Woods.

A Gift of Pigeons

In 1961, Geoffrey Zimmerman was a handsome, fit fourteen-year-old with dark hair, a skinny build, and a huge smile. He played on the rugby team for his Standard 7 (ninth grade) class at Selbourne College, a public all-boys high school in East London. Geoffrey raised pigeons and often gave birds to his friends. His parents and teachers described their son, the younger of two brothers, as "studious" and "home-loving."[17] Geoffrey had many friends, none closer than Desmond Schultz, fifteen, and Robert ("Nuts") Nuttall, fourteen.

On Wednesday, February 1, 1961, Geoffrey, Desmond, and Robert went swimming together at Nahoon Beach. They entered the water at the precise spot where thirteen-year-old Shannon Ainslie would surf his first exhilarating wave thirty-seven years later.

When Geoffrey and his friends arrived at the beach that afternoon, the water was an astonishing 25.5°C (78°F), a near record-high water temperature for the area. About thirty-five people were enjoying the wide, dune-backed beach that day.[18] The three youths spent their time body surfing, each boy using his body as a surfboard and chest-grinding to a tumultuous stop in the shallow sands.

Shortly after 3 p.m., Desmond rode a wave into the beach. As he stood and turned to wade back out, Geoffrey and Robert were still awaiting waves in chest-deep water about ten meters apart. Another boy, Barry Kreusch, fifteen, was in deeper water just seaward of them.

Barry was the first to see it—a fin, coming straight at him. He yelled "Shark!!" and the animal veered away, heading straight inland toward a second youth. Seconds later, Geoffrey began screaming and pounding the water in frenzied terror. "Nuts!! Nuts!!" he shrieked, begging for help from his friend. An adult close to shore saw the boy's mad flailing and thought Geoffrey was "playing the fool," but the crimson froth around the boy's torso told a very different tale.[19] The onslaught was unrelenting. The huge shark bit Geoffrey over and over, ripping deep punctures in his thigh, lower legs, and left arm.[20]

Robert plowed toward him but was slowed by the deep water. Desmond, who was wading out from the shallows, was able to reach his besieged mate first. In a widening pool of bloody brine, Desmond used one arm to support Geoffrey and used the other to punch the animal.[21] Roy Simpson, a lifeguard, saw it all from the beach and was astonished. "It was the bravest thing I ever saw," he later told a reporter from the *Daily Dispatch*. "He deserves a medal."[22]

When Robert was able to join the fight at Geoffrey's side, the shark broke off its attack and circled the boys three times before vanishing in the deep. The two boys dragged their injured mate toward shore, leaving a highway of blood in their wake. Geoffrey mumbled something to his mates, but his words were unintelligible and he fell limp in their arms. Roy Simpson and fellow lifeguard Geoffrey Cook met the boys halfway, pulled the wounded lad the rest of the way to shore, and began administering chest compressions.

Twenty minutes later, during a frenetic ambulance ride to East London's Frère Hospital, Geoffrey's massive blood loss took its final, terrible toll. The boy's blood pressure crashed. He drew one last shallow breath and then breathed no more.[23]

Over 400 people attended the Friday funeral at St. Alban's Church in East London.[24] Nearly 300 school kids created an honor guard at the cemetery. Desmond and Robert, who were pallbearers, cried inconsolably. One of the fifty-eight wreaths laid that day took the form of a giant rugby ball.[25] Today, few seem to remember this boy who lost sixty birthdays and Christmases for the simple pleasure of swimming with his mates.

Geoffrey's death was the first recorded shark fatality in the Nahoon area. Witness reports and a post-mortem examination of Geoffrey's injuries revealed that the boy had been taken by a ten foot long blue pointer—a short-fin Mako shark.[26] Makos, the fastest of all sharks, have been clocked at speeds of 74 kilometers per hour (46 mph) and are believed capable of bursts of up to 100 kph (62 mph).[27] They have a reputation for inflicting multiple bites when they attack humans. The unusually warm water at Nahoon on the day of Geoffrey's attack was almost certainly a factor. Makos are among the few warm-blooded sharks in the ocean, and they prefer temperate waters.[28] Local authorities considered a ban on swimming at all East London beaches whenever the water temperature exceeded 22°C (72°F), but nothing came of it.[29]

After the attack, locals mounted an effort to kill the offending shark. Several candidates were spotted, but none were caught or killed. Such endeavors are useless anyway, somewhat akin to killing a bear for protecting her cubs. Sharks, like bears, are part of the natural order. In the ocean—in even one meter of it—humans are at risk of a shark attack. Indeed, wading depth is exactly where the majority of attacks occur. The International Shark Attack File reports that, of 253 unprovoked white shark attacks studied between 1900 and 2014, fully 92 percent occurred in five feet of water or less.[30]

If Geoffrey Zimmerman's attack was unusual in any way, it was that he was a swimmer. Most of the Nahoon area's victims—fully 75 percent of them—were surfers. Time would pass before Nahoon's reputation began to darken. Shannon would play a role in that shade.

6
A World Lit by Candles

Shane and Michelle Ainslie recovered some economic stability after moving to East London, but they were living with Shane's mom, Elaine, and their marital difficulties continued. Finally, in 1994—the year Nelson Mandela became president of South Africa—the couple divorced, and Shane gained custody of the children.

Shane and the kids decided to leave Elaine's home so Michelle would have a place to stay. She was the mother of Shane's children, after all, and, according to Shane, she was adored by all:

> Everyone loved Michelle. She had no enemies. My entire family loved her. She had a fantastic personality. When Michelle was around, everyone laughed and smiled. Everyone was drawn to her. She was a very warm, loving, and caring person. She would help anyone in need whether she knew the person or not.

For ten-year-old Shannon, his parents' fighting and ultimate divorce were brutally traumatizing. He went into a tailspin that affected his relationships with family, friends, and even God:

> The unhealthy relationship between my parents made me feel so insecure. Parents are your source and your resource. They make you feel loved, secure, protected, confident, and purpose-driven, or the total opposite in an unhealthy situation such as mine. The fact that my parents fought all the time and then divorced after their separation broke something in us all. It broke all of the things that parents are supposed to do and provide. And it goes way beyond physical needs.
>
> The fighting and divorce killed me emotionally, mentally, relationally, and socially. It made me not ever want to talk to my parents about my struggles and weaknesses. It made me a closed book with anger and resentment inside that was about to explode!

The divorce made me ask myself questions like, "Where did the person who carried me in her womb, and fed me, and raised me go to?" "Why did our family break apart?" "Is mom gone because of me?" "Was I bad?"

When there is no unity between your parents, you tend to fight with one or the other because you almost have to take someone's side. So it breaks your bond and relationship with both parents. The divorce isn't just between the parents but also between the parents and the kids. I felt divorced too! But why?

Even though the situation got a little better after the divorce, I was still deeply hurt. I felt as if two pieces of paper that had been glued together had been just ripped apart from one another. This made me feel a lot of resentment and pain, and I felt anger toward everyone, even God. The divorce seemed to break the bonds in my family and made me feel that I had no consistency or control in my personal life.

Because I was young and didn't understand why Mom was not with us, I felt betrayed. I ended up struggling to relate to women and felt shy, scared, and embarrassed around them. It took me a really long time to ever get along with women and to share close friendships with them. This could be the reason why I was so aggressive towards my sister.

The divorce also affected my school work. My school marks were really bad, and I struggled to work, pay attention, and behave in class. I wanted to take control of my life, so, whenever I felt threatened by family, friends, or others, I retaliated with anger, aggression, and force. But nothing ever worked. No matter how hard I tried to take things into my own hands, it never worked out for me and left me feeling useless, weak, and vulnerable. I felt worthless because now my mom was gone and maybe I was to blame.

I also felt betrayed by this God I kept hearing about at Sunday school and wondered where He was in my situation. Did God care? Did God see and feel what I was going through? Did God really want to help me, or was I not good enough for God either?

I felt alone and useless because of my bad school marks, my

lack of friends, my mother's absence from my life, and my dad's struggles as a single parent during apartheid. I felt that life was not worth living. I went out of my way to be naughty and rebellious. I stole, smoked, fought, swore, and cursed at people. I even cursed at God. I went to church because I was supposed to, but nothing seemed to help me. My depression and loneliness made me think about taking my life several times before I turned twelve. If my life sucked and nothing ever worked for me, what was the point of living?

For Shane, too, life was extremely stressful. He was left with sole responsibility for three children and needed space for them, but renting a house in the city was too expensive, and good jobs were scarcer than ever. By 1994, the lingering effects of international sanctions had driven the extended unemployment rate in South Africa to a cataclysmic 45 percent![31]

Return to the Land

To manage costs, Shane leased a farm in the Glengarriff area about twenty kilometers east of the city. In a way, the move marked a return to his childhood. Shane had lived on a farm at age five and had dreamed of farming again someday. He loved being close to nature, being outdoors, caring for animals, and being self-sufficient—qualities he always tried to instill in his children.

The farm, which overlooked an earthen dam in the Bulera district, was home for two years. Shane raised some 8,000 tomato plants while living there, and he needed help tending them:

I had no help except for the kids. They helped me fertilize the plants and spray the plants after rains to prevent disease. I used to promise them pocket money for helping but was never able to pay them. When the fruit ripened, a bird colony of yellow finches would attack the plants. They nested in a huge dam in front of the house. I always taught my kids never to kill birds, but I had to offer them one Rand for every bird they shot with a pellet gun.

As tough as Shannon was, he had what his dad describes as "a soft spot for animals." So, shooting the birds was not fun for the boy, but the family needed to protect its tomato crop. There were fire risks, too, as Shane explains:

> We had a huge veldfire one night. It started in dry grass at about 10 or 11 p.m. and burnt our farm and a neighbor's farm. The boys and I joined other farmers and neighbors in trying to beat it out with big branches. There was no water close by.
>
> After the fire, Shannon brought an injured male fawn to me. The fawn's mother had been killed in the fire. Shannon was crying, so we took the fawn to Queens Park Zoo near my mother's house, and they rehabilitated it, saving its life. Shannon was so happy.

Shane bought his youngest son a horse when the boy was ten. "Shannon was madly in love with the horse, a mare named Thunder," Shane remembers. "He always joked that he was going to marry her."

Shannon rode her endlessly, often to the beach eleven kilometers away. Thunder wouldn't allow another soul to mount her. If anyone tried, she would pin her ears back and buck them off. The horse would nuzzle Shannon's neck as he stood in front of her and would lower her head to his knees so the boy could scratch her head. She would let the boy ride her bareback.

One night, Thunder disappeared. Tearful and desperate, Shannon enlisted his father and brother to search for her with torches. They found Thunder standing in a copse of trees in obvious distress. The mare's breathing became labored, and eventually, she just lay down. "Shannon had his arms around the horse, crying his eyes out," Shane remembers. "Shannon was about ten years old. I gave Thunder an injection for tick fever. Our ticks carry diseases like red water, hot water, and gall fever that can kill horses. If I could have given Thunder the shot sooner, she might have survived, but she didn't."

"It seems like all of my animals died during those years on the farms," Shannon laments. "Brandon, Candice, and I each had a German shepherd, but mine died from a snake bite when it was very young. My next two dogs died in less than a year as well. I had two horses, and they both died. My cat died. Even my pet rat and hamsters died." But conditions would get worse before they got better.

Shane began working as an agent for an insurance company in 1994 and traveled up to 8,000 kilometers a week while developing clients. Financial challenges continued, however, mostly due to the unreliability of his insurance clients. "Most of my clients were employed by the government (education, health, etc.)," Shane explains, "and many of them let their policies lapse due to an inability to handle their finances."

In 1996, Shane's lease ran out on the farm, and the owner decided to sell the property to the neighboring Inkwenkwezi Private Game Reserve, a huge African wildlife refuge for lions, zebras, giraffes, elephants, and other native animals. Shane found a new farm in the Cefani/Chintsa East district and signed a one-year lease.

They lived in a one-level white house high on a hill in the bush. Grapevines adorned one side of the house. The other side featured a strawberry patch and orchards. Shannon and Brandon shared a room at the front of the house. From their window, they could peer out over a valley full of free-ranging chickens, turkeys, and cows. Life on the second farm, however, was intensely Spartan and only exacerbated Shannon's emotional burdens. He was nearly forty kilometers from the few friends he had in East London, and for nearly a year, he had to eat, sleep, and read by candlelight. They had no electricity.

Like most sensitive teens, Shannon was acutely aware of things his friends had that he didn't have—things like lights, cars, mothers, and computers. While living with his grandmother before the divorce, he had rarely invited friends over because of the less affluent Albany Street neighborhood. His parents' fighting and ultimate divorce had taken a toll on his emotions and his relationships. He had become angry and rebellious and felt useless. By the time he ended up on a remote farm, serious depression was inevitable:

> When we lived on the farms we struggled so much. We had no electricity for nearly a year!! We showered after swim or water polo practice during the week and had to take cold water baths on weekends unless we could heat some water over the wood stove. We lived, worked, studied, and kept warm by candlelight and stove fires. Fortunately, it never gets really cold in

South Africa during the winter. I never saw snow until I went to Norway at the age of twenty-four.

On some of the farms, there were vegetables. My dad was able to grow them and cook them over a fire for supper at times. On one farm, we had avocado pear trees, pawpaw trees, apple trees, grapefruit trees, mango trees, and pecan nut trees. We also grew cabbage and lettuce, raised chickens, and had cows for milk. Often we went to gran's house for supper or Sunday lunch. At breakfast, she would cook a huge pot of mielie meal that would feed all of us so dad wouldn't have to cook before taking us to swim practice at 5:25 a.m. With the early swim practices, we often didn't have time to make lunch for school, but Travis Naude's mom would make sandwiches and have Travis bring them to me so I had something to eat there.

My brother never really showed his emotions. It is hard to say how he dealt with it. When he got to high school he started partying a lot, like most of his friends, and maybe he used that to fill his emotional tank. He never really did too well at school either, because he was quite rebellious too, but as soon as he got out of school and got his current girlfriend, I think he started taking life a bit more seriously. He studied and worked super hard to pay for his studies and now both he and his girlfriend have their law degrees.

My sister, on the other hand, seemed to battle a lot. She had it the hardest in my opinion because she was the youngest. She seemed to get sad and depressed very easily, and she and I used to almost hate each other when I was young. And she has had so many other struggles as well. Her boyfriend got into an automobile accident and passed away.

Life just seemed to be against me.

7

THE DAY THE CANDLE FLICKERED

Boys enter puberty at eleven or twelve years of age. They are years of rapid change, growth, and surging testosterone. The arrival of this powerful hormone creates not only sexual drive but also emotional turmoil—moodiness, unexplained bursts of anger, clouded judgment, and unacceptable risk-taking. Add external trauma, like parents getting divorced and financial hardship, and the mix can become explosive. For Shannon, the mix was nearly catastrophic:

> One day about two years after the divorce, it all came to a head. I was twelve years old and had an argument with my dad. My school marks were really bad, and I had not been doing my homework. My dad challenged and rebuked me very hard that day about not studying and not being diligent. He told me that if I didn't study and do my homework, I would grow up to be uneducated, would fail multiple times, and would become useless and possibly homeless. His words cut me so deeply that I will never forget them. He was not trying to be mean, of course. He had been naughty and rebellious in school and had not pursued his education either, so he knew the dangers that I would face if I did the same. I understood him, but I had no drive in me to do what he asked. Perhaps my dad could have challenged me in a different way, because, at the time, his words made me feel that he didn't care about me either. Did he also not love me?
>
> After that conversation, I ran out of the house for a while, sobbing and balling my eyes out. I was so over life and over trying. When I got back to the house, I was in a terribly dark place. I went straight into my dad's room and grabbed the pistol that he kept under his pillow. I put the gun to my head and wanted to blow my brains out. I wondered if anyone would care if I was even alive or not. I wondered if I would miss out on anything in life. I

wondered if I had a purpose in life and if I would ever amount to anything.

To this day, I don't know what made me put the gun down. I just remember coming to my senses and thinking how stupid I was for even thinking about doing it, much less almost actually doing it!!

I remained depressed and angry over life, though. The depression felt like a spiritual, mental, emotional, and social burden, and it made me feel very heavy. I struggled to fight it and could not free myself from it. I felt that I needed the help of someone who was much bigger and stronger than me. I didn't know it at the time, but, in less than two years, just such a Person would enter my life.

Better Days

In 1997, Shane moved to a third farm that was next door to the second one. The new farm was less hilly, was better suited for growing, and mercifully, had electricity. The family stayed there for two years until Shannon turned fifteen.

The kids, of course, made the best of farm life. They rode horses, surfed, played with pellet guns, and raised and cared for animals. Candice and Shannon often played in wooden go-karts. Candice remembers the day Shannon got going too fast, broke the plank that served as a brake, and rode the go-kart right into a giant bush. She also recalls a time, years earlier, when Shannon rode Thunder toward a gate so fast that he had to jump off. "He sat there on the ground crying," Candice remembers, "with that big open mouth of his." Shannon broke his hand that day but never saw a doctor. Too expensive, the boy felt.

Times were hard to be sure, but Shane spared no effort to support his kids and make life rich and exciting for them. He encouraged his kids in their competitive swimming, surfing, water polo, lifesaving, and karate. He drove them to 5:25 a.m. swim practices five days a week and picked them up after their various afternoon sports activities. He attended their swim meets, mile swims, surfers' marathons, karate competitions, water polo matches, and Nippers training. He took them on surfing tours to South Africa's best breaks and drove them over a dozen times to Hogsback, a spectacular locale that inspired J. R. R. Tolkien to write his *Lord of the Rings* trilogy. He took them on two-day canoeing trips up the Kowie River near Port Alfred. He took his boys on hikes along the amazing Strandloper Trail. He bought them horses and surfboards, dropped them off at surfing beaches on non-school days, and made sure they had food, school fees, and shelter. He pushed them in their studies and made sure they attended church. He was always there for them.

Shane would drive to the beach with the surfboards and set up a braai while the kids rode their horses to the beach. A braai, or barbeque, is hugely popular in South Africa. While the boys surfed, Shane and Candice grilled the food—boerewors or other meats like beef, lamb, ox kidney, or pork sausage. Sometimes they would make kebabs. Always they prepared pap, a thick cornmeal concoction made from white corn and covered in tomato and onion gravy. Your cardiologist would not approve.

In the last analysis, Shane's kids enjoyed a far richer life, and far more support, than other kids who whiled away their time away watching big screen TV, playing Xbox, and smoking weed. And if the true test of parenting skill is the quality of one's kids after they become adults, Shane passed his tests with flying colors.

Harbinger

In 1998, Shane took his sons and his nephew, Russell Annesley, to Glengarriff Beach for a braai and some surfing. Five or six locals were in the line-up that day, and Shane watched his boys surf from a vantage point on the rocks at the side of the bay. A strong rip current was pulling water out to sea along one side of the bay, and the boys used the rip for rapid transit back to the wave break.

Suddenly, the locals bolted for shore in a dog pack. And a dog pack of surfers racing for shore is never a good sign. Unfortunately, the Ainslie brothers were not experienced in these things. They had been surfing for only a few months and did not appreciate the significance of the locals' abrupt exit at Glengarriff.

Worse, once they were on shore, the locals began waving frantically. Thinking the gestures friendly, Russell and the Ainslie brothers waved back. Russell, though, sensed a deeper meaning and paddled ashore to investigate.

Then, he too started waving at his cousins. Getting no response, he signaled Shane instead.

The delays continued to compound. Shane misunderstood Russell's gestures and waved back. Quickly, though, Shane realized that his nephew's semaphores were a warning, and a warning on the Wild Coast usually means only one thing. Instantly, Shane whistled and shouted at his sons and pointed emphatically at the beach. The brothers obeyed the order without delay, and within seconds, Brandon knew why it had been issued:

> As we were paddling to shore, I looked back and saw a huge dorsal fin following us about fifteen or twenty meters behind. And when we got up on the beach, one of the local kids showed us his surfboard. It had a huge bite mark!

The Glengarriff episode augured dramatic events to follow. Over the next four years, Shannon would have three more encounters with one of the planet's most feared creatures—far more intimate encounters to be sure.

Return to East London

During the farm years, Shane brought his kids to town for Sunday school so regularly that they won awards for attendance. Afterward, he drove them to the beach for Nippers and took them to Sunday lunch at his mom's house. Elaine Ainslie, "Ganna" as the kids called her, was the constant force that held the family together. She was a heavy-set woman with fair skin, curly gray hair, a bad hip, and a wonderful sense of humor.

By 1999, life on the farms was no longer feasible for the family. The Chintsa East area was a forty-kilometer drive from East London, and Shane had to have his kids at swim practice by 5:25 a.m., meaning 4:45 a.m. departures at the latest. Shane was also working with a new insurance company and needed to travel more. Having only a few days to renew his farm lease and no time to search for a house in town with reasonable rent, Shane decided to return to his mother's for a few months. By then, Elaine had moved into a nicer home across the street—a bungalow-style house on a walled corner lot at 15 Albany Street. Michelle was no longer living with Elaine; she had moved back to Cape Town.

After the kids settled in, Shane began traveling to Johannesburg to develop his insurance business. Johannesburg and neighboring Pretoria, the capital, were more promising markets for him. Many government employees lacked insurance, and the two cities were less saturated with insurance agents than white-dominated East London.

While in Johannesburg, Shane researched his ancestry and eventually changed the spelling of his last name to Annesley. It seems that his great-grandfather, an Annesley, had sired nine children. Four of them, including his grandfather, had been raised by other family members who had misspelled the family name, morphing it to Ainslie. Shannon and Brandon never followed their dad's lead on the name change, though Candice did.

As Shane succeeded in developing more business in Johannesburg, his family's stay with Elaine extended beyond a few months. They stayed for three full years, with Shane contributing support. During her son's absences, Elaine was in charge of the kids, of course. Fortunately, Shannon was fourteen when they moved back from the farms, and he had calmed down a bit. He was not as combative anymore.

Shannon and his brother had fought constantly when they had lived with Elaine at 22 Albany Street in the early '90s, and it had often fallen to Elaine to enforce the ceasefires.

"Ganna had her grumpy moments and hated fighting," Candice remembers. "She used to hit Shannon over the head. But we're a male-dominated society, and Ganna loved the men, so she put up with a lot more from them." Given Shannon's depression and anger levels in those earlier days, she probably needed to.

8

TEMPESTUOUS YOUTH

During his pre-teens and early teens, Shannon was, in Brandon's estimation, "a naughty little chap." Shannon was anything but physically imposing, though. Entering his first year of high school—Standard 6 or eighth grade—he and one other kid were tied for the hardly coveted title of smallest boy in their entire grade. Just 5-feet 2-inches tall and scrawny as a dried reed, he was easy to underestimate. That fact, coupled with his family's limited financial resources and his parents' fighting and divorce, brought out a chippy side in the youth.

Shannon definitely had to work through anger issues. He was not a big dog, but he had big dog fight in him, and he released the hounds constantly. "He was very aggressive and extremely energetic," Brandon attests.

The fighting started in Cape Town when he was in Sub A or first grade. When a female classmate was bullied, Shannon came to her aid as a bodyguard. He would beat up anyone who messed with her. The girl turned him into a paid mercenary, plying him with candy for his protective services. None of that came as a surprise to Brandon:

> Back in primary school, Shannon got into a fight with a mate of mine named Terence who was one year older and quite a bit bigger. This occurred after school hours while they were waiting for transport. Shannon got a lot of bruises, but I think Shannon won. He just would not back down. I would often be at home and Shannon would come in with his white school shirt dirty, muddy, and even bloody.

Shannon estimates that he got into "about 20 fights" in his primary school years, a source of constant frustration for his dad. "I used to fetch him from school in grades two and three," Shane remembers, "and there he would be on the pavement, fighting, with his arm around some kid's neck, his buttons torn off, his shirt out. I would tell him that his mom would be

42

furious and ask him what the school would think of his fighting. He always told me that he was 'just playing.' Shannon had no fear of anything. Despite his small size, he would have taken on the biggest guys at school."

As Shane predicted, the school didn't think much of Shannon's pugilistic tendencies. More than once, school authorities threatened the boy with "jacks," a brutal butt-hiding with a thick meter-long leather whip. Several of Shannon's older friends and even his father had received plenty of them—usually five strokes per offense—and none had spoken highly of the experience. When angry at Shannon, teachers would pull out the whip and crack it on the wall or the floor in front of him. The boy was just cheeky enough not to care whether he got whipped, but he never had to bend over the table. By then, public sentiment had soured on corporal punishment. Instead, he ended up in detention or at the school's weekend sports camps, performing chores and clean-up work.

Shannon even institutionalized his combativeness. He pursued *kumite*, a fighting discipline within karate, and made the Border (Eastern Cape Province) team. Brandon made the Border team in the *kata* discipline, which centers on technique. Both boys had their brown belts—the last belt before black, but soon they both quit. Brandon was unwilling to wait to age fourteen, the minimum age to qualify for his black belt. Shannon was deemed "too violent" for competition after bloodying an opponent in a match.

Shannon's combative and belligerent nature erupted at home too, and Brandon did little to help. "Brandon was very stubborn," Candice remembers. "With Brandon, it was always 'my way or the highway.'" Like many older brothers, he bullied his younger brother shamelessly.

Shannon recalls it all too well. "Brandon would punch me in the shoulder, and I hated it so much. I would tell him to stop it, and he would do it again. Then, if I punched him back, he'd give me ten or twenty punches. I'd get madder and madder, and finally I'd just go crazy."

Being two years older, Brandon got his growth spurt before his brother, and Shannon paid the piper for the size differential. "I remember one time really well," Shannon says. "I got beaten up so badly, in front of my dad too!" Brandon recalls the day quite well—sometime in 1994—mostly because it was the only fight that the boys' father refused to stop:

We were living at my gran's old house at 22 Albany Street. I was probably eleven or so, and Shannon was nine at the time. I don't recall why we were fighting, but I was usually the one who was bullying Shannon, you know, trying to get my way as usual...being the older brother. Back then, I loved slugging Shannon in the shoulder to prove my point.

I guess Shannon got extremely cross one day after I had punched him, and he started coming at me throwing punches, so I punched back. This happened in the afternoon, and my father was in the house at the time. He must have heard the commotion, which was in the kitchen. He came in, moved us out of the kitchen area into the lounge, had us stand about three meters apart, and then told us that, when he said 'go,' we could start fighting. My father was strict and did not like us to fight, so it is strange that he let this happen...way out of the ordinary.

Truly, Shane did not approve of the fighting, but he had finally reached a point where he let this one dust-up continue:

They fought weekly for about two years, going at each other hammer and tong. It was a boy thing, I guess. The father, of course, is the master, and I suppose they were fighting over who was number two. They both had blue belts in karate at that time. Anyway, I just got tired of it, so I decided to let them fight this one out.

Brandon remembers the events that followed:

My dad eventually said "go" and Shannon, being as brave as he is, came at me with punches blazing and moving forward at a pace. As he approached me, I threw a punch and he walked straight into it. He was crying in agony, and my father then stopped the fight and made us shake hands. No apologies were made. We never apologized after our fights.

On another occasion, two years earlier, Shannon and I had a fight in our room. I was probably trying to push Shannon around, and he must have hurt me somehow or punched me which obviously hurt (not in the face, on the body somewhere). So, I started going for him, and then he crouched and I started elbowing his back. (I know...I feel very guilty, but we were lighties.) Then he threw himself from a crouched position into a standing position with me being almost on top of him, and his head hit my face and chipped one of my middle bottom teeth. Shannon also used to terrorize our little sister, Candice, who is five years my junior, and I always protected her.

Candice needed Brandon's protection, too. "He could be such a mean boy," she recalls. "I once got this doll for Christmas—one that cried, drank milk, and talked—and Shannon took it and hit it against a door and broke it. Brandon would often protect me from Shannon. He would put me in the bathroom and guard the door to keep Shannon away from me."

"Shannon couldn't stand Candice," Shane agrees. "Shannon wouldn't allow her to sit next to him, talk to him, say hello to him, or say goodbye to him. I think it was a boy thing, brother versus sister." More likely, it was the middle child fighting for status. In fairness, though, there were other more caring moments.

"Shannon could be very loving too," Candice confesses, smiling. "Even when he was ten or eleven years old, he would sometimes play 'tea set' or play dolls with me, just because it made me happy."

Shannon often paid the price for his less caring moments. "I got grounded a lot, and Dad gave me spankings so often it was ridiculous. He had a branch and wrote on it, 'For Shannon's bum.'"

Even when they weren't fighting, the brothers went at each other at full tilt. They used to have brick fights in the driveway out back. Yes, bricks...the red kind. The fights started out as simple rock-throwing wars, but boys, like great nations, love a good arms race. They each took cover and began lobbing larger and larger stones over a small tree in the back of the house near the loft. Eventually, Shannon picked up a full brick and launched it, hitting Brandon in the forehead. Brandon bled profusely and still complains about it today, albeit with amusement. He carries a reminder of the battle—a scar at his hairline. But he gained a measure of revenge. A while later, the boys launched a missile war again, hurling rocks from behind cover. This time, Shannon drew the short straw. "I saw what I thought was a bird out of the corner of my eye," Shannon remembers, "and then, BAM, a brick hit me right in the forehead. I bled all over the place, and the scar is easily visible on my forehead today."

Chipped teeth, fights, scars...surviving brotherly love is not for the faint of heart.

Shannon was even disgusted by his own hair—curly blond locks that, left uncut, could have challenged Angela Davis in a 'fro contest during the 1967 Summer of Love. He was known to pull one of Candice's stockings over his head at night in an effort to flatten out his mop. Eventually, he stopped worrying about it and occasionally spent time in front of the mirror trying to fashion two horns from his curls—suitably emblematic of his temperament.

Shannon liked to swear a lot in those days too, though he never cursed in front of his parents or grandmother. His dad would not tolerate it. But he loved to unleash the four-letter stuff when speaking with his brother or his friends.

Shannon's temper erupted during his sports endeavors too, especially in the roughest of his sports, water polo, which he took up in his first year at Hudson Park High School, at age thirteen.

Even if you've watched a lot of water polo, you cannot begin to appreciate the feral nature of the sport. You take fourteen boys, each awash in testosterone, throw them in a pool virtually naked, and tell them to fight like hell for every position, possession, and goal. Naturally, they try to handle their opponents by fouling, and the only "handle" out of official view is rather personal. In September of 2001, an ignominious month to be sure, precisely such a foul became a big issue for Shannon.

He was participating in the third game of the South African Coed Nationals, a national water polo tournament for males attending coeducational high schools. Shannon ended up "cap off"—ejected from the game:

> It all happened because a guy fouled me. The team we played against that day had a really big center-forward, and he was aggressive and strong and also a dirty player. They had possession of the ball and their center-forward managed to break away from our center-back. I managed to break away and catch up to him and mark him as he got to our goal. He was in the right position to get the ball and attempt to shoot for goals.

His teammate passed the ball to him, and as I defended him, he hit me in the groin and then stuck his hand down into my Speedo and grabbed my privates, pulling me down under the water.

I managed to get his hand out but, by this time, I lost my temper because I hate it sooo much when guys grab or hit me there. If there is anything that makes me angry easily and quickly, it's that! Anyway, he was ready to shoot for goals and I managed to get his hand out my Speedo. As I got to the surface of the water, I forgot about trying to defend and get the ball off him. Instead, I punched him in the ribs like three times and then pulled him under the water so the refs couldn't see me punch him in the face. I held him under the water and gave him about three shots in the face. By this time, the ref was blowing his whistle and trying to get my attention. Once he did, he kicked me out the water.

I was so angry, I didn't care how big, good, or strong this guy was. All I wanted to do was fight with him and beat him up. Fortunately, by the end of the game I had cooled down and when both teams shook hands, he apologized to me with a smile. We ended up beating the team and won the tournament.

With maturity came less fighting, and Shannon ultimately reached a point where he didn't even want to fight at all. One day, he punched a family friend in the face, and the friend wanted a proper rematch the next day. When they got together, Shannon chose not to punch him at all; he just walked away. "Everyone thought I was scared," he recalls, "but I just didn't want to get in trouble with my dad for beating up a family friend. Besides that," he notes rather proudly, "I never lost a fight to anyone except Brandon."

Shannon and Brandon would grow far closer in the winter of 2000. Affection among brothers grows rapidly, it seems, when one of them almost loses the other forever.

9

PRELUDE TO AN ATTACK

The Antarctic Circumpolar Current is like the ocean on spin-cycle, a massive west-to-east rotation of water around Antarctica. In the Drake Passage—the narrow gap between South America and Antarctica—the current generates legendary storms. The gap between Africa and the ice continent is much wider, allowing sailors to pass the Cape of Good Hope in comparative safety. Still, winter storms generate radical surf all along South Africa's 2,500 kilometer-long coast, a shoreline longer than the entire western seaboard of the United States. From April to September, the country's many bays, beaches, and reef breaks become surfing paradises. That makes winter break—a three-week school holiday—a joyous time for young surfers.

Spooked

Winter break in 2000 ran from June 25 to July 16, and Shannon, then a 5-foot 6-inch 130-pounder, nearly wore out his wetsuit. He surfed two or three sessions a day and spent the last weekend of his vacation at Nahoon Reef under clear blue skies and bright sunshine. The usual suspects joined him there—his brother Brandon, seventeen, his close friend, Alistair Cokayne, fifteen, and Brandon's good friend, Ryan Fox, eighteen. Shannon and Alistair attended Standard 8 together—tenth grade in American parlance. Brandon and Ryan were in their "matric" (pronounced "muh-TRIK") or senior year.[32]

Shannon's close friend, Travis Naude, would have been there too, but the two boys were having a bit of a spat... or perhaps we should say "spit." A few days earlier, Travis had "leached" at Shannon. Leaching is kind of like spitting, only you use the clear water that forms under your tongue when you press your tongue to the roof of your mouth. Shannon reciprocated in good humor, but Travis thought Shannon had used real spit, so Travis spat back. Shannon countered, moods soured, and a full-out spitting war ensued. Fifteen-year-old boys...what can you do?

On Sunday, July 16, the last day of the break, Shannon bumped into his friend Leslie Hempel in the car park at Nahoon Reef. Leslie seemed preoccupied.

"I've seen a lot of fins during the break," he said wistfully, staring out over the reef. "But I guess if it's your time, it's your time."

"Yeah, but I don't ever want to be attacked!" Shannon interjected.

"Well, then," Leslie answered, "maybe you should pray before you surf!"

"I do!" Shannon insisted.

Shannon had a profound fear of sharks and never surfed with fewer than four or five friends. This practice has nothing to do with strength in numbers. Surfers can't gang up on a great white. Rather heartlessly, the practice has to do with improving your odds. The cold truth is that it's safer to be one of five entrées on the smorgasbord than to be the only one. Shannon's younger sister, Candice, had nightmares about the "men in gray suits," and she didn't even surf! Shannon's mom, Michelle, had a sense of foreboding about sharks as well, often warning her sons about "what lies beneath." His father was a more adventuresome sort—a "Come on, let's do it" kind of guy. He had, after all, put his youngest son on a surfboard before the kid knew how to multiply.

Back to School

For more than a year, Shannon, Brandon, and Candice had been living with their grandmother in her new home at 15 Albany Street in the North End Central District of East London, just north of the city center. The street features a few homes, some apartments (called "mansions"), a chicken distribution company, a couple of food stores, a school playground, a daycare center, the East London Zoo, and the East London Private Hospital.

The urban neighborhood was not the safest in the world. About twice a month, Shannon would hear gunfire coming from the Porter Street taxi rank 150 meters to the southeast. "You had to be aware of your surroundings," he says, though he says he has never been the victim of a serious crime. Once, when he was nine, a local kid pulled a knife on him and stole his new bicycle, but Shane borrowed his mother's car and drove around with his cousin until he found the young thief. A few years later, another of Shannon's bicycles was stolen during swim practice. And Elaine's car was broken into once. But that was it. You could do worse in Muncie, Indiana.

Elaine Ainslie's home had five bedrooms, a kitchen, a lounge, and a dining nook in front with wide windows and sunny northern exposure. A large tree, tropical shrubs, and honeysuckle bushes adorned a narrow front yard guarded by a gated fence with stone posts and an overarching trellis of roses. Tall stone walls, ubiquitous in South Africa, protected the other three sides of the home. In the back, a gated driveway exited onto Wolseley Street. A deck-like structure extended from the back of the house adjacent to some small trees at the edge of the driveway. Shannon and Brandon often played on the deck despite Elaine's best efforts to stop them. She once warned them that there were snakes in the trees, but that merely enticed the boys to go look for them.

While the kids lived there, Elaine rented bedrooms to other boarders to help make ends meet. She kept the home neat as a pin and would not tolerate mess. If the kids left clothes on the floor, she would throw them on the sidewalk in front of the house. In her strictness, she would sometimes contradict herself. "She would tell me to wear a short top," Candice laughs, "and then, when I put one on and my middle was showing, she would tell me to take it off!"

The boys shared a small bedroom in the front of the house. They had bunk beds with Shannon drawing lower tier. Older brothers usually take lowers, but when Shannon was nine, he banged himself up pretty badly falling out of the upper berth. Brandon gave him a break and took the top, accessing it by climbing a wardrobe.

Winter Break ended on Monday, July 17, 2000, the boys' first day back to school. The morning dawned sunny and cool, and Shannon and Brandon arose at their customary 6 a.m. Shannon was in a rosy mood. School was to let out two hours early that day—at noon—leaving six hours for surf team practice and time for free surfing afterward.

Clad only in boxers, a yawning Shannon wandered into the kitchen to wolf down a bowl of mielie meal—essentially cornmeal—and returned to the bedroom for fifteen minutes of stretching that has become a lifetime habit. He had showered before bed, preserving a night's worth of male pheromones for the girls at school. He just needed to brush his teeth. His mop of astoundingly curly blond hair needed no tending, and shaving was still off his radar.

By 7 a.m., the brothers were nattily attired in their school uniforms—

white shirts, blue ties, red blazers, gray pants, and black shoes. The prevailing theory in former Commonwealth nations, and many American schools, is that uniforms improve deportment, but it's only a theory. Shannon's uniform was sullied in so many fights it could have featured an "Everlast" logo.

The boys threw their books and surfboards into Elaine's red Mazda 323. Elaine hated surfboards inside the car because the fins shredded her ceiling liner. But Shannon says the car wasn't that clean anyway. "It stunk from Ganna's two bulldogs."

Brandon drove his brother and sister to school, illegally as usual. Brandon had only a learner's permit, but Elaine, 74, had a bad hip and didn't care to drive. Fortunately, the police don't fret very much about underage driving. "People do it all the time," Shannon says, suggesting that he probably did too.

Arriving at Hudson Park High School, the boys left their boards in the car. Shannon's six-foot Town & Country three-fin thruster cost R2,500, about $350, but surfboards were not high theft items even in the theft-prone environment. Nonetheless, Alistair Cokayne stored his board inside the school.

The Hudson Park campus features two complexes, a primary school, and a high school separated by a road and a large field. The school boasted 2,200 students when Shannon attended, 1,200 of them in the high school. Despite the end of apartheid, about 70 percent of the students were white, mostly due to the monthly student fees of approximately R350 ($45 to $85 during that era).

Of the 600 boys at the high school, Brandon estimates that only 30 boys surfed with any regularity. You could always tell who they were. Teachers would catch them staring out to sea from their shared two-seat lift-top desks. The school sits 100 meters above sea level and a mere 2,500 meters from the coast, offering panoramic views of the ocean.

Peering out the windows that Monday, Shannon was excited to see clear blue sky and a moderate break—good enough for surf team practice that afternoon. Decent surf would arrive with the high tide later in the day—"waves in the four- or five-foot range," he estimated. (Even in metric countries, the foot remains oddly popular.) The air outside was a pleasant 24°C (75°F). The water was chilly, probably 15°C (59°F), but warmer than you might expect given the mid-winter date and Antarctica's looming presence five flying hours over the horizon. Still, wetsuits would be needed.

Moods soared when surf team practice was abruptly canceled, opening the entire afternoon to free surfing. At noon, the Ainslie brothers and Alistair raced from the school, loaded their boards atop the Mazda, and gave one of Brandon's classmates, Ryan Fox, a lift home to retrieve his board.

Shannon's Wave

The foursome arrived at Nahoon Reef at half past noon and found two older friends, Brad Coetzee (kuht-SEE'-uh) and Karl Smit, already in the water. Karl had bunked his college classes that day, and the pair had been surfing for nearly two hours. Two Aussie surfers, both bearing dreadlocks, had entered the lineup as well. And a Canadian backpacker had arrived to watch the action.

Shannon pulled out his board wax—the world's leading brand, marketed shamelessly as Sex Wax—and gave the middle of his board a new coating of grip. Then he stretched to regain flexibility lost during the school day. Performing a towel-trick, he dropped his pants and boxers and stepped into his Reef wetsuit—black with dark blue stripes around the shoulders. Like many surfers, he wore nothing underneath except a chafe vest to prevent underarm irritation and provide some added core warmth.

Shannon was never the serious sort except when he prayed, but Alistair and his friends thought it was cool when he did. Something about Nahoon's ominous reputation makes everyone a bit more spiritual. So, for a brief moment, they all bowed their heads as the fifteen-year-old spoke over the sound of the rolling surf:

> Thank you, Jesus, for the privilege and opportunity to surf. We commit our surf to you and ask that you keep us safe and protected in the water. We ask that you help us to respect each other and to have a good surf with our friends and the other locals and that in everything we do, we would represent and honor you. Amen.

Yes, he forgot to pray for the foreigners on the break that day, but localism was not the reason. It was an innocent omission. He was a good Christian, after all, and so were most of his friends. He wished no one ill.

Like many young people, though, the fifteen-year-old probably harbored unspoken questions when he prayed. Faith is the suppression of doubt, and, in his weaker moments, he may have wondered whether God heard his prayers. When he arrived at Nahoon that Monday afternoon, he had no way of knowing that he would have his answer in less than two hours.

At 12:45 p.m., the boys were ready. The four made their way past the big boulder at the base of the cliff and plodded barefoot down the slipway. They didn't have far to walk. A full moon on the far side of the earth was pulling the planet out from under the sea, raising a spring tide. Only the upper third of the slipway was exposed. As they reached knee-deep water, they noticed the fishy scent, common during the sardine run, and dropped their boards into the rock-strewn lagoon.

A quarter-mile to the east, beyond Nahoon Corner, Ashley Grimmer and Devon Swart were sprinting westward along wide Nahoon Beach, anxious to join their friends at the reef. The Nahoon River mouth didn't slow them. Without losing a step, they simply dropped onto their boards and paddled across. As they did, they noticed the odor too.

"Devon and I remarked about how 'fishy' the water smelled," Ashley recalls. "That happens sometimes when natural oil from the sardines accumulates on the water's surface."

Ashley and Devon climbed to the top of Nahoon Corner using the stairs and descended to the car park mere minutes after Shannon had taken to the sea. Ashley's brother arrived too, along with another mate.

The triangular route followed by the surfers that day never changed. They would paddle straight out along the left side of the reef, ride waves in a diagonal trajectory away from the tip of the reef and toward the car park, and then paddle back along the shoreline to the base of the reef. Most of them planned to surf until dusk, a bit more than four hours, but good sets were scarce. With the rising tide pushing water over the reef, they had hoped for stronger swells. Poor waves meant no exercise. No exercise meant dwindling body heat. Frustrations mounted.

Brandon and Ryan were the first to call it quits. At 2:15 p.m., they surfed in on some waves just behind Shannon and Alistair, but Brandon and Ryan didn't follow the younger boys back out. Instead, they veered right to shore. As they left the water, they paid little heed to Canadian backpacker Sean Smith who was perched atop the large boulder at the top of the slipway. Reaching the Mazda, they peeled their wetties down to their waists and stood shirtless in the breeze.

Brad Coetzee and Karl Smit left the water a few minutes later, but not because of poor waves or cold bones. Karl was bothered by the foreigners in the water that day. Brad was bothered by the foreigners too but also by something else:

> The whole session, I had a real uneasy feeling, but I couldn't pin-point what it was. There were a few foreigners in the water, and I felt maybe they had brought a bad vibe...either that or I was just having a bad surf. I had just hit a wave and Karl was on the one behind it. About thirty meters from shore, I stopped paddling, turned to Karl, and said "I'm getting out...I don't feel right out here." Karl told me he was actually feeling the same. We didn't give it much thought and caught the next wave in.

Brad came by his uneasy feeling honestly. In June 1997, he and a friend had suffered a fright while surfing at Palm Springs about twenty-five kilometers west of East London:

> A set approached us and just ahead, in the swell of the first wave, we saw a hammerhead swimming parallel to the shoreline. If I remember correctly, it was about 1.5 to 2 meters long—not massive, but it scared us enough to scramble for shore. I actually caught the wave it was in! So did my friend.

In December 1998, Brad had another close encounter at Plettenberg Bay on the Garden Route, South Africa's answer to California's spectacular seaside motorway, Highway 1:

> I was surfing Roberg Beach with Karl Smit, and after searching for ages—Roberg is a big beach—we found a fun little peak. We had a wave or two each and then, to our right about three meters away on the surface, was a lovely ragged-tooth shark watching us. We got out immediately. They say those sharks are docile, but they look super mean, and when you see a shark in the water, you don't want to be near it.

They—whoever "they" are—would be wrong. Ragged-tooth sharks, known as sand tigers to the rest of the planet, have been responsible for about 40 percent of all East London-area shark attacks in which species could be positively identified.[33] From 1900 to 2014, ragged-tooth sharks were associated with twenty-seven unprovoked human attacks.[34] If you think that passes for "docile," then you're well on your way to understanding surfers. Indeed, 61 percent of all shark attacks involve surfers and board riders.[35]

So, we can excuse Brad and Karl if they occasionally get the creeps while surfing. Very possibly, though, their disquiet at Nahoon that Monday was linked to something more tangible, perhaps an official warning that Brad recalled being issued earlier that winter:

The Natal Sharks Board representatives informed Border Surfing that they had flown between East London and Coffee Bay and had been blown away by the number of sharks in the water, the most they had ever seen. Obviously, the sardine run makes this happen every year, and we all carry on surfing because that's what we do, but they urged us to keep an eye out during the next few weeks. They said that if we see fish or bird activity, particularly at point breaks, it may be better to stay out of the water.

Whatever the source of their concern, Brad and Karl felt better back on dry land. The younger boys, though, continued their quest for rides in the weak swell. "Shannon was getting irritated because he couldn't catch a good wave," Alistair recollects, "but we kept trying."

At 2:30 p.m., Shannon, Alistair, and Ashley paddled out along the reef one more time. When they reached a point 130 meters from the slipway, Shannon and Alistair stayed together, both facing out to sea looking for waves. The reef was sixty meters to their right, Ashley ten meters to their left. Soon, they spied a pretty line of two-meter swells rounding the point.

As the first wave approached, Alistair had a clear view of Shannon who was in front of him and five meters to his left. Suddenly, Shannon snapped his board around toward shore and began paddling hard.

"This is Shannon's wave," Alistair thought to himself. "I'll take the next one." Turning his gaze back to the onrushing breaker, Alistair prepared for a duck dive. As the green wall reached him, he flexed his arms and prepared to push down hard on the front end of his board. The move was routine. He had plowed under oncoming waves a thousand times.

But he had never plowed under a wave like this one.

10
ATTACK!

"Oh, God, no…"

Alistair's spine snapped into a reverse arch, his upper body bracing itself on steeled arms. The face of the oncoming wave—a green wall within touching distance in front of him—had come terrifyingly alive:

> A massive shark—the size of a car—flew from right to left through the face of the wave directly in front of me. He was black and I could see his eye and fin. His mouth was open and his teeth were visible. He was very round with a huge girth. He was at least four meters long, and I could see scars on his body. He was so close that I could have touched him as he raced past me. In my head, I was screaming, "Oh, God, no, not this!"
>
> Just after it passed me, I heard the shark hit Shannon's board. It made a loud thud, and I heard Shannon make an "Ooof!" sound. I instinctively turned my board to the left, toward shore, just as the wave reached me. As I did, I looked back over my right shoulder at Shannon and saw his legs flying up in the air. Then the wave broke right on top of me, and I lost sight of him.

Preparing to catch the wave, Shannon had matched speed with the on-rushing water and had just risen to all fours. He never made it to his feet:

> I was at the top of the wave and about to stand up when I felt a massive impact from my back left. The force just lifted me up. It was as if someone took me out of reality in that split second. I felt like I was in a different life where time slowed down.
>
> The impact flipped me and my board around. My right hand must have gotten caught in the shark's teeth when it bit my board and tossed me upside down in the air, though I didn't know I was injured at the time. I never felt any pain. I landed on the back of my neck in the water and plunged fairly deep. I ended up deep under the water in an upright position. It all seemed like a dream.

Shannon found himself two meters beneath the surface, his feet some-where near the boulder-strewn bottom. He had plunged deep in the water countless times before...but never like this. Directly in front of him loomed the massive head of an adult great white. The animal's long body curved away to the left, most of it obscured by the turbid water:

I was face to face with the shark. He just stopped and stared right at me. He was no more than two feet in front of me, easily within arm's reach. I could see his huge right eye, his open mouth, and his teeth. My hand was extended and almost touch-ing his mouth. He was massive, and I couldn't see the rest of him because he was too close to me and the water was murky. I was fairly deep and don't remember seeing the bottom, but it had to have been just beneath me. I wasn't paying attention to my sur-roundings, so I don't remember seeing any rocks.

I didn't have any feelings, emotions, or sense of fear. It seemed like my senses weren't even working. It was so weird. I was in a dream state. I felt nothing. I don't remember struggling for air either. I was just...there! The only thing I remember while staring at the shark was that it looked confused or disappointed.

I never struggled for oxygen and have no idea how long I was under the water, but it felt like a long time. After about five sec-onds, the shark began moving. He swam rapidly by me on my right side and just after he passed me, I felt a hard bump from behind. I was shoved forward through the water for several meters. Then I swam a few strokes to the surface. I still didn't know what was happening.

Once on top, I saw my board floating in front of me, between me and the shore. I remember thinking, "Why is my board floating there?" I reached out and grabbed it, still in my dream state, and then looked all around. Other guys were just staring at me with their mouths open, and I thought, "Why are they all staring at me like that?" Then I felt something odd with my right hand and lifted it out of the water. As I did, I saw blood pouring out of my hand. I stopped and looked carefully at it and saw a huge hole in my hand, a tear in my wetsuit over my wrist, and bones sticking out from my last two fingers. The fingers were loose and dangling from threads of skin.

My dream state shattered. I suddenly realized that this was real and started freaking out and panicking! I remember that my heart was pounding out of my chest and I was shaking. Fear was controlling me. My diaphragm seemed to lift up into my chest, and I had trouble taking breaths. I yelled, "Shark! Shark!" but I guess everyone knew already because I saw them all disappear over the last wave in the set. They were all gone, and I was just floating there alone. I wasn't mad at them for rushing to shore without me. Even I wouldn't have had the guts to help me!

My first thought was that the shark was going to come back for me. Nahoon was my very favorite wave, but it was the scariest place for me to surf because of its reputation for shark attacks. I kept looking in front of me, behind me, to my left, and to my right, expecting the shark to take me at any second.

Alistair Cokayne had eluded the shark's trajectory by a single meter. After turning for shore, he was struck in the back by the full weight of the breaking wave and was rolled by the cascading water for nearly eight seconds. When he surfaced in white chop, he glanced over his shoulder again and saw the shark's huge tail fin flip into the sky and then submerge. At that moment, Alistair's life was reduced to two simple vectors—the terrible risk beneath him and the astronomical distance in front of him:

My first thought was, "Get out of the water!" I just panicked at that time. As I was paddling in, I tried to take white water so I would not be visible to the shark. While I was in the white water, though, I got knocked off my board. Then I totally panicked. I balled up in the water to try to look small until I could rein in my surfboard with my leg rope and get back on.

Ten meters down-wave from Shannon, Ashley Grimmer didn't see the attack, but he quickly heard about it. "I saw Shannon climbing back onto his board," Ashley remembers, "and he shouted to me, 'There's a shark! Get out of the water!' He did not appear to be injured."

Shark strikes board, catching Shannon's hand underneath (Courtesy of Screen-ocean/Reuters)

Shark wrenches board violently as Shanon falls head first (Courtesy of Screen-ocean/Reuters)

Shark's pectoral fin appears as shark rolls in wave and continues attacking surfboard (Courtesy of Screenocean/Reuters)

Surfers race to shore ahead of Shannon who is furthest out and mired in flat water (Courtesy of Screenocean/Reuters)

Back in the car park, confusion reigned. The surface attack had lasted barely a second and had taken place 200 meters away. At worst, the sight of a surfer somersaulting in the air was merely puzzling. Ryan Fox didn't see the strike at all, but his friends did.

"Pierre Strauss was standing behind Brandon and me," Ryan recalls. "Pierre said in kind of a puzzled tone, 'Did you see that? It looked like someone was attacked!' I looked up quickly, but I couldn't see anything."

Brad Coetzee did see it:

> I was standing in the middle of the car park with Karl Smit. It's slightly elevated and you have a good view of the lineup. We weren't out of the water five minutes, and I saw a good set approaching. Then I saw someone trying to catch the first wave. It looked like he was on top of the wave and about to stand up. All of a sudden, he went flying through the air from right to left in a cartwheel fashion.
>
> Ryan and Brandon were standing near me, and I almost said to them, jokingly, "Either he was punched by someone or that's a shark attack." I really wasn't sure what had happened, nor could I figure it out by just seeing it. It only lasted a second and was pretty far away. But, when I saw fifteen guys on the same wave all racing for dry land with nobody standing up, it became clear."

"No one knew who was involved," Brandon recalls. "There were fifteen surfers in a line, and they were paddling for shore like a pack of wild dogs."

Ryan sprinted to the end of the car park and scrambled on all-fours to the top of the bluff overlooking the reef. "I could see chunks of polystyrene floating in the water where the shark had ripped pieces out of someone's board," he recalls, "but I couldn't tell who had been hit."

Shannon surfaced amid the chunks, alone and 130 meters out.[36] Treading water in a pool of blood, he feared renewed assault from the aggressive shark lurking beneath—the kind of shark that kills 26 percent of its human victims and maims a majority of them. Shannon knew he had to escape the water quickly, but the wave sets had passed. He was marooned in flat water:

I was so scared. I was shaking badly, and my adrenaline was surging. I wanted to catch a wave to shore but the ocean had gone dead flat and I was still far from the shore. I was afraid that if I started sprinting for shore, the splashing sound would attract the shark, and I worried that blood in the water would attract it too. I was certain the shark was going to hit me at any second. As hopeless as it seemed, I told myself I would go down swinging and fight the shark with my fists if I had to. I knew there was no way I was going to escape.

There were no waves at all, so I started paddling with my left arm. The last two fingers of my right hand were dangling by skin, and I was afraid they'd fall off if I paddled with it. But it was taking forever, so I started paddling with both hands. I could feel the water surging up into my bones, muscles, and tendons. It was totally disgusting. With each stroke, I thought I'd bring my arm out of the water with no fingers. And every time I lifted my right arm out of the water, blood poured out of it. The thought of my blood attracting the shark would not go away.

As I paddled, I kept glancing wildly to my left and right which caused my board to jerk wildly in the water as I braced for the hit. Thoughts of death, of losing an arm or leg, or of being severely savaged played over and over in my mind. I remember thinking about the Carter-Corby attack that took one of their lives, and nearly both, at the same spot six years earlier. I thought about how I was too young to die and that it was so unfair that, out of all the people who surf, the shark had chosen me. I felt like this was just another bad thing happening to me...like life was just against me.

On the shore, Ryan, Brandon, and Pierre raced down the slipway to the water, their eyes riveted on each surfer arriving in the shallows. Ryan remembers the moment vividly:

Brandon was saying, "Gosh, I hope it's not my brother." Those moments of waiting to see who had been attacked, and how badly, were things that I'll never forget. It was scary. We didn't know what to expect.

They knew what they could expect. They could expect a boy coming ashore with a missing arm or leg, a kid's blood squirting in fountains from a severed femoral artery, an ashen youth issuing his last blood-choked breaths in their arms. They knew that, in mere moments, they could cease being carefree teens enjoying a day of surfing and become, instead, para-medics fighting through blood, gore, and war-zone agony trying to save a friend's life, using skills that none of them possessed. Such scenes had played out at Nahoon Reef before.

Six years earlier, at the precise spot where Shannon was struck, a single great white had attacked Andrew Carter and his friend Bruce Corby within thirty seconds of each other. Carter had suffered catastrophic wounds to his back, buttocks, and thigh, only barely surviving after five hours of sur-gery and the reattachment of all of his leg muscles. Corby had lost his right leg above the knee, and two days later, his life. Memories of such tragedies linger. Surfers remember. Swimmers remember. Towns remember. "Your heart just sinks at moments like these," Karl Smit confesses, shaking his head. "You imagine the worst."

Soon, Brandon's fears for his brother proved justified. "After a few sec-onds, I saw one person lagging about twenty meters behind the rest in a black and blue wetsuit and with long blond hair," he remembers. "He was paddling with just his left hand, with Shannon's style. I was so worried."

He had good reason to worry. Surfers with mortal wounds often make it to shore while bleeding out, only to expire later from cardiac arrest, brain death, or massive organ failure. Bruce Corby had managed to reach shore after his attack in 1994. Stumbling in the shallows, the doomed youth had calmly informed a friend, "I lost my leg." They are believed to have been his last words.

Shannon paddled toward the slipway but was still stuck in quiet water. Ashley Grimmer took a different trajectory, toward the car park, and arrived on the rocks nearly 100 meters east of the slipway. He estimates that he needed "four or five minutes" to hobble across the treacherous rocks to Shannon. (It was probably more like two minutes. Adrenaline surges and poetry readings slow time with equal effect.) However long it took, Ashley managed to get to the slipway before Shannon reached shore.

Just as Ashley arrived at Brandon's side, Shannon caught a break. "Sud-denly, a nice sheet of white water picked up his board," Brandon marvels, "and washed him right into the shore!"

More than anything else, Shannon remembers that solitary white wave—that final shoreward thrust that moved him quickly out of harm's way. It would become a life-altering experience for him:

> I was getting nowhere, so I decided to pray. I knew I had no strength or ability to defend myself against the shark. I knew that I needed help from someone greater than the shark—namely the One who created it! I remember thinking, "'If there's a God, let me pray and see." So, I prayed out loud. I said, "God, if you're real, please get me out of the water."
>
> The instant I said that, all of my fear and panic just seemed to disappear. I felt calmer and stopped shaking. Thoughts of getting attacked stopped racing through my mind. I knew I would make it out. The best thing ever is when you are in a hopeless place but you are given hope! Then, I looked over my shoulder, and there it was!! The wave I longed for so desperately just popped up out of nowhere. It was not there, and then it was. I was confused by it, but flippin' stoked! I couldn't figure out where it came from because there was no set coming over the point, but I knew this wave was my ticket out of there. I said, "Thank you, God!" out loud and rode the wave on my belly all the way to shore with my right hand up in the air. It was the most amazing thing.

As he neared the shore, he steered a few meters left of the slipway and toward reef rocks that were a little closer to him. He reached waist-deep water, with his board floating behind him, and tried to stand as friends negotiated the slippery rocks trying to reach him. As they did, incoming waves repeatedly rammed the board against Shannon's backside and knocked him down. Shannon was pale and in shock but grateful to be ashore. Partly due to the surfboard knocking him down, his benevolent emotions were short-lived. Adrenaline highs are notoriously followed by dramatic mood swings.

"Suddenly, I was really bummed," he admits. "I got very, very angry and was certain I was going to lose my hand or two of my fingers. And it was my right hand—my stronger, dominant, and more coordinated hand. I felt I might be disabled, unable to write, wrestle, catch, or punch. As I stood up in the shallows, my brother and friends gathered around me. I was shaking blood from my hand, and I threw my board down into the water in frustration. Then a small wave picked up my board and slammed it against my butt, knocking me down."

"Oh, my word, oh, my word, Shannon, are you all right?" Alistair yelped as he and three others surrounded their wounded mate. "Shannon was cross," Alistair recollects. "He was saying, 'Damn it! Damn it!' as he looked at his arm. He seemed calm, but I don't think he realized the magnitude of what had happened."

As Brandon phoned for an ambulance, Ryan Fox, his wettie pulled to his waist, assumed the role of medic. He conscripted the leg rope from Devon Swart's board to use as a tourniquet and affixed it to Shannon's arm just above the elbow. Shannon held his arm above his head as others disconnected him from his surfboard. The undercarriage of his thruster bore a huge bite mark that encompassed the entire width of the board in the fin area. Brandon, with a phone at his ear, led four other surfers as they escorted his brother up the slipway.

"I kept telling him everything would be okay and that I had called an ambulance," Brandon recounts. "Shannon was extremely distressed and frustrated, and he was making audible 'Ahhh!' sounds. When we got to the car park, he was losing a lot of blood, so Pierre Strauss wrapped a towel around the injured hand and wrist. Shannon complained about the disgusting feel of the cotton on his exposed bones and muscles."

Everyone thought Shannon was in pain. Oddly, he wasn't.

"I had no pain whatsoever," he insists, "not when I was bitten, not at the hospital, not the next day, and not the next week."

But in the car park, Shannon's frustrations were quickly matched by those of his brother and his friends. For whatever reason—perhaps because of Brandon's description of the injury—medical assistance was not dispatched. This became a lasting sore point with Brad Coetzee.

"Shannon's brother was on the phone to the emergency hospital and the people there were not helpful," Brad recollects bitterly. "They never sent an ambulance, and I know that because we stayed at Nahoon until dusk. It pisses me off to this day."

With a worse bite, of course, Shannon's life might have depended on that ambulance. The timely arrival of an ambulance at the same car park in

Ryan Fox maintains tourniquet on Shannon's arm and escorts him ashore. (Courtesy of Screenocean/Reuters)

Shannon elevates injured arm to reduce bleeding (Courtesy of Screenocean/ Reuters)

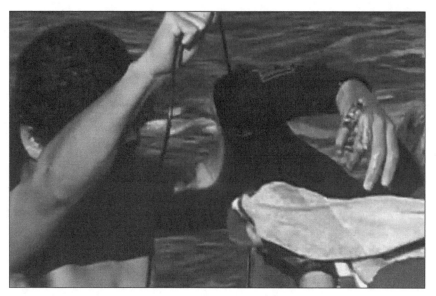

Shannon suffers nearly-amputated fingers and broken wrist. (Courtesy of Screenocean/Reuters)

Shannon awaiting ride to hospital (Courtesy of Sean Smith)

1994 had allowed medics to rescue Andrew Carter from the very brink of cardiac arrest. He had needed plasma desperately. Even a five-minute delay might have doomed him.

After a seemingly interminable thirty minutes, Brandon resorted to self-help. He bundled his brother and Ryan into the back seat of his grandmother's Mazda, spun out on the sand-glazed asphalt, and raced to the hospital. Alistair, Brad, and others stayed behind to guard the surfboards.

"After they left, it was really calm," Brad reflects. "We all stood around the car park and retold the story. We stayed until dusk, describing the attack to everyone we saw. Nobody went close to the beach after that, and it was closed the next day."

The shark flags were up for ten days, but some boys surfed there the next day...just as they had after the Carter-Corby attacks in 1994.

That evening, in the gloaming, Brad surveyed the bleak gray reef and reminisced about all of the warnings that he and his friends routinely ignored when they surfed Nahoon:

> I thought of the plaque that is mounted next to the slipway. It lists the names of seven Nahoon surfers who have died. I thought about the Natal Sharks Board warning. And I thought of something that Brian and Ashley Grimmer's father told us once. He's a scuba diver who explores the reef regularly. He always told us that we were absolutely mad to surf Nahoon Reef. He said there are almost always enormous sharks in the water there.

Was it this combination of warnings that had prompted Brad to leave the water just before Shannon's attack? Was it the oily scent of sardines? Was it the subconscious awareness of a gull diving for silvery treats? He isn't sure. Whatever it was, Brad had left the water early.

"I'm only nervous about sharks when I see them," Brad insists, "but I've learned to listen to that feeling."

11
REPAIRS

Brandon needed less than seven minutes to negotiate the five kilometers of afternoon traffic between the reef and the Medicross Medical Centre on Pearce Road. He sped, veered, honked, flashed headlamps, and ran robots (stop lights) while making cell phone calls—hardly recommended for a seventeen-year-old with a learner's permit and an impermissible carload of people.

Shannon grumbled the whole way, disgusted by the feel of cotton fibers touching bones and tendons laid bare by the bite. The fabric of the towel was soaked in blood, much of it clotted and tugging uncomfortably at the carrion that, an hour earlier, had been a healthy hand and wrist. Ryan was seated to Shannon's right, behind the driver (South Africans drive on the left). He supported Shannon's elevated right arm and maintained tension on the makeshift tourniquet.

Brandon called his dad first. Shane was in Johannesburg with his daughter and mother to attend one of Candice's swim meets in nearby Bloemfontein. Shane was driving alone on busy Rivonia Road when he got the call from his eldest.

"Dad," Brandon blurted, "are you on medical aid?" The boy forgot the good-news-first protocol when reporting family emergencies.

"Why?!" Shane demanded, pulling off the road instantly. His heart rate was soaring.

"Don't worry; everything is okay," Brandon assured him, restoring the protocol. "Shannon was attacked by a great white shark."

And there went the protocol again. Shane entertained images of his son's severed limbs drifting to shore on a crimson tide.

"Take him to Medicross," Shane told him, "and I'll phone Sandra to meet you." Shannon's aunt, Sandra Leigh Quirk (nee Ainslie), lived in East London. Shane peppered Brandon with questions about Shannon's condition, but his eldest was too consumed with his cross-town motor derby. He tossed the phone to Ryan in the back seat.

"He's okay," Ryan reiterated. "We're taking him to hospital."

"Can I speak to Shannon?" Shane asked, his tone bearing an air of insistence.

"He's fine," Ryan reassured him, clumsily trying to manage the phone, the tourniquet, and his friend's arm.

"Yes, but I'd like to speak to Shannon!" Shane urged. Shane was irritated, but Ryan kept the phone.

"He's okay, really...he just got bitten on the hand and arm, and..."

"Let me speak to Shannon!" Shane yelled. Brandon could hear his dad from the front seat.

Parents don't want to hear squat from other people when their children are hurt. They want to hear from their children. They know that people always minimize a child's injuries when communicating with parents. Ryan finally relented, handing the phone to his injured mate.

"I'm fine, Dad," Shannon assured his father, his left hand fumbling awkwardly with the phone. "It bit my fingers and arm, but I'm all right." In reality, he wasn't as confident as he sounded. He still thought he might lose those two fingers, but he knew he would live. Bad news could wait.

Brandon screeched to a halt in front of Medicross and sprinted inside. An attendant saw Shannon in less than five minutes and escorted the boy in his still-damp wetsuit to a trauma room. A nurse wearing the white garb of a nun met him there and pulled the blood-clotted towel from his wounds, its loose threads tugging nauseatingly at raw flesh. Shannon fretted aloud about his dangling digits, but the Sister offered encouragement. "I wouldn't worry," she assured the wide-eyed lad, her smile exuding confidence and reassurance. "You won't lose your fingers."

One thing you always notice about health care professionals is that they don't react to blood with nearly the same degree of alarm as those who are leaking it. In 1982, ski patrollers at Keystone Ski Resort in Colorado were unable to help me stop a severe nose bleed that had all the earmarks of a water main break. I opted to ski the two miles and 2,300 vertical feet down to the medical clinic rather than bother Ski Patrol with a carry. They gave me a medium-sized white towel that turned solid red during the descent. At the base, a fifteen-year-old boy was visibly shocked by the bloody sight. Noticing this, I jokingly said to him, "Deer hunter!" "You were SHOT?!" he yelped. Inside the clinic, however, the doctor, a thirty-something from Chicago, merely smiled, summoned up his best Swedish accent, and regaled me with Sven and Ollie jokes. After seeing real gunshot wounds at Chicago General, he probably rated my exsanguinations somewhere in the boo-boo category. Chemical cautery fixed the problem.

Shannon needed treatment to stop blood loss too, so the Sister began cutting away the arms and sides of Shannon's Reef wetsuit so they could peel it down to his waist. The wettie had been a gift from his friend, Nick Pike, and just that fast, Shannon's day had become as expensive as it had been traumatic—to the tune of $550 in lost gear. He couldn't have cared less.

"I had already decided I would never surf again," he laughs, "so the board and the wetsuit didn't matter to me at all."

Brandon and Ryan waited patiently while the Sister spent ten minutes cleansing and disinfecting his wounds. Then she gave Shannon a pain shot that he didn't need. He truly didn't feel pain from his injuries, and more oddly, he suffered no nervous reaction either, at least not that day.

Uncontrollable shaking is a common byproduct of strong adrenaline surges, but only after they subside. Right after I took the bar exam in 1977, I drove to Delaware to visit friends at Dover Air Force Base where I had been stationed in the early seventies. After a softball game, several of us went to a McDonald's in Smyrna, Delaware. A close friend of mine, Tom, and his wife and baby were in the car with me, Tom in the front passenger seat. Suddenly, a group of Pagans motorcycle gang members drove up and the leader, a huge bearded and tattooed sort, walked over to my open driver's side window, pointed at Tom, and threatened him. I shooed Tom's wife and baby out of the car on the passenger side and cracked my driver's side door open in case the man drew a weapon. The threats continued until Tom, who probably weighed all of 130 pounds soaking wet, finally got upset and started to get out of the car to confront the man, forcing me to grab Tom and throw him back in his seat. The gang leader's beef with Tom was a case of mistaken identity, but the threat was fearsomely real. Eventually, he uttered one last "I'll getcha" to Tom and drove off. Only after the police arrived did Tom and I begin shaking uncontrollably. (The police knew the gang leader involved and advised us not to file charges. Four of Tom's friends and I stood armed guard inside of his home for the better part of a week.)

Similarly, Shannon's shakes didn't come until well after his attack. Twice in 2002, while paddling back out to a lineup, his hand touched something under his board that felt like a shark. He flashed back to his shark encounter, panicked, shook like a leaf, and fled the water. While standing onshore at the South African Surfing Championships that same year, he started shaking while merely discussing his shark attack with friends.

After his pain shot, though, Shannon's manic Monday became a pleasant float through Fantasy Land. "I slept a lot and don't remember much after that," he says. "Somewhere along the way, a physician attempted to sew up my wounds but quickly determined that my fingers required more extensive surgery. He re-bandaged my hand and scheduled me for surgery at another hospital later that evening."

Medicross personnel recommended a highly-skilled plastic surgeon, but he was operating that day at East London Private Hospital. The surgeon agreed to squeeze Shannon into his evening schedule.

Brandon continued notifying family members. He reached his mother, Michelle, in Cape Town, and a bit later, talked to his grandmother, Elaine, who was with Candice in Johannesburg. "Shannon's been bitten by a shark," Brandon told both ladies, "but he's okay...the shark bit his hand and arm, but he's having surgery to repair it tonight."

Elaine Ainslie was sure she was taking delivery of a giant load of hooey.

"You tell me how he is right this minute! You're not lying to me, are you? Is he okay? I want the truth! Tell me!!"

Finally convinced that Shannon would live, Elaine launched into a tirade about the sport that no mother—or, in this case, grandmother—can love. "How can you boys surf?" Elaine asked rhetorically. Brandon attempted no reply. Why would he? He was wondering the same thing.

Shannon's aunt, Sandra Quirk, reached Medicross at 3:30 p.m., less than thirty minutes after taking Brandon's call. When she arrived, Brandon and Ryan drove back to the reef to retrieve their gear.

Sandra was amazed when she saw her nephew. The lean, blond-headed youth was sitting shirtless in the trauma room wearing a tired but happy smile. There was a mellow air about him, something akin to a youthful burglar enjoying his fourth beer after a clean getaway. And truly, Shannon had gotten away with something that day.

"Shannon was sitting on the edge of the bed with his shredded wetsuit pulled down to his waist," Sandra recalls. "Brandon had run off with his clothes, so he had nothing to change into. I was amazed that he looked so calm and happy. I will always remember that happy, peaceful look on his face."

The pleasant look was opiate-aided, of course, but Sandra detected other reasons for her nephew's equanimity.

"He told me he had been fascinated by how small his hand had looked in the shark's mouth," Sandra remarks. "He stared the shark in the face, and the shark stared back with his big enormous eye. He told me that God had saved him. After the attack, he prayed over and over again for God to get him safely back to shore. He kept talking about the shark's huge eye."

At 4 p.m., Sandra followed the ambulance that transported Shannon to East London Private Hospital, but she made a detour to pick up her daughter, Denra Friess, along the way. The surgical hospital proved to be unusually convenient. Located on Albany Street, the facility's front entrance was little more than a 9-iron shot from Shannon's home.

Shannon talked to his cousin before surgery. "I was excited to see Denra," he remembers, "because I was relieved to know that I would not lose my fingers or my hand." Denra was also relieved. "You are extremely blessed and lucky to be alive or not to have lost an arm or leg," she asserted. "Most shark attacks are more serious!"

Denra has another recollection:

A moment I remember in the hospital is when I saw Shannon in a wheelchair with bloodied dressing around his wounds and I asked him why he surfed. His reply was simply, "I love it." It is so profound that a young boy still had his love and faith after being in such a horrifying ordeal. His simple answer has stayed with me for all these years, and I think it speaks volumes about his character and the man he has become today.

Down at hospital registration, Sandra was providing her injured nephew with another blessing. "My brother had no medical insurance," Sandra explains, "and the hospital required a substantial deposit before they would complete the admission. I left Medicross at about 4:30 p.m. to get money for the deposit and returned at 5 p.m." Later, Shane worked hard to pay her back for the expensive procedure.

"The surgeon agreed to operate on Shannon later that evening after his last scheduled case," Sandra adds. "Shannon went into surgery at 8:30 p.m. and came out at 10 p.m."

At 4 a.m. on Tuesday morning, South Africa's newest shark victim awoke from his post-anesthetic sleep. Alone in the dark, he could feel something solid—something awkward—on his right arm. An elbow-to-fingertip cast secured a broken wrist. Beneath the cast lay a skillful reconstruction of the bones, muscles, and ligaments of his two fingers and a thirty-stitch repair of a large laceration on his forearm. He got a bigger surprise when he turned on the television. Just fourteen hours after his attack, Shannon was on *BBC World News*.

The Morning After

With the help of an aide to South African president Thabo Mbeki, Shane was able to catch an early plane to East London on Tuesday morning, arriving at the hospital at 7:30 a.m. "Shannon was all smiles and relaxed when I arrived at his side," his father reflects. "He told me he thought another surfer had hit him. Then he said he went flying through the air and ended up face to face with a shark. He said he had to stick his hand in the shark's mouth to push it away."

Candice and Elaine arrived at the hospital half an hour after Shane, having made the nearly 1,000-kilometer trip from Johannesburg via overnight bus. Candice was overjoyed to see her brother. "I kissed him on the lips for the first time, and he allowed me to! I was very, very happy. He was smiling a lot," she remembers of her sibling. "He was just happy to be alive, I think."

Brandon tried to convince his mom that she didn't need to make the long flight from Cape Town...that Shannon was fine. But Patton's Third Army couldn't keep a mother from her injured child. Michelle made the 1,000 kilometer trip on Tuesday as well. "She was stressing out and overreacting to the max," Shannon says. "She told me the attack was a sign from God that I should stop surfing. At the time, I more or less agreed with her."

By late morning on Tuesday, the lean little kid with the curly blond hair and the huge arm cast had become a national celebrity. The Tuesday morning edition of the East London Daily Dispatch featured a photo of Shannon and Alistair. Then, Radio ALGOA FM and one of the newspaper's reporters interviewed him in his hospital room. Shannon kept wondering why there was so much fuss.

Brandon and Ryan already knew why. They had known since Monday afternoon.

12
ENTERING THE PANTHEON

When Brandon and Ryan returned to the reef to retrieve their boards that Monday afternoon, Alistair, Brad, and Karl greeted them with extraordinary news. The news involved the two foreigners who had been at the reef that day—Canadian backpacker, Sean Smith, and Aussie surfer, Nathan Millett. During the attack, the Canadian had been sitting atop that huge boulder at the head of the slipway.

He had been up there for a reason.

Visitors

Sean Smith arrived in East London on Friday, three days before the attack. He and a friend, David Files, were at the end of a six-week-long bicycle tour that had begun in Cape Town. Sean's visa was expiring that very day, but he arrived at the Department of Home Affairs office just as the office was closing for the weekend. He returned to Sugarshack Backpackers, a popular hostel on the Eastern Esplanade, and hoped to extend his visa the following Monday.

While at Sugarshack, Sean met Nathan Millet, an Aussie who was on a planned four-month surfing tour. Nathan had been in South Africa for three months and had only eleven days left on his visa.

On the following Monday morning, while Shannon was still in school, Nathan surfed at Nahoon Reef, and Sean tended to his visa extension. Both men returned to Sugarshack at around noon. After lunch, Nathan planned to join a group of Aussies back at the reef and invited Sean to come along. Sean was not a surfer but was interested in seeing the sport in action. Riding in the van together, Sean noticed Nathan's Sony High-8 video camera and offered to video him surfing. Nathan happily accepted.

The View from the Water

At 2:30 p.m., Nathan finished riding a wave and began paddling back out. Two locals, Shannon and Alistair, were about fifteen or twenty meters to his right. Nathan happened to be watching as Shannon was preparing to catch a wave. That's when Nathan noticed something else:

> About five meters on the other side of Shannon, between him and the point of the reef, I saw the snout of a huge great white come vertically out of the water by about one and a half meters and take a look around. I heard someone scream, but I don't know who it was. Then the shark submerged, and I remember thinking, "Who's it going to be?" Then, just a second later, I saw Shannon launched upside down in the air and taken down by the shark.
>
> Moments later, I saw Shannon pop up on the surface. He was shaking his arm which was mangled. His wrist was dangling and he was clearly in shock. I yelled to him, "Get on your board and paddle in!"
>
> I remember, also, that there were two Aussie surfers that were further out than Shannon. They had to paddle in through the very area where Shannon was hit.

Shannon had been totally focused on catching the wave. He had not seen the breaching shark and had not heard the initial scream.

Nathan remembers the moments that followed:

> I was with Shannon as he stumbled onto the rocks. Other surfers were waiting to assist him. Someone applied a leg rope to Shannon's arm as a tourniquet. I remember thinking to myself that this might be a bad idea since there was no arterial bleeding. Tourniquets can cause harm to limbs when applied improperly or needlessly. I pulled Shannon's board out of the water and noted a huge bite mark over the fin area.

The View from the Rock

For Sean, who was videoing surfers from the top of the boulder, events unfolded less dramatically…at least initially:

> I was at loose ends for the afternoon. I ran into Nathan Millett as he was about to leave for a surfing session at Nahoon Reef,

and he invited me to join them, so I grabbed my camera (a 35mm SLR...2000), and we caught a ride in a VW Van full of Ozzies. Noticing that Nathan had a camcorder with him, I asked if he'd like me to shoot some footage of him while I hung out at the beach. As I recall, he said that would be great, gave me a quick rundown on the controls, and headed for the water.

The large boulder at the south end of the parking lot provided an ideal perch to sit and film from, so I set up there and started shooting and experimenting with the camcorder. The view was amazing but the break where the surfing was happening was too far away for me to tell which surfer was which, so, instead of Nathan getting some footage of himself, he was going to end up with a bunch of random riders doing their thing.

When Shannon was hit, my perception through the very small viewfinder was of two surfers paddling for the same wave, colliding at the peak and crashing as the wave passed by them. So that was that—a bit of commotion on the wave, two boards up in the air, two riders down, not an uncommon occurrence. So I pressed the red button and stopped shooting.

No one was attempting to stand up, just paddling hard for the beach. This was my first indication that something strange was happening; surfing is a somewhat solitary endeavor and an entire break full of riders heading in simultaneously was odd, so I started shooting again. I believe I caught a shot of every single surfer paddling for the beach in a "V" formation.

As the first guys hit the rocky shore, I thought I heard the word "shark," and then noticed one of the surfers struggling in the shallows. I focused on that guy as he started to receive some support from the other guys, one fellow improvising a tourniquet around his arm with a board leash and a couple of others helping him out of the water and up the shore. As the surfers helped Shannon past me and into the parking lot, I got a little self-conscious about filming this fellow in distress. Strangely, still photos seemed alright, so I swapped cameras and snapped a few 35mm shots of the scene as Shannon was helped to the ground, and someone wrapped a towel around his arm and hand.

"Shannon's face was white," Sean recalls. "His wetsuit was ripped, and his arm had significant damage and was dripping blood." Sean also marveled at the huge bite mark on the board and recalls a moment of revelation:

> People were debating what to do at this point. I believe someone called an ambulance, but Shannon's brother showed up with his car—I think he ran from us to get it from the upper part of the lot. They took off for the emergency room. Somewhere in there, just after Shannon left I think, one of the guys said something like, "Did that guy with the camera film it?" That's when the light bulb went off in my head and suddenly the whole event coalesced into a totally different context. I wasn't sure what I had on tape but thought I'd caught some of the incident. The footage would reveal that the second "board" that I saw flip into the air was actually the left pectoral fin of the shark as it rolled into the backside of the wave, with Shannon's forearm in its mouth. There was a second surfer though, and he must have had a front-row seat as Shannon was hit and dragged under.

The "front row seat" had been occupied by Alistair, and by now, everyone at the reef knew about the attack. In mere hours, everyone in the world would know. Sean recalls events that followed their return to Sugarshack:

> We hustled back to the Sugarshack to watch the footage on a bigger screen and see just what I had captured. The whole hostel and a local reporter (word traveled fast!) crowded around as Nathan hooked the camera up, and holy sh-t, there it was! We watched it a bunch of times—slow motion, backward, forward. As I said, big shark fan here, and the talk was of the rarity of this footage. I was pretty sure I'd seen everything there was on great whites, and this was totally unique.

Revelation

Early on Tuesday morning, when Shane arrived from "Joburg" to join his son at the hospital, news of Sean Smith's boulder-top activity awaited him. Stunned, he raced from Shannon's bedside, and with Brandon and Ryan in tow, drove to Sugarshack.

Catching that unexpected wave to shore may not have been the most amazing thing that had happened to Shannon that day. More amazing, perhaps, was the fact that Shannon Ainslie had possibly become the first surfer in history to be videotaped while under attack by a great white shark...and perhaps only the second human.[37]

Shane raced back to the hospital to pick up his son before noon checkout. When SABC-1 Television and a throng of reporters ambushed the boy at the exit, the fifteen-year-old finally understood all the fuss—there was a video of his attack.

Shane drove all three of his kids and Alistair Cokayne back to Sugarshack to view the video. Shane fretted that the images might be too much for his son. "I don't think you should watch this," he said in an exploratory tone, "it may be too hectic."

One Word

When you get to know the wonderful people of South Africa—and they truly are such—you will detect that they use the word "hectic" more than Westerners. Oh, sure, it's a common English word, but in South Africa, it is used far more frequently and carries far broader meaning. "The meeting was hectic." "The traffic was hectic." "Exams were hectic." These are normal usages everywhere. But in South Africa you hear it used in the context of a harder life: "The riot was hectic." "The house fire was hectic." "The shark attack was hectic."

"Hectic" sums up life in South Africa today, a life rife with challenges both in the sea and out of it. The vast, wild, and beautiful country has weathered gas shortages, international isolation, racial strife, political change, limited services, high unemployment, government corruption, elevated crime, and the difficult task of re-emerging on the international economic, political, and athletic scene. Even today, militant sects threaten suppression of whites in the country while the nation's ruling party fumbles in its pursuit of the racial unity and fairness so magnanimously sought by Nelson Mandela, a man who had 10,000 days' worth of reasons not to be magnanimous.

It's funny how words differ in their meaning in different cultures. Shannon describes another South African peculiarity—the use of the word "now." If you say you'll do something "now," that means you'll do it right now. If you say you'll do it "now now," that means you'll do it soon. Saying you'll do it "just now" means, well, you'll try to get around to it.

Anyway, one can hardly fault a South African, regardless of race or age, for finding life exciting, unpredictable and, yes, a bit hectic. It's certainly hectic when you watch a video of an Audi-sized shark trying to make a meal out of you.

A Tale of Two Circles

Shannon watched in rapt silence as the video played. The magnitude of his peril became instantly clear. He watched it over and over, sometimes in slow motion. The size of the beast roaring out of the wave was shocking. It resembled a submarine ripping the surface after an emergency blow. "Look at the size of that fin!" someone exclaimed. With each replay, the dark, towering fin, probably a pectoral, rolled seaward at the top of the wave as Shannon somersaulted in the air and disappeared behind the crest. Visible just under the face of the wave was the surfboard being wrenched violently from side to side by the immense animal.

Starting at 8 a.m. on Tuesday, Sean and Nathan were bombarded by a constant stream of phone calls from reporters, news agencies, and television stations wanting to purchase the video rights. On Tuesday afternoon, Reuters representatives flew in to meet with the two men. They met in a pub initially and then moved the meeting to the East London Aquarium where the video could be reviewed more easily.

Willie Maritz, Curator of the East London Aquarium and a marine biologist, was present, and he saw something in the video that no one else had noticed. "What's that?" he remarked, with a keen eye for things aquatic. A day or so would pass before the world would learn what Willie had seen.

Following the viewing, Reuters agreed to pay $10,000 for the video rights, a sum that Sean and Nathan agreed to split 50-50.

Because Shannon was a minor, Reuters also sought a model release from his father. Shane signed the release without negotiating for it, a move questioned by his sister:

I had an argument with Sandra in her car. Reuters was negotiating with Sean Smith and Nathan Millet, and Reuters wanted me to sign something. Sandra felt I should be negotiating too, for Shannon's benefit, but I don't usually operate that way. I felt guilty about it later and made inquiries with an attorney back in Johannesburg. He told me that Shannon had no rights in the video, that it belonged to Smith and Millett.

Shane's legal advisors were correct. When a person photographs or videos someone in public, it is the photographer and sometimes the camera owner, if different, who hold the copyright interest. The owner is free to use the images as long as they are not used to slander photo subjects or cast photo subjects in a false light. There are exceptions to this free use, of course. You cannot use photos or videos of people taken in places where they have a reasonable expectation of privacy or taken where photography is prohibited. And you cannot make commercial use of people's recognizable images without their permission, especially minors. Reuters sought the release after interviewing Shannon on camera at the reef.

Reuters' initial distribution of the video to its worldwide affiliates opened a whole new dimension to the story. Late in the week of the attack, the *Daily Dispatch* published a screen capture from the video. In the image, Shannon was upside down in the air. On the right side of the image was the attacking shark, circled by the editors.

But there was something else in the photo. There was a second circle… on the left side of Shannon in the image and very close to him. The circle marked the anomaly that Willie Maritz had noticed at the East London Aquarium earlier in the week. There had been two sharks in the wave, one on each side of Shannon. He had been simultaneously attacked by two great whites—highly unusual given their solitary hunting style. By week's end, the video had become a worldwide media sensation, as had the boy who survived it.

Return Home

Shannon spent two days recovering at home. Shane occasionally propped Shannon's arm on a pillow to offer comfort, but again, his son was in no pain. The real pain was served up by the media. They gave the youth no quarter. News of the attack continued to run on national and worldwide television even before Reuters released the video. ETV and several other television stations came by the house on Tuesday and Wednesday for interviews. Radio stations from around the world were calling "every five or ten minutes" Shannon recalls. Friends were calling and dropping by. He wondered about his return to school. Would his 1,200 classmates want to hear the story? Would they ask, "What's it like to dance with the devil...or two devils?"

Video captures a second shark in the wave. (Courtesy of Screenocean/Reuters)

Candice and Brandon found out first. They returned to school on Wednesday and were mobbed. "It was hectic," Candice recalls. That word again! Candice, who was in her last year of primary school, Standard 5 or seventh grade, even found a way to benefit from Shannon's shark encounter in a non-monetary way. "I did a school project about the attack using Shannon's [badly bitten] surfboard, the attack video, and TV footage as props," she recalls gleefully. "And I got an 80 percent on it!"

Shannon didn't run the gauntlet at school until Thursday. "I was like a TV star," he laughs. And, indeed, he was. He had been featured on national television every single night that week. Kids and teachers alike mobbed him with questions—attention so persistent that, one week later, Shannon had to take evasive action when he arrived late for a school assembly. As he started to enter near the front, students began ignoring the speaker, pointing at the youth, and murmuring audibly. Not wishing to be a distraction, Shannon returned to the hallway and re-entered the auditorium from the rear.

School officials quickly realized that students needed to get the affair out of their system. So, two weeks after the attack, a special assembly was called. Shannon, Brandon, Alistair, and Ryan sat on the front edge of the stage and fielded student questions read aloud by a school prefect.

The fin-area of Shannon's surfboard bore a complete upper jaw imprint of the shark's teeth. Willie Maritz measured the bite radius and concluded that the bite was that of a great white of "between 4 and 4.5 meters in length." That's roughly 13 to 15 feet...about 2,000 pounds of fish or fifteen times Shannon's weight at the time. As it happens, the plastic fins of Shannon's board may have saved the boy's life. "The fins had to have injured the soft upper palate of the shark's mouth," he insists.

His lower arm cast stayed on for six weeks, a non-surfing window that produced a degree of introspection about his sport and near-certain proof that surfing is, in fact, an addiction. "For two to three days, I swore I would never surf again," he remembers. "After five or six days, I swore I would never surf at Nahoon again. Then, after a week, I was excited about surfing again, and it didn't matter where!"

Shannon at scene of attack after surgery (Courtesy of Sean Smith)

Even Shane, the man who had so tirelessly encouraged his sons to surf, wanted Shannon to wait. His youngest son, however, yearned for the waves.

"Everyone in the family was upset that he wanted to surf again," Candice recalls. "But Shannon's attitude was, 'It wasn't God's will that I die.' He kept pointing out, 'It's the shark's ocean, not mine.'"

On the latter point, the entire family agreed.

Reality Star

Shannon's attack became instant newsreel fare worldwide, and soon, television producers were after the story. The video was featured on *Impact: Stories of Survival* (2002) and later in the decade, enjoyed an energetic revival on *Animal Planet* (2004), *Headline Attacks* (2008), *After the Attack* (2008), *Untamed & Uncut* (2008), *Weird, True, & Freaky* (2008), and *When Animals Strike* (2009).[38] His encounter, of course, is annual fare on *Discovery Channel's* Shark Week. Only one other person, a swimmer, had been videoed while being attacked by a great white.

Perhaps the strangest post-attack media intervention came when one television producer set out to prepare a computer animation showing the

Alistair Cokayne, Brandon Ainslie, and Shannon Ainslie at Nahoon Reef following attack (Courtesy of Shane Annesley)

attack sequence from underwater—an animation readily available on You-Tube. The only information that the producers had about the attack, of course, came from the Reuters video, from Shannon's recollections, and perhaps from family members to whom Shannon had spoken about the attack. Shannon and the two great whites were the only ones present during the attack, however, and the two sharks weren't talking.

Shannon explained exactly what had happened—that he had been hit from his back left side by the shark, had been knocked upside down in the air with his right hand caught in the shark's teeth, had ended up underwater with a giant predator two feet in front of him, had seen his hand look small in the shark's mouth, had been bumped from behind, and had surfaced with a shredded hand and broken wrist.

The resulting animation reflects each point. In it, Shannon gets hit while riding a wave, flips upside down in the air, and lands in the water. In reality, he wasn't riding a wave when he was hit; he was paddling to catch one and in the process of popping up—but, so far, so good.

Next, the animation shows Shannon in an upright position underwater with the shark clutching Shannon's right arm in its teeth and dragging the boy backward through the water. Suddenly, a second great white appears from behind Shannon and tries to bite the boy's head off. The interloper misses, collides with the snout of the first shark, and causes the first shark to release the boy's arm. Thus freed, Shannon makes his escape.

This sequence seems to comport with Shannon's comments. In reality, though, his arm was not clutched in the shark's mouth except during the initial impact at the surface. He has no recollection of being dragged through the water by his arm, and he never knew there was a second shark in the water until he saw the circled photo in the *Daily Dispatch*.

"I thought it was pretty cool when I saw it," Shannon laughs, "but if my arm had been in the shark's mouth, I would have had bite marks on both sides of my arm, or I would have lost my arm, and I don't even remember being bitten. I'm sure the bite happened when I first got hit while on my board. And I'm pretty sure the shark that I was face-to-face with under the water was the same one that swam past me under the water and then bumped me from behind."

In all fairness, the producers accurately captured the essence of the boy's predicament as reported to them. Shannon had been underwater, bleeding,

Nahoon Reef and boulder from which Sean Smith videoed attack (Courtesy of Brandon Ainslie)

Shannon sitting on surfer's walk at Nahoon Reef (Courtesy of Travis Naude)

eye-to-eye with a one-ton shark, and in the presence of two sharks. As for the hand in the shark's mouth, Sandra and Shane both recall Shannon commenting about his "hand looking small in the shark's mouth"...probably because he extended his hand to ward off the beast two feet in front of him. Anyone hearing this comment and seeing Shannon's cast would assume that a shark had held the boy by the arm. The video also shows Shannon flipping upside down with his hand likely caught, at least momentarily, in the shark's mouth.

One thing is certain—Shannon's situation didn't need any embellishment. More than a decade after the attack, images of that black submarine ramming Shannon and that second shark closing in from the opposite side still bring gasps. The producers were also entirely correct in their principal conclusion: Shannon was in the presence of two great whites that day, was attacked, and was in most extreme peril.

The docile shark that had stared at Shannon under the waves, by the way, was almost certainly not the animal that had attacked him on the surface. Shannon never fully focused on this fact until ten years after the event. Confronted with video evidence that the attacking fish had violently wrenched his surfboard back and forth at the surface, Shannon agrees that the docile shark must have been the second animal in the wave—the second circled fin in the *Daily Dispatch* photo. To be sure, the boy's underwater confrontation with sheer death was astonishing. As the staring contest unfolded, Shannon was too stunned to think, saving him from panic and sudden movement that might have cost him his life. A shark's usual prey, a seal, always bolts rapidly. This prey just floated there, staring at it and reaching toward it. So, we are left to wonder what the second shark was thinking as she peered at the youth.

"Ugliest seal ever?"

Or perhaps she was trying to apologize for her mate.

"Sorry," she might have been saying. "He gets this way when he drinks."

13

TRADING PLACES WITH MICHAL

While Shannon was recovering from his attack, hundreds of people—family, friends, students, teachers, reporters, and strangers—wanted to know about the *last* time the boy had surfed. A few, though, most notably the producers of a brand new television series called *Ripley's Believe It Or Not*, were interested in the *next* time. They knew Shannon would surf again. It's an addiction, remember? They wanted to tape a segment about a kid who goes back to the sea after a tangle with two great whites.

Ripley's film crew arrived in East London three or four days before Shannon's cast came off in September and worked with him on the shoot. "I was weary and scared, and I was nervous about surfing and about appearing on television," he remembers. "I was excited too, but I wasn't at all excited about surfing at Nahoon. I just couldn't face Nahoon quite yet, so I decided to go to Yellow Sands."

Yellow Sands Point lies fifteen kilometers up the coast from Nahoon Reef—a twenty-two minute swim for a motivated great white. *Ripley's* crew was happy with the choice. As the swell breaks around the tip of the Point, the waves flow into the bay at close to right angles, giving land-based camera crews the ability to film surfers at close range.

Shannon's decision to travel up the coast was understandable. When a black-button spider bites you in a closet in the back bedroom upstairs, you're always leery of that closet in the back bedroom upstairs, even after you kill the spider. Still, you use other closets without a single thought.

Shannon felt he would be safer at Yellow Sands, but his sense of security there was illusory. The Wild Coast offers no haven from marine attack, and, as one of Shannon's former Border teammates can attest, Yellow Sands certainly does not.

Yellow Sand, Red Water

On Tuesday morning, February 16, 2010, 19-year-old Michal du Plessis (me-KHAL dew-pleh-SEE) emerged from his home near Yellow Sands

Caravan Park to survey the morning sea. "Yellows," as locals call it, is a popular vacation spot where visitors can rent a caravan home (mobile home) and enjoy a quiet week of swimming, surfing, paddle skiing, and braais.

From the bluffs, the curly-haired youth took in the panoramic view of the bay below him. His eyes followed the gentle arc of the beach to the right where the beach ends at the mouth of the Kwelera (Kweh-LEGH-ah) River. On the far side of the bay, a promontory called Yellow Sands Point extends into the sea, sheltering the bay. A foggy overcast had started to lift, and small patches of blue sky gave safe passage to beams of sunlight. A light breeze wafted in from the ocean, driving pleasant rollers around the Point and into the bay. The water was clear and free of river silt, a gift of the on-shore winds.

The sea beckoned, and two of Michal's best mates, Rodger Berkhout and Logan Philpott, talked Michal into surfing that day. Michal then called Aiden Leppan and Oscar Miller. Michal, Rodger, and Aiden hiked down the bluff from the Caravan Park, paddled across the Kwelera, and hiked out along the Point to drop in. Oscar Miller, who lived ten kilometers away, joined his friends twenty minutes later, driving out onto the Point in his red "bakkie," a covered pick-up truck.

Yellow Point sets up a bit like Nahoon Reef. Surfers catch waves coming around the Point from the west and ride them into the bay and toward the beach. There are differences. Yellow Sands Point is elevated dry land with paths and roadways affording access to the take-off area near its tip. Nahoon Reef, on the other hand, is low, rocky, often submerged, and backed by a cliff. Yellow Point's waves tend to be tamer than those at Nahoon too, but they're still excellent.

Shortly before 11 a.m., the boys dropped in at a large rock formation on the lee side of the Point and paddled out to a take-off area fifty meters from the tip. They had the bay to themselves that morning. The younger kids, including Michal's sixteen-year-old brother, Jean, were all in school.

Jean du Plessis didn't want to be in school, of course. His life too was focused entirely on surfing. Possessed of even curlier hair than his brother (if that's possible), the winsome youth has gone by "Shorty" or "Shorts" since early childhood because, like Shannon, he had been one of the smallest boys in his class. Still, he was a competitive wunderkind. A member of the Border surfing team from age eight through his late teens and a skilled aerialist, he won the Border Under-18 Championships in 2008, 2009, and 2010. He also finished an impressive third in the South African Under-16 Championship in 2009.

"Shorts" would have the last laugh. A late-teen growth spurt would rocket him to a lanky 6-foot-1 (plus two inches of curls), and he would tower over many of his former classmates. Indeed, he would go on to win his nation's intercollegiate surfing championship in 2014.[39] So, it's safe to say that, as Jean sat in his 11 a.m. Afrikaans class at Merrifield College, a high school in East London, he wasn't thinking about conjugating Afrikaans verbs. His mind was on the water.

Back at Yellows, Michal and Rodger had finished riding waves and were paddling back out to sea. Rodger was navigating the shallower channel closer to the Point. Michal was in the deeper channel further out. Aiden, Oscar, and Logan were out at the take-off point waiting for waves. Logan then caught a wave and surfed inward between Michal and Rodger. As Logan surfed by, Rodger spotted big trouble:

A shark was riding the vortex of Logan's wave. It kicked off the back, gave three solid waves of its tail, and covered about fifty meters in two seconds, knocking Michal clean off his board. There was a bit of splashing. I saw Michal climb back on his board and catch a wide set toward Logan on the inside.

Michal had been unaware of the charging animal:

I never saw it coming. The shark hit me from my right side under the water with a really hard thud. It bit my right leg hard, getting more of me than my board. It pushed me to my left and then underwater. There was no pain, probably because of the adrenaline. I knew right away it was a shark. The shark never shook me from side to side, though, and after one or two seconds, it let me go. I could see the silhouette of the shark while I was underneath the water. It was three meters long, definitely longer than me, and I could see its huge eye and dark skin. I then surfaced in bloody water and started yelling to my mates, "Shark! Shark! Get out of the water!" Then the shark surfaced in front of me and slowly swam next to me. It seemed curious.

We all raced to shore and arrived on the rocks at the same place, about 100 meters from the end of the Point.[40] I was bleeding badly. I had left a huge trail of blood in the water, and there was blood all over the rocks near me. Aiden removed his surfboard leash and tied it around my right thigh, and that stopped some of the bleeding right away. Aiden and Logan then carried me over the black, slippery rocks to the grass. They both sliced up their feet badly.

Oscar and Rodger ran to get Oscar's bakkie. Then, after lifting me into the truck, Aiden and Logan stayed with me in the back as Oscar drove. Rodger stayed behind with our gear and had to swim across the Kwelera River with all of our boards to get to his car. I have no idea how he did that.

The rear of the bakkie had a metal floor with a plastic cover. Aiden and Logan were kneeling next to me, and a puddle of blood was swishing back and forth under us. Twice, Aiden's hand slipped completely into my gaping wounds, once while carrying me across the rocks and a second time in the truck when I asked him to tighten the leash around my thigh. I felt no pain either time. The wetsuits that Aiden and Logan were wearing were covered in my blood and had to be cleaned several times. Aiden has blond hair, and even his hair was red!

They drove me to Crossways Pharmacy about six kilometers inland and the people there bandaged my leg and gave me morphine which made me kind of high. There was a delay of 20 to 25 minutes before the ambulance arrived. Oscar called his dad to get the ambulance for us, but Oscar is quite the prankster, so his dad didn't believe him at first!

A doctor whose office was next door to the pharmacy raced to Michal's aid. He pressure-bandaged the boy's wounds and gave him shots for pain and shock. The news was good. Michal's blood loss was under control, and his leg bones seemed intact; he would live and keep his leg. He was lucky. Of all great white victims worldwide, only 73 percent live to tell about their experience. An even smaller percentage avoids permanent disability.

Throughout his ordeal, Michal kept his cool. He even had the good sense to call his mother himself, instantly satisfying those unspoken protocols about communicating family emergencies. "Mom, don't panic, I've been bitten by a shark, but I'm okay," he told Marietjie ("Maria") Müller du Plessis. "Please phone Dad and Jean." Maria didn't call anyone...not right away. She raced to Crossways instead, arriving before the ambulance did. The doctor assured her that Michal would not lose his leg. She marveled at Michal's calm demeanor. "My friends," he told her, "prayed like mad in the bakkie on the way to the pharmacy."

Aiden busied himself trying to reach Michal's brother but had no success. Because he was in class, Jean merely checked his caller ID, whispered to Aiden that he couldn't talk, and hung up. When Maria arrived at Crossways, she called the school. Soon, Jean was headed to the front office to return an "urgent call."

"When I got called out of class, I knew something was wrong," Jean insists. "I had that feeling, that sensation one gets in the gut. But, when I called my mom, I did not expect to hear what I heard."

"Michal's been attacked by a great white," Maria told her youngest— here, yet again, a major telephone protocol failure.

"I totally and completely freaked out," Jean recalls. "I was so shocked. I accidentally unloaded a few f-bombs without thinking about my mom or the school staff around me. My heart dropped to my knees. I had all of these horrible images in my mind, and I didn't know if Michal would live."

"Try to relax," his mom added quickly, sensing her mistake. "He's apparently okay. He's on his way to St. Dominic's. I think everything is under control." Of course, "I think" was not what the loyal younger brother wanted to hear. Nor was Maria's assurance necessarily justified.

Alderson's Ambulance Service rushed Michal to Life St. Dominic's Hospital in East London, an 18-kilometer journey from Crossways. During the ride, shock began to set in due to blood loss. He suffered from a rapid, shallow heartbeat and had great difficulty breathing—the only truly emotional time for him. "That was the worst part, not being able to breathe," he remembers. "It scared me, but the medical technicians told me I was breathing just fine." Of course, paramedics would tell you this if you were hearing harp music.

In reality, Michal's inability to breathe was concerning. With severe blood loss, respiratory distress is often the very last symptom before cardiac arrest. On September 12, 2003, for example, nineteen-year-old David Bornman suffered catastrophic destruction of his entire left thigh, left buttock, and left kidney region while body-boarding at the Dunes surf spot on Noordhoek Beach just south of Cape Town.[41] Two other surfers saw an enormous great white take Bornman under the water and then toss the boy into the air. On a solid red wave, one of the surfers accompanied the gruesomely mauled youth to shore. As they entered the shallows, Bornman told his escort that he couldn't breathe. Those were his last words. Bornman was given CPR for thirty exhausting minutes but to no avail. The youth had lost his entire blood volume in less than two minutes.[42]

So, the paramedic's calm indifference to Michal's breathing difficulty may have been for show—to keep him calm, slow his heart rate, and in so doing, slow his blood loss.

Back at Merrifield, a distraught Jean du Plessis sought transportation from a friend:

> When I asked my mate for his motorbike, he looked at me funny, laughed, and said, "No, you mad." I didn't tell him what had happened. I just said I needed to get to the hospital as soon as possible. I was sixteen at the time and didn't have a license, but he knew I could ride a bike because I was the one who taught him how to! My instant reaction was, "You know what, screw this guy; he's not willing to help me out, and I'm unsure if I'll make it to the hospital in time." At that time, I was still unsure of the intensity of the wounds. I didn't want to get there and my bro had already died, you know?

Instead, Jean raced into the school office and begged a ride from a staff member. He reached the hospital before the ambulance arrived and paced back and forth under the awning at Trauma Reception for fifteen interminable minutes, his reddened eyes fixed on St. Mark's Road. When he heard the first faint trills of the siren, his heart nearly skipped out of his chest.

"When they opened the door of the ambulance," Jean remembers, "I saw all of the blood-soaked towels. Michal was pale as a ghost. I could see a bite near his ankle and it looked bad, but it was only a small wound that wasn't even wrapped. It was nothing compared to the two giant wounds that I couldn't see under solid red towels. I was crying, and Michal was in shock. But he looked fairly good considering what had happened!"

From the time of his attack to his arrival at Life St. Dominic's, a full hour had passed. Another hour passed in the emergency ward, albeit with an IV, while hospital staff obtained needed information and found a qualified surgeon. In the meantime, Jean busied himself keeping his brother occupied:

> With fluids, Michal gained a lot more strength and courage. I remember that Oscar Miller, Logan Philpott, and I laughed and told jokes to keep his mind stable. Our emotions had subsided by then. All we felt was relief...a whole lot of relief. He was alive—a miracle now that I am rethinking this.

When Michal's wetsuit was cut off, the femur, knee, and tibia of his right leg could be seen deep inside two gaping soda can-sized holes on the lateral aspect of his lower thigh and his upper calf. Surgeons needed two and a half hours to clean the deep lacerations, assess possible bone damage (there was none), and repair severed and torn muscles. The shark's teeth had missed the femoral artery by less than an inch. If a single shark tooth had nicked it—if the shark had shaken Michal even slightly—any account of the youth's experience would be a tribute to a bright and talented lad who had died far too young. But Jean remembers that the news was all good:

> After surgery, the doctor came out and told my parents that Michal would be fully functional within the next six weeks, and we couldn't believe this. There were tears of joy amongst us all, and when we went to see him after the anesthetic wore off, it was laughs all around. It was like we were celebrating his life in a hospital ward.

Despite the physical damage that Michal suffered, his recollection of the shark is not what you might expect. His mom recalls a discussion with her son:

While we were waiting for surgery, another side of my boy surfaced. He said, "Mom, for a split second under the water, the sight of this magnificent animal looking me straight in the eye was without a doubt the most beautiful picture I've ever seen...better than on *National Geographic* channel. Then I realized I had to get away!!" I'm extremely proud that Michal had time to appreciate nature and not condemn all sharks as man-eating beasts.

And they aren't man-eating beasts. The shark that attacked Michal was clearly acting in error. Seeking a seal's delicious blubber but ending up with muscle and polystyrene, the shark released its unsavory prey in two seconds, looked at the youth under the water, eyed him curiously on the surface, and moved on.

Michal is endlessly grateful to his four mates—"my heroes" he calls them—who worked tirelessly to save his life that day. Invested so suddenly in their unexpected roles as paramedics, they slashed their feet carrying Michal to safety, created a makeshift tourniquet to stanch the boy's blood loss, knelt in pools of blood to keep his leg elevated and his tourniquet secure, kept pressure on his wounds, calmed him with assurances, prayed with him, phoned his family, and raced him to the nearest medical professional. Rodger, who stayed behind with the boys' gear had difficult tasks as well—worrying from afar about the survival of his fallen mate and returning the boys' gear to the Caravan Park. Swimming across an open river mouth with four surfboards and a bodyboard cannot be easy.

A week or so later, Michal's deep thigh wound became infected, and he required additional surgery. Jean, frustrated by his older brother's continuing plight, punched his bedroom wall and broke his hand. Later, Jean sought permission from his mom to have the word "Faithful" tattooed on the interior aspect of his upper arm, one of the most agonizing tattoo sites on the human body. "I am against tattoos and piercings," his mother says, "but I signed because he convinced me that this was his way of thanking the Lord for saving his brother's life." It's odd with brothers, isn't it? Most of them fight tooth and nail, but let something happen to one of them, and the carbon steel bonds snap into place.

The Natal Sharks Board examined the tooth marks on Michal's leg and determined from the spacing that he had been attacked by a great white.

Three days earlier, that same animal might have caused even greater trouble. On the Saturday before Michal's attack, Yellow Sands had been packed with surfers and runners for the start of the Surfer's Marathon, an annual 18-kilometer beach run in which Michal participated. Dozens of surfers and bathers had been in the water that day.

Shannon was twenty-five years old and working as a surf coach out of the country at the time of Michal's attack, but he knew Michal from their days together on the Border surfing team. He wrote Michal a Facebook message wishing him well.

Michal's attack is another testament to the addictive nature of surfing. After recovering from his surgeries, he was on crutches for five weeks. The day he set them aside, on March 23, he was just eight days from the start of a long-planned, once-in-a-lifetime "surfari"—a ten-month-long yacht-based fishing and surfing odyssey across the entire Indian Ocean. But he was still limping, and he had no surfboard or wetsuit.

He had prophesied the solution to his gear problem. While awaiting his initial surgery, Michal shared with his mom one of his first thoughts after the attack. "When I was on the rocks waiting for the bakkie," he told her, "I remember thinking that if I come out of this ordeal alive, someone might offer me a free wetsuit and board!" With some prompting from Oscar Miller, two companies did exactly that. XCel gave Michal a brand new wetsuit, replacing the one cut off in the emergency room, and Bilt Surfboards shaped the boy a brand new ride. He had the gear he needed for his trip, but he didn't know if he had the legs. So he decided to go surfing on March 23, his very first day off of crutches. The question was where to surf, and this is where Michal's story merges with Shannon's.

Michal couldn't summon the nerve to return to the site of his attack. "I may never surf at Yellow Sands Point again," he told his mates, and that is hardly surprising. More surprising is where he did decide to surf next. He traveled to Nahoon Beach! Ten years apart, Michal du Plessis and Shannon Ainslie had independently adopted the same philosophy: If you get attacked in one end of the shark tank, don't swim in that end. They effectively swapped places.

Michal felt comfortable at Nahoon Beach despite its proximity to infamous Nahoon Reef and the fact that Geoffrey Zimmerman had died of a shark attack there in 1961. He had learned to surf at this beach, and he

Michal and Jean du Plessis after Michal's shark attack (Courtesy of Maria du Plessis)

Michal du Plessis's scars (Courtesy of Maria du Plessis)

had the support of fifteen or so mates when he took to the water again. He found out quickly, though, that five weeks without walking takes a severe toll on leg muscles and lungs.

Surfing is a vastly greater test of strength and cardiovascular fitness than non-surfers imagine. It's right up there with cross country skiing and wrestling. When you spend all day duck diving, paddling, and popping up onto a board, you put enormous strain on your arms, shoulders, and abs, and you test your lung capacity. Riding a surfboard places even greater demands on the large muscle structures of the legs, butt, and stomach, and hence, the heart. If you doubt this, try to pinch some skin on the stomach of a dedicated surfer (being sure to ask nicely first). You'll have better luck pinching a ceramic tile.

On his first day back, Michal barely managed twenty minutes on the waves, but it was a good start. Young people bounce back quickly. Just eight short days after his post-attack debut at Nahoon Beach, and right on schedule, Michal flew to Tanzania for the start of his Indian Ocean adventure aboard the *Abundant Life*, a 58-foot catamaran owned by a friend's father. For ten months, Michal fished, scuba-dived *sans permis* (he later qualified), and surfed the breaks of Tanzania, Zanzibar, and Seychelles. Toward the end of the year, fully recovered and stronger than ever, he surfed the famous Mentawai Islands, a 500-mile-long chain of world-class surfing meccas west of Sumatra in Indonesia. The islands drape southward from the epicenter of the great tsunami of December 26, 2004. It was there that another tsunami awaited him—an emotional one.

14

DEADLIEST BEACH IN THE WORLD

When Jean du Plessis's summer break began in December, he and his dad hopped on a plane and joined Michal on the *Abundant Life* for a joyous month of surfing, fishing, diving, and sightseeing. It was the kind of month you dream about—deepening tans, perfect waves, spectacular vistas, warm water. But all of that ended for Jean early on January 16, 2011.

That morning, a Sunday, the *Abundant Life* was anchored in Telaga Harbour on Malaysia's spectacular Langkawi Island. Easily one of the most beautiful settings in the world, the natural outer harbor is surrounded on three sides by palm tree-lined beaches and verdant hills. Its seaward exposure is sheltered by a pair of manmade islands laid end-to-end, each measuring about 50 by 250 meters.

At dawn, Jean awoke first and went topside to perform any popular teen's initial morning ritual—checking social media. Shirtless, relaxed, and yawning, he plopped onto a deck couch and nimbly clicked through to his timeline where he found a brief Facebook post from his friend Bradley Dalbock. Written in teen text-speak, the post bore news about Zama Ndamase, Jean's teammate on the Border junior surfing team:

zama just died 4wom a shark attack just wanted u 2 no :(

The blood drained from Jean's face. For the second time in less than a year, a shark had dealt a horrible blow to someone close to him. Zama had just turned fifteen, and, this time, the outcome was forever:

My heart sank into my feet, and then a wave of anger swept over me. I remember thinking, "This is the last straw, and stuff surfing...I'm staying out of the water." I threw my phone on the deck, jumped off the back of the catamaran, and swam really hard toward a secluded little island about 200 meters away. The island was one of two manmade islands built to shelter the harbor.

101

Once I reached the beach, I was balling my eyes out and didn't know what to do with myself. I felt helpless—for Zama's older brother Avuyile especially—because I was on the other side of the planet from him. I was thinking to myself that this so easily could have happened to my own brother, and that made my heart ache even worse. I jogged up and down the little stretch of beach and kicked and punched the ground trying to release my anger— anger that I guess I have for sharks even though we cannot blame them at all. I feared for Avuyile's life. What if he was next? I even remember thinking, "When is it going to be my turn?"

Jean's anger eventually gave way to resignation, and he swam back to the boat to share the awful news. He then called Avo, as Avuyile likes to be called, completely forgetting the six-hour time difference. Avo took the call in the middle of the night, but the grief-stricken sixteen-year-old hadn't been able to sleep. He deeply appreciated Jean's call and tried to explain the tragedy to him.

The day before, Zama, only four days past his fifteenth birthday, had gone surfing with Avo at Second Beach near their home in Port St. Johns, a rural black community of 5,000 in the Transkei District.

Second Beach, just three kilometers east of Port St. Johns, lies near the mouth of the Umzimvubu River in the heart of the Wild Coast.[43] The beach, about 10 meters wide at high tide and 300 meters long, is tucked in a spectacular crescent-shaped cove and is bookended by two tidal lagoons. Because of silt expelled by the Umzimvubu, the cove at Second Beach is shallow out to a considerable distance and raises magnificent surfing waves over 200 meters from shore.

On pretty days, because of crowding, the west end of the beach is reserved for swimmers and the east end for surfers. Saturday the fifteenth, Avo recalls, was one of those days:

It was just a beautiful day, and no one expected anything bad to happen, even though the beach has the history. It was cooking hot and the beach was crowded. There were almost a hundred swimmers at the west end of the beach and in the car park. We were surfing at the east end of the beach, just off the lagoon mouth. It was late morning, and we planned to go home at mid-day because we were having a family braai for Zama's birthday. He had turned fifteen on January 11th, but we had delayed the celebration to the weekend.

As Zama was heading back out to catch another wave, I left the water and ran back to our house to swap boards. I remember that another friend, Anele, had come by and left a Shark Shield device on the beach. An English tourist was also there taking pictures of us surfing.

When I returned to the beach, I saw Zama surfing fairly close to shore in chest-deep water. Another relative, Karabo Tieli, who was my brother's age, was in the water just beyond him. Zama made a series of really good turns, and we were all cheering him. As he pulled out of the wave, he waved at us, dropped into the water, and crawled onto his board. He was lying chest down with his feet dangling off the back.

Another friend and I started wading out into the water. Just as we did, I saw Zama get yanked off of his board by the leg and saw his leash snap. I saw some blood come up and knew it was a shark. Zama came to the surface and tried to pull himself back onto his board. We were all yelling "Paddle! Paddle! Paddle!" but then the shark came up between his legs and bit him again, this time hitting the artery in his left thigh. It looked like a huge ball of blood exploding.

Karabo, who was closest to him, bravely ran toward Zama through the chest-deep water and tried to pull him, but Zama refused. He told Karabo, "Everything will be okay." Then he waved his hand at us and stuck his face in the water. That's when we knew he was gone.

I lost it. I was crying and screaming. Our former coach heard our shouts from the beach and could see that the whole peak of the wave had turned red. He and the English tourist ran to get the lifeguards who managed to get Zama onto a wave runner and bring him to shore, but he was lifeless. He had died almost instantly. About a hundred people gathered around us. It was just so intense, losing my only brother and trying to figure out how I was going to tell my mom and my sister.

Karabo Tieli, who was Zama's cousin, cannot shake the memory of that day. He was talking with Zama when the shark struck:

> I was sixteen at the time of the attack. We were in waist-deep water about 45 to 50 meters from shore. Zama had just caught the last wave of a set, and we were all cheering him on because he performed so great. He paddled toward me at the back of the queue. We were chatting and about three meters apart. Zama wasn't sitting on his board; rather he was lying on it with one leg in the water.
>
> All of a sudden there was this thing moving fast in the water. I saw it before Zama did. Before I could even communicate, the shark went under and attacked him like three times. It would attack, leave, and in about five seconds, attack again. I reached my arm at him while he was being attacked, but the shark kept pulling him under the water. I panicked and paddled toward shore to get help. When I realized that I was in water just above my waist, I stood and looked back. I could see that Zama was hanging half on his surfboard and struggling to paddle, so I waded back to him and grabbed his hand to pull him ashore. Along the way, he said, "Let go, bro, everything is gonna be alright." I could feel his hand move slowly out of mine. Then he lowered his head under the water and raised one hand with a fist in a salutation manner.

Michal du Plessis remembers Avo telling him about the dark history of Second Beach:

> Jean introduced me to Avo a few days after my own attack in 2010, and Avo told me about the four fatal attacks that had occurred at Port St. Johns over the previous three years. Then he witnessed his brother Zama pass away right in front of him. Avo was very traumatized by his brother's passing and did not want to surf anymore. My brother invited him to stay with us at Yellow Sands for a week or two so that he could get away from Port St. Johns and all the grief that surrounded him there. Jean, Avo, and

Zama Ndamase (l) with older brother, Avuyile (Courtesy of Richard Johnson)

The "deadliest beach in the world" (Courtesy of Richard Johnson)

Zama were all very good surfers and provincial surfers for the Border Junior Surfing team from the East London area. The Border Team takes part in the annual South African Championships that are held in different venues around the country. In 2007, I was also a part of this surfing team, and that was also the first year that Zama was on the team.

To the casual eye, Second Beach appears to be a surfer's paradise, and for over twenty years, it was exactly that. Then, in 2007, everything changed. Nature unleashed a six-year reign of terror in the little cove. In those six years, sharks attacked seven young swimmers and surfers. All seven were local males. All seven were in their teens or twenties. All seven were killed. The frequency of attacks and the 100-percent death rate earned Second Beach a reputation that no one could have imagined—the deadliest beach in the world.

Locals think the beach is cursed, and good luck trying to prove them wrong. The cove's bright, beautiful shoreline has become a dark event horizon between life and death.

The carnage began with the death of Sibulele Masiza, twenty-four, who was taken by a tiger shark while bodyboarding on January 14, 2007. Two years later, on January 24, 2009, Sikhanyiso Bangiliswe, twenty-five, was torn into three pieces by a suspected bull shark. Less than sixty days later, on March 21, 2009, sixteen-year-old Luyolo Mangele was killed. On December 18, 2009, Tshintshekile Nduva, twenty-two, was hit while kneeboarding. Zama Ndamase's death followed thirteen months later. On January 15, 2012, a suspected bull shark took the life of Lungisani Msungubana, twenty-five, who was merely swimming Finally, on Christmas Day in 2012, Liya Sibili, twenty, was killed by a tiger shark, also while swimming.[44] In all, the sharks involved in these attacks robbed their young victims of more than three centuries of expected life.

No one knows why the death toll is so horrendous at Second Beach. Avo believes the nearby river and reef are responsible:

The Umzimvubu River is just a few kilometers from the beach, and Zambezi sharks breed in the river. The river is a hot spot for them because it is a protected stream and is not dammed. Also, there is a reef and a big drop-off about 200 meters off the Gap, a rocky peninsula and blowhole about 500 meters from the east end of the beach. Sharks swim in circles there, feeding off the reef. The area off of the Gap is so infested that it has become a hot spot for shark fishing in the summer. Ninety-nine percent of the attacks are in the summer.

The Umzimvubu carries a great deal of silt toward Second Beach, making the water shallow and dangerously murky. The river also carries dead animals to the sea, and like many rivers, is a breeding ground for baitfish.

With each tragedy, the problem at Second Beach becomes a subject of national debate. Shark nets are considered. Beaches are closed. Warning signs are erected. Electronic tagging is evaluated. In the end, though, little is done. People oppose the nets because they kill marine animals. The beaches reopen. The warning signs are ignored. The tagging idea is deemed impractical.

The KwaZulu-Natal Sharks Board does its best to come up with answers, but the answers are elusive. Several good-hearted countrymen donated electronic Shark Shields to the surfers at Second Beach—one was present the day Zama was killed—but there aren't enough of them to do any good.

Second Beach's perfect fatality record (if not its brutal reputation) came to an end on March 13, 2013, when a thirty-nine-year-old businessman was attacked by a Zambezi and suffered injuries to his arms and hands after bravely fighting the shark.[45]

Sadly, though, the grim saga of Second Beach resumed on March 22, 2014, when sixty-six-year-old Austrian tourist Fredrich Burgstaller was fatally attacked by a two-meter shark while swimming.[46] That two-meter shark, most likely a Zambezi, inflicted the eighth fatal attack at Second Beach in less than seven years.

Back Home Again

Michal and Jean du Plessis returned home in late January to resume their education. Jean started his matric (senior) year at Merrifield, and as Michal noted, invited Avo to spend time at the Du Plessis home at Yellow

Sands. The Du Plessis boys were raised to be decent, faithful, and caring young men. Jean wanted to give Avo some relief from the trauma and gloom that hung thick over his home. Jean's kindness and that of his family is the essence of Nelson Mandela's dream—a country in which whites and blacks embrace one another and emerge together as a united nation. Avo needed the respite. "I fell into heavy depression and felt nothing but emptiness," he recalls, "and two years later, I was still struggling with concentration."

Michal pursued an architecture degree at university. He could just as easily earn his living behind a camera. The lad with the half-meter-long scar on his leg is a digital Michelangelo. He doesn't merely photograph a church, for example; he photographs it at night in the glow of car headlights with the back-lit shadows of himself and his friends hauntingly superimposed on the edifice. He doesn't just photograph a fellow surf photographer; he photographs him in high contrast black and white against the backdrop of a dramatic sunrise. He doesn't just photograph the arc of a colorless sandy beach; he photographs it from a foot above its surface with a solitary sandal, ablaze with the colors of his national flag, in the foreground. Not surprisingly, he started winning visual arts gold medals when he was six years old. One can only imagine the power of his architecture, a profession that he began pursuing with a firm in Berlin, Germany, in 2021.

After working for several years, Jean moved to Port Elizabeth in early 2014 to pursue his own undergraduate education at Nelson Mandela Metropolitan University.

Hearing the shark-related experiences of the Du Plessis brothers, one wonders if anything can justify the risk faced by surfers as they challenge an alien domain in which humans hold little sway. The surfer's answer, of course, is predictable. "Nothing could keep us from surfing," Jean says matter-of-factly. Jean acknowledges, though, that he and his older brother still have serious reservations about Yellow Point:

> I know for sure that I will never, ever, in my life paddle out there again, even though I used to love that wave so much. Michal wouldn't surf there after his attack either, and I originally doubted that he ever would, but he did paddle out at the Point in 2013. He was in board shorts because the water was warm, and he

thought he would give it a go. He was out there only briefly and didn't even wait for a wave. I still have not been back out, but I often go there to relax and watch the waves roll in.

The brothers do surf along the beach at Yellow Sands and several secret breaks away from the Point. Those spots, though, are barely 500 meters from the site of Michal's attack—less than a one-minute swim for a great white. Still, the boys feel safer there. Jean even managed to get Avo back on his surfboard within a month of his own brother's tragedy. Three months later, Avo began competing again for the Border team. His first contest after the tragedy was the South African Under-20 Championships where he ran into Shannon.

The former teammates spoke, and Shannon offered his profound sympathy. Remarkably, Shannon saw no deficit in Avo's surfing performance. "He surfed quite well!" Shannon recalls. That is especially impressive given that the contest was held at a place bearing a rather ominous name if avoiding sharks is important to you. It's called Seal Point.

Such is the lure of the green room.

15
BACK ON THE HORSE

Filming day was nearing, and Shannon's anxiety over returning to the waves was growing. Six weeks had passed since his terrifying day at Nahoon, but he faced problems. He lacked physical conditioning and surfing gear. His thruster, bearing an enormous bite mark, had been reduced to a museum exhibit. His wettie had been cut to shreds in the emergency room. Fortunately, help was on the way. Nathan Millet and Sean Smith, the foreigners who had produced their dramatic video of Shannon's attack, paid for his new surfboard and wetsuit.

Shannon's surfboard purchase, as it happens, was an ironic testament to the familial nature of the surfing community. He bought his new ride from Andrew Carter, a man whose body bears enormous scars from the most horrific shark attack in Nahoon history.

Finally, the day arrived—a hot, cloudless day in early September. "It was blue, blue, blue," Candice recalls of Yellows that spring afternoon. Some of Shannon's friends joined him for the shoot. Brandon, Candice, and Shane were there of course, as were Ashley Grimmer, Devon Swart, and Travis Naude. Despite the support of his friends, Shannon was a nervous wreck:

> The cast had just come off my arm, and I had not surfed in six weeks. I was out of shape, nervous, and scared, but also very excited!! *Ripley's Believe-It-Or-Not* was there to capture my first surf back in the water. All my family and friends were there too, so the hype on the day was huge. I felt like I was in a movie. I had only seen these things in movies, and now it was happening to me! I wanted to surf really badly, but I didn't know if I could because the six-week layoff was my longest time out of the water. And having a TV crew there filming and interviewing me put a lot of pressure on me to act, perform, and surf well, and I wasn't used to that. So, I felt intimidated and excited at the same time.

I didn't know how to react or respond to all of the people who were treating me as some sort of celebrity, sticking cameras in my face and asking me about my shark attack. Having *Ripley's* there was such a privilege and honor, but I was nervous speaking in front of the camera. It was all kind of overwhelming, especially for a young kid who didn't have much and who felt like he was at the bottom of the social scale. Some of my friends said I was getting a big head about it. I didn't ever want to be an arrogant, proud, or lofty person, though, so I tried hard to be normal and humble.

Because of his questionable conditioning, Shannon chose to surf on the sheltered east side of Yellow Point, about 100 meters from the tip—the precise spot where Michal du Plessis would be attacked a decade later. Indeed, Shannon entered the water from the very same rocks that Michal would later redden with his blood:

I remember standing on the rocks about to jump into the water, wondering what it would feel like to face my fears again. My wrist had been out of the cast for only three or four days, and I wore a plastic-covered pack on my arm and hand to keep my bandages dry. By then, my fingers were quite sore. I didn't know what to expect. Just a few weeks earlier, I had almost died and now I was about to enter the water again knowing that it could all happen again. My experience with God had enlightened me to the fact that He would keep me safe, and if not, be with me. He had given me a new confidence and the courage to face both giant beasts and life.

Finally, I jumped in the water. Brandon and some friends surfed with me. It was cool to have them share this great experience with me. Everyone cheered me on and shared waves with me. I felt so loved and cared for that day. *Ripley's* put a video camera on the front end of Brandon's surfboard and asked him to surf behind me.

I was so out of practice that I could hardly surf. Thinking about my shark attack and knowing that crews were filming me from a boat and from the beach caused me to "cook out" on most of the waves, though I did catch one nice ride. I had so many thoughts and emotions racing through my mind. I was scared that I might get attacked again, but I took comfort in the fact that there were a lot of people around to help me. As I surfed, I kept telling myself that I had already been attacked by two sharks and that the odds of it happening to me again had to be extremely small. It was only wishful thinking, but it calmed me down a bit!

I only stayed in the water for half an hour because my hand and fingers were aching, I was out of shape, and I felt weird. I also wanted to get out alive and in one piece. I didn't want to overstay my welcome!

Ripley's producers got what they wanted. They broadcast Shannon's return to the sea two months after the attack. Shannon got what he wanted. He remounted the horse that had thrown him. He stole his sport back from those two great whites. But there was one thing left for him to do. He needed to return to the scene of his attack. And if you need evidence of the transformative power of testosterone, Shannon Ainslie might be your proof.

At age seven, Shannon-the-child waded with his father into a knee-deep rock pool at Gonubie Beach. Suddenly, the boy froze and started crying and screaming at the top of his lungs—"that big mouth of his wide open" as his sister would say. Shane asked what was wrong, but the boy just kept bawling and yelling. With constant prodding, Shane finally convinced his wailing son to point to the source of his fear. It was a clump of seaweed wafting back and forth in the foot-deep lagoon.

At age fifteen, Shannon-the-man confronted two fifteen-foot great whites at Nahoon Reef, got bitten by one and bumped by both, and seven months later, confronted his worst fears head-on. He returned to Nahoon Reef—the very site of his attack.

He went to the reef on a Saturday morning in February 2001. The sky was partly cloudy, and an off-shore wind was holding up some pretty two-meter waves. He did a towel trick to slip on his wet suit, though his modesty was unnecessary. Only his brother and one other friend were present. At first, he didn't know if he could even enter the water, but a prayer replenished his courage.

Finally, he walked down the slipway, whistled past the plaque memorializing those seven dead Nahoon surfers, and stepped into the rocky lagoon. Cold water lapped over his feet, but it was the chill of his last experience there that caused him to shiver. He knew, better than anyone, what lurked beneath those cold dark waves. He knew that sharks patrolled the reef with regularity. But he was there on a mission of faith and courage. There was no turning back.

Shannon dropped his board into the rock-strewn lagoon, laid down on his board, and slowly paddled into deeper water. He watched the black, slimy rocks of the reef drift by on his right as he pressed seaward. Nearing the reef's tip, he veered left, away from the rocks and toward the exact spot where he had been ambushed in 2000...the exact spot where Andrew Carter and Bruce Corby had been so tragically stricken in 1994...the exact spot where the waves begin to break after rounding the submerged tip of the reef. His mind was racing:

> As I waited for the next line to arrive, my entire body was unusually rigid. I felt like my hands were clutching my board with vice-like grips. I arched my back and bent my knees to keep my legs out of the water. I was so incredibly tense. Finally, a promising swell approached. As the water began to lift me, I snapped my board shoreward and paddled hard, preparing to stand.

Popping up on a surfboard is a precisely timed and graceful act that takes a surfer from flat on his chest to a standing position in the blink of an eye—the end product of leg, arm, shoulder, butt, back, and stomach muscles working in powerful synchronicity. The move requires balance worthy of a rocket gyro and takes less than one second. This time, though, it seemed to take much longer:

> When I popped up, it seemed like time stood still. The whole attack came rushing back to me. I felt like I was reliving a horror movie in slow motion. This was the exact moment. This was the exact place. I could almost feel the terrible impact all over again.

This time, the dragon slept.

As Shannon dropped in, his rigid body and grim mental image softened. He dragged his badly scarred hand along the rising green sheet to his right. He glided smoothly away from the reef, angling gently toward the car park as the wave rolled shoreward. He rode the billow for fifty meters and then bailed out, quickly paddling back to the rocks. One run was enough. He had remounted yet another horse—this time, his home break—but he still needed time.

As he stumbled over the treacherous rocks to the slipway, the boy who had always prayed *before* surfing embarked on a new tradition. He prayed *after* leaving the water. His supplication consisted of two simple words, spoken quietly and repeated once as he cast his face heavenward with eyes closed. "Thank you," the boy mumbled. "Thank you."

Shannon would be the first to tell you that surfing is more than a sport; it's a quest. It's a quest for warm sunshine on your shoulders, fair winds at your back, and sea spray in your face. It's a quest for adrenaline rushes, beautiful coves, youthful revelry, skillful athleticism, new countries, and lifelong friendships. It's a courageous, insular, and unique lifestyle. And it's a lifestyle worth understanding.

16
SURFERS

According to UNESCO, an estimated three million ships lie at the bottom of the sea.[47] Among them are the wooden hulks of ancient Phoenician war galleys, the long canoes of Māori warriors, the rusted frames of German U-boats, and the severed halves of the *Titanic*. Each sinking represents tens, scores, hundreds, or even thousands of lives lost. Add to this human toll the countless individual tragedies—star-crossed swimmers, fishermen, divers, boaters, explorers, crime victims, storm victims, and sailors who have met their fates at sea—thousands each year for thousands of years. The sea is the unkindest of places, one that seldom spares the unprepared who enter her vast expanse. The sea is harsher still for those who choose to challenge her when she is at her most violent—like surfers, for example.

You know them. They come in all races, colors, nationalities, and genders. Many of them are sun-bleached males like Shannon Ainslie. They use words like "dude" and "bru" a lot and raise laid-back lifestyles to art forms. They're the kids you saw in *Endless Summer, Big Wednesday, Point Break*, and *Newcastle*—timeless tales of cash-strapped youths sleeping on beaches, mooching for food, toking on roaches, and caring less about unplanned futures. They seek only one thing—the perfect wave. Even competitions are more about waves than winning. The most strident of surfing competitors hang together socially, a universe unto themselves. And they're an interesting lot, these surfers.

Big Sur

In 1991, I traveled with two friends to an astronomy convention in San Jose, California. We had a free day and drove down Highway 1 to Big Sur on California's rocky and beautiful south-central coast.

The "town" of Big Sur is little more than a wide spot in the road and has the feel of an Oregon logging camp. When we arrived, veils of coastal fog were drifting through the tops of the lofty redwoods on both sides of the two-lane highway, and the crash of water on distant rocks was faintly audible. Nestled at the feet of the massive trees, a little surf shop beckoned.

Inside, I was overpowered by unexpected splashes of color—surf posters, racks of brilliantly colored surf shirts, and rows of brightly designed surfboards for rent and sale. A line of wetsuits hung on a rack at the back of the store. They were the exception; most were black.

The kid in charge looked like an escapee from a boy band. He was about eighteen, dimpled, and blond, and he had that "hey dude" manner of speaking. His nametag bore the name "Jeff," and he could have landed a role in *Fast Times at Ridgemont High*. When we walked in, Jeff was chatting up a family of three and giving directions using one of those colorful maps you find at tourist spots.

"Well, it depends on what you're looking for," Jeff told the visitors. "This is the family beach here, and this one's for lovers."

He was just getting started. There are countless secluded coves and rock-sheltered beaches along the coast of Big Sur.

"This one's the nudist beach," he added, "and this one here is Gay Bay." Everyone was laughing as Jeff described the various spots. Then there was a tone change. "This one," Jeff warned with uncharacteristic solemnity, "is only for local surfers, so you need to avoid that." The warning surprised me a bit. I didn't know about localism at the time. I was wondering what he would point out next—a cross-dressing beach perhaps or maybe a stoner cove. On reflection, I realized that most coves in Cali are probably stoner coves.

When the family left, Jeff started chatting up a surfer buddy who had a distinct South African accent. "Bru," said Jeff's friend, "I'm pullin' to the bay tomorrow, bru! We've got to shoot the Point, the lines are crankin', yeah, fully!" And there I stood, not a portable translator in sight.

I wanted to buy a t-shirt, and being the polite sort, I waited for Jeff to finish his conversation. But after five minutes of "bru" this and "dude" that, I got a little chafed. "Excuse me," I interrupted, "but could I buy this t-shirt sometime this month?"

Jeff's happy air evaporated. With downcast eyes, blond hair flopping over his eyes, he gently lifted the t-shirt from my hands and turned toward the register. Then he spoke, and as long as I live, I will never forget what he said.

"Wow, man," he mumbled, "there's no reason to be *hos*-tile."

And there I stood, awash in the harsh light of pure epiphany. I...was hostile. Midwest lawyer, meet California surfer. In a matter of seconds, an eighteen-year-old had made me feel like a complete ass.

I'm pretty quick on the draw, though. I asked Jeff if he would help me pick out a surf shirt for a young cousin of mine who was exactly his size. The spectacularly colorful long-sleeve shirts ran about $55, a bit pricey for that era. "Pick one that you would wear," I said. His mood brightened. With unexpected enthusiasm, he looked around and pulled from the rack a yellow shirt with a blue and red surfboard design wrapped around one side. "This one's totally radical," he said, a smile creasing his face. So, I purchased the shirt. And then I gave it to him.

Thus did I make amends with the surfing gods. And in the years since I visited Big Sur, I have learned even more about the ethos of surfing.

On land, surfers seem carefree and chill, like nothing bothers them...like nothing excites them. They move slowly, talk slowly, and live life in the slow lane. They seem to worry about nothing, at least openly. No bed? No money? No problem. They even fashion their own distinct language and speaking style to increase their sense of brotherhood and affection. I have a theory that many surfers seek a life on the waves because they don't fit in very well on land. The waves are an escape for them...an escape to a hostile kingdom but a kingdom where, among humans, they rule.

They rule with authority too. When they are in the water, they are all business. They face drowning, sharks, jellyfish, rip tides, rocks, and pummeling waves. At sea, they are deadly serious athletes risking everything they have, or ever will have, against a prodigious array of dangers. Really, they're quite brave.

Surfing is a love affair with nature and with risk—a love affair that has the power to bring a kid back to the water every single day if circumstances permit, and even if they don't. It's like a guy falling in love with a beautiful girl at school. He can't spend enough time with her. He sees her before school, between classes, at lunch, after school, in the evenings, all weekend long, and even after curfew. That's how surfers are with the sea.

The non-surfing world never sees much of the sport. It's not top fare on sports television, though the addition of surfing at the Tokyo Olympics may change that. Still, we usually only hear about surfers when they are killed or when they are attacked by sharks.

Surfers don't seek fame-by-shark, of course. They have no interest in crawling out of the water minus a leg or thirty pounds of flesh. They're thin enough as it is. The fact that they risk such inconveniences, however, speaks volumes about their love for the sport.

The Atlantic and Indian Oceans meet along the South African coast. To the northeast, in Durban, Indian Ocean waters dominate and are relatively warm. To the southwest, however, Atlantic waters rule, and surfers at prime spots like Nahoon Reef, Port Elizabeth, and Jeffrey's Bay endure waters that run 8° to 18°C (46° to 65°F) in prime winter surfing season (June through August) and that rarely reach 27°C (81°F) even in summer. If you stay active in the water, you can surf there in summer wearing only board shorts—"baggies" as South Africans call them—but wetsuits are generally needed year-round.

Despite their wetsuits, surfers have to keep moving to retain warmth. The particular advantage of a wetsuit is that water infuses through the four millimeter suit thickness (just three millimeters in the arms and legs) very slowly, giving a heavily exercising body time to warm the water trapped inside.

Shannon's friend Brad Coetzee describes another technique for staying warm. Brad is a strong lad. Three years older than Shannon, his dark good looks and powerful frame give him the distinct appearance of an Italian rugby player, a comparison to which he takes amused offense. "We pee in our suits quite often," he says, "because it's easy to do, and it increases warmth in the suit...gross, but true." "When you surf in cold water," he adds, "you're stoked when you need to schwaz."

It's called a "wettie warmer," and Shannon becomes almost transfixed when describing the relief that the warm release brings as it creeps across the stomach, back, and legs. There's nothing to impede the flow. Most surfers wear nothing under their wetsuits except, perhaps, a rash vest to protect their armpits from abrasion. Wettie warmers, though, raise a couple of issues.

One issue is sharks. Are they as attracted to urine as they are to blood? Some experts argue that any odd scent can draw their attention. Others aren't so sure. Anyway, surfers drain the well and take their chances. Shannon often surfs for four to six hours without once touching dry land. (The emphasis here is on "dry" land because he does get mashed into the seabed now and then.) During such sessions, peeing in the wetsuit is the only way to avoid a tedious trip to the rocks, a long walk, and the awkward peeling down of the tight garment with its zipper in back where it can't damage delicate surfboards and, of course, can't be reached. This practice is of possible relevance to Shannon's story. In the several hours before his shark attack in 2000, he had urinated in his wetsuit about five times.

Another issue—more embarrassing perhaps—is who might be nearby when you take off your wettie. "It can really stink if you take it off shortly after peeing in it," Shannon laughs. Mercifully, this was not an issue when the nurse peeled down the fifteen-year-old's wetsuit at Medicross.

Surfing isn't entirely cheap, but unlike skiing or snowboarding, access to the venue is free. Boards cost about $300 for generics and $500-$800 for top-line models, and wetsuits can run from $150 to over $600 (2022 prices). As with all sports, there are the dreaded accessories. You need wax, of course, to keep your forward foot from slipping off the board. Add a leash, a rash vest, some booties and gloves for extremely cold water, a tail pad, and a fin system, and you're all set. The real expense is replacing broken or creased boards. They're made of various components, usually epoxy resin, polystyrene foam, and fiberglass cloth, and the sea trashes them with wallet-draining regularity.

Then there's the language. South Africa recognizes eleven official languages—Afrikaans, English, Ndebele, Northern Sotho, Sesotho (Southern Sotho), Swazi, Tswana, Tsonga, Venda, Xhosa, and Zulu. Even the country's beautiful national anthem, *Nkosi Sikelel'iAfrika* ("God Bless Africa") consists of four stanzas sung in two keys and five languages—Xhosa, Sesotho, Zulu, Afrikaans, and English, in that order. Afrikaans, of course, is a West German dialect and a close relative of Dutch: "Wanna go surfing?" "Lekker!"

In reality, though, there is a twelfth official language in South Africa—the one I learned the hard way in that little surf shop at Big Sur. No sport has a more well-developed vocabulary than surfing, a lexicon that has spread seamlessly into the cultures of snowboarding and skateboarding worldwide. Consider a few examples.

A "grommet" or "grom" is a teen-aged surfer, usually under sixteen, and a pre-teen rider is, rather amusingly, a "microgrom." "Grommet" most likely derives from the English word "gremlin."

Surfboards are known as "sticks." They have noses, tails, footpads, skegs (center fins), rail fins, and leg ropes, and come in a variety of shapes, lengths, and multi-fin arrangements. The most common board among good surfers seems to be the "thruster" that Shannon rode during his attack. Thrusters are thin, pointy-nosed, three-fin boards designed for high-performance in difficult and critical sections of waves. Generally, thrusters are too small for massive waves. Shannon discovered this the hard way at Supertubes in 2007.

Good things in surfing are Kelly Slater (the winner of an astonishing 11 ASP[48] (now WSL) world surfing championships, "styling" (surfing even remotely as well as Kelly Slater), "cranking," "firing," or "macking" waves (big waves), offshore winds (winds that blow toward the sea and hold up the faces of the waves), surfing "in the green room" (in the barrel with a wave breaking over the top of your head), and being "lank stoked" (very excited). "Brah" and "sick" need no explanation. And if a South African surfer says "Shot!" to you, the polite response is "You're welcome."

Bad things in surfing are "getting snaked by foreigners" (having your wave stolen by someone from out of town), "family or party waves" (too many people on a wave), taking a "rail-bang" (catching a surfboard in that special place), getting "caught inside"(when you get stuck in the impact zone of a breaking wave and have to duck dive under it), getting "locked in" (getting too low on a wave and having it crash on top of you), ending up in the "washing machine" (when you fall off the wave and it takes you with it, tumbling you every which way), "eating it" and "getting nailed" (having a big wipe out), doing an "acid drop" or "going over the falls" (falling from the top of a tall wave which usually happens when you get stuck in the lip of the wave that then drags you to the bottom of the wave), suffering "noodled" arms and legs (having muscle fatigue), and of course, running into the "men in gray suits." Those would be the sharks.

Surfers come in two flavors. About 70 percent of them, including Shannon, are "naturals" or "regular" surfers who place their controlling right foot on the rear footpad of the board and place their left foot forward. Naturals prefer right-handed waves—waves that break from right to left as seen from shore—because naturals can face the waves as they surf and execute stalling maneuvers by dragging their right hands in the wave faces. "Goofy footers" control with their left foot in back. They prefer left-handed waves. Good surfers love trying both.

For all of the laid-back and mellow attitudes that seem to be associated with the sport, however, those who go down to the sea with surfboards are engaged in an intensely serious enterprise. They face a serious array of risks and problems, some natural, others manmade. Shannon has faced most of them.

17
THE PRECIOUS PRESENT

Snow skiing doesn't appeal to everyone. Non-skiers watch with amazement as skiers tote heavy boots and skis through airports, rent pricey vans and condos, buy $100 lift tickets, sit in chairlifts while gale-force winds freeze snot-lines across their faces, brave driving blizzards, blunder into double-black-diamond chutes, suffer painful frostbite, endure high-altitude nose bleeds, thrash in bed with mountain sickness, and return home in leg casts. Who needs such fun? Once you get past those first few days on the slopes, however, that cold white stuff on the mountains becomes an addiction. To a skier, nuclear winter sounds like a good thing.

Surfing is the same. Once you keep your balance on that first wave, there's nothing else you want to do. Well, okay, there's one other thing, but even that's a close call. Riding waves is a mix of excitement, exercise, and athleticism immersed in the beauty of nature. On the face of a wave, life is stripped of all regret and concern. Failure, worry, loss—all of these things become meaningless. On the face of a wave, the only thing that matters is now. The problems of yesterday and the worries of tomorrow vanish in a rush of white spray and green water.

For those who find themselves wrapped in surfing's unyielding embrace, no problem or risk associated with the sport is too great to overcome. And Shannon Ainslie would be the first to tell you that surfing's risks are plentiful indeed. He's experienced them all.

Drowning

Surfers occasionally ply their sport in the kind of waves you saw in *Perfect Storm*, waves that can drop ten tons of water on them and drive them mercilessly into the rocks or coral on the sea bottom...all beyond human help or visibility. Worse, they don't wear life vests unless they're challenging ridiculous 15 to 20 meter-high waves in places like Tahiti—and then only because the vest will bring their body to the surface for a remote chance at resuscitation. Normally, a surfer's only means of flotation is the surfboard, and as Shannon's Victoria Bay experience revealed, monster waves can reduce a board to popcorn. Even if a surfer's leg rope holds, the board can become a sea anchor that keel-hauls the surfer over coral or rocks. Surfers' leg ropes often become entangled in rocks, reefs, and piers with fatal results.

Surprisingly, there's very little information about the drowning risk associated with surfing, but we can estimate the risk using some arcane data kept in Hawaii in the 1990s.

Sharks are presumably indiscriminate about the ages of their victims, and the average age of all South African surfers attacked by sharks is twenty-one years.[49] The youngest victims tend to be about fourteen and most victims are under thirty, so we can surmise that prime surfing years are somewhere in the fourteen to twenty-eight age range. In Hawaii, 260,000 people fall in that age group. About 80 percent of surfers are male, and there are 130,000 males in Hawaii between the ages of fourteen and twenty-eight. We can reasonably assume that about 100,000 of those males are disability-free and financially capable of surfing. An informal survey of several high school surfers in South Africa suggests that about five percent of healthy high school-aged males who live in surfing towns regularly participate in surfing. If it's double that in Hawaii, we can infer that there are probably 10,000 dedicated surfers among Hawaiian males. Factoring back in the 20 percent of surfers who are female, we would expect to find about 12,500 dedicated surfers there.

Here's where the arcane data comes into play. During the five years from 1993 to 1997 inclusive, seventeen Hawaiian surfers lost their lives to drowning.[50] That's an annual rate of 3.4 deaths per 12,500 surfers and places a regular surfer's annual risk of drowning at 1 in 3,600. Shannon has been surfing for well over thirty years. Over that length of time, therefore, he has faced a lifetime risk of drowning of almost exactly one percent. That's a risk 2.5 times higher than the lifetime risk of dying in an auto accident.

Now consider Shannon's conservatively estimated 23,000 lifetime hours on a surfboard, approximately twenty hours a week for fifty weeks a year since 1998. That's easily twenty times the norm! Suddenly, his experiences at Nahoon and Victoria Bay seem almost inevitable.

Stingers

Jellyfish tend to "bloom" in the warm waters of the world each summer, and with a warming global climate, they have become an international scourge. Surfers and swimmers take the brunt of the onslaught, and Shannon knows the beasts all too well:

> A jellyfish sting feels like you're taking a hard lick from a paddle. They sting soooo badly and the beach can be packed with them. They are just loads of trouble. I got hit twice in the forearms, about a year apart. After the stings, I had big bad itchy rashes that lasted two months.
>
> Another time, I was surfing in shorts and a vest and I got a bluebottle under my vest. It stung so bad I could barely breathe. I got nauseous. Then I got stomach cramps and the lymph glands in my groin and underarms swelled up.

Shannon's bluebottle friend is also known as a Portuguese Man-of-War, so named because its marine float, or marissa, resembles a 16th century Portuguese fighting ship called a caravel. Bluebottles float on the surface where surfers and swimmers easily encounter them. They often have one large tentacle, but sometimes multiple ones, that range from two to ten meters in length.

In reality, a bluebottle isn't a jellyfish at all. It's a *siphonophore*, a pelagic colony of highly specialized and psychologically integrated polyps or zooids responsible for defense, digestion, reproduction, contraction, and flotation. Essentially, it's like a boat full of armed sailors accompanied by engineers, cooks, and spouses.

Steven Sawyer can tell you something about Portuguese Man-of-Wars and their tendency to arrive in armadas. Stevie, whom Shannon taught from age ten, went on to win the WSL world longboarding title in 2018 after a runner-up finish in 2016. One evening, the tow-headed youth went for a quick surf wearing only baggies. He couldn't see well in the gloaming and found himself smack in the middle of a bloom of bluebottles that had drifted in with the on-shore breeze. Suddenly, thousands of nematocysts discharged into the boy's legs, arms, feet, and hands. He might as well have been strapped to a table in a medieval dungeon.

"It felt like someone was whipping me with molten wire," he says with a descriptive flair matched only by his singing and surfing skills. The exquisite pain drove him from the water and produced red welts and terrible itching that persisted for weeks.

Real jellyfish, which are single animals, can be even more problematic. Some are lethal.

Spreading down the Queensland coast of Australia and arriving in warm waters elsewhere in the world are the dreaded *Irukandji*, tiny translucent jellyfish with bells no larger than the tip of your pinky finger and four thread-like tentacles that can be mere inches long. Nets cannot keep them out, and they are currently threatening surfing on Australia's Gold Coast in southern Queensland. The nearly invisible creatures are so fragile that they die if they bump into the glass walls of an aquarium. For that very reason, they have venom designed to incapacitate rapidly before their prey can flail and endanger them. For a human, though, the immediate sting of the Irukandji feels like a mere bug bite. The aftermath is another story. Starting from several minutes to two hours after contact, Irukandji syndrome sets in. Some victims remain in writhing agony for three to seven days and require hospitalization. Pain medications are of little use. Two deaths in Australia have been attributed to Irukandji envenomation, both involving contact with several of the organisms.

If the Irukandji sounds like fun, consider the chirodropid box jelly, *chironex fflickeri*. Known as the "sea wasp," it is hailed by numerous scientists as the most venomous creature on earth and is listed in everyone's top five. Extensive contact with a box jelly can cause cardiac arrest and death in less than two minutes. Even if cardiac arrest is avoided, the pain can be so severe that victims lapse into shock, lose the ability to swim, and drown. Box jellies have been blamed for hundreds of deaths in the Indo-Pacific region. There are box jellies in South African waters too, but their agonizing stings are not as lethal as those of western Pacific cousins.

After competing in World Qualifying Series events along the Galician coast of Spain, Shannon's friend Dylan Lightfoot traveled to Ibiza and Formentera with his girlfriend for a holiday. While swimming at a beach in Formentera, Dylan noticed jellyfish in the water but thought little of them because other swimmers were present. Suddenly, a purplish noctilucent jellyfish known as a mauve stinger grazed his bare back. The mauve stinger is one of the most studied of all jellyfish because of its impact on beach tourism and the fishing industry. The agonizing effect of the jellyfish's stinging cells, called cnidocytes, was immediate and acute. "It felt like a hot iron branding me," Dylan recalls with no fondness in his voice. For two hours, he had to have vinegar applied to the huge welts on his back. He suffered pain and swollen glands for days. The whole affair seemed a bit odd to the youth:

> It was just strange that, in my twenty-two years of surfing, I had never been stung by a jellyfish...just some bluebottle stings, and then I went for a little swim on holiday and got nailed by the jellyfish.

Sea urchins aren't to be ignored either. Shannon's older brother, Brandon, managed to step on one of the spiny creatures at Nahoon Reef. He suffered throbbing pain and temporarily lost the feeling in his limbs. "The evening after he was stung, Brandon slugged the metal part of our bunk bed really hard," Shannon remembers. "His hand was bleeding, and he just showed it to me and said, 'Look, I can't even feel that!'"

Rail Bangs

Even the best of surfers end up going a few rounds with their surfboards or the sea bed. Shannon is no stranger to the problem:

> I had a broken nose once from hitting my board. The board has hit my head many times, leaving bumps or cuts. My board has hit me in my shins, groin, and arms. I have surfed over shallow sandbanks where I have fallen head first, hit my face on the bottom of the ocean, and bent my back and neck. One time, it was so serious that I got out of the water and just lay on the beach for twenty minutes, nauseous and in agony. I have cut my feet plenty of times on the rocks. I have scars on my feet and have had to have stitches in my feet from surfing over the reefs and rocks.
>
> Another time, I wiped out and my leash somehow wrapped

itself around my neck. I got pounded by the wave and into the rocks on the seabed. The wave was pulling my board one way and me the other, and the leg rope was strangling me all the while. It was pretty hectic.

Hectic, indeed!

Seals

Surfing, it seems, is a bit like running through a Rottweiler pen wearing bacon shorts. Even the seals, those friendly circus animals with the balls balanced on their cute little noses, want a piece of you.

In September 2010, Shannon was surfing at Point, an excellent point break at the north end of Jeffreys Bay. The waves were running at a respectable two to three meters, and Shannon had been in the water for several hours. Finally exhausted, he headed for the lower channel, a deep water exit through Point's ubiquitous shoreline rocks.

As he entered the rocky channel, he saw a large seal drop into the water about ten meters in front of him, heading out to sea. The canal-like space was narrow. They were destined to meet. "It was a big fat seal too," Shannon remembers:

> I knew that the seal would feel threatened and that I should prepare myself for something to happen. So, I climbed off my board and hung onto it from one side with my arms across the board, holding the opposite rail. My feet were hanging off the board in the channel, and I was ready to defend myself if the seal came at me...which it did.
>
> The seal opened its mouth, barked at me, and tried to bite me. As it came for me, I dodged it, shouted at it, and tried to hit it with my board. As I did that, it came back for me a second time, and I again shouted at it and tried to hit it with my board. It was so quick and fast...way faster and quicker than me. After it tried to bite me the second time, it disappeared under the water, and I finally made it up into the rocks and to the shore.

Seals are seldom seen in J-Bay. Shannon runs across one every six months or so. They're scary but not solely because they're big and prone to bite. They're scary because of what loves to dine on them. Where you find seals, you also find...

Men in Gray Suits

When a surfer lies on a board and paddles, feet dangle off the back and arms off the front. From below, the surfer's limbs look like flippers extending from the oval body of a seal. And sharks think of seals the way some people think of Big Macs.

The three most notorious sharks—responsible for 65 percent of all unprovoked human shark fatalities in which a species was identified—are great whites, bull sharks, and tiger sharks.[51]

Bulls and tigers tend to inhabit tropical waters, but the king of all sharks, *Carcharodon carcharias*, more popularly known as the great white or the white shark, prefers colder water. It is found in especially great concentrations in three areas of the world—the seal-rich waters of western and southern Australia, California's Red Triangle[52], and Shannon's homeland. South African waters also play host to the bull shark. Bulls are responsible for only a third as many deaths as great whites, but if you're going to be attacked, you'd be better off with a great white.

Florida has more shark attacks each year, on average, than Australia, Hawaii, California, Brazil, and South Africa combined, and Volusia County—the justifiably self-appointed Shark Capital of the World—has more attacks than any other part of Florida. But only about 5 percent of Florida attacks are fatal and less than 9 percent of U.S. attacks result in loss of life.

South Africa, on the other hand, experienced a 19 percent fatality rate and played host to eighty-four fatal attacks from 1900 to 2022.[53] Indeed, in the span of less than one year, from January 24, 2009 to January 12, 2010, five South African surfers and swimmers: Sikhanyiso Bagilizewe, nineteen; Luyolo Mangele, sixteen; Gerhard van Zyl, twenty-five; Tshintshekile Nduva, twenty-two; and Lloyd Skinner, thirty-seven, lost their lives to sharks.[54] Three were surfing or body-boarding at the time of their attacks. The other two were swimming.

In all of South Africa, few places pose greater shark risk than the lee side of Nahoon Reef. There, in 2000, a pair of great whites launched their attack on a single human, Shannon Ainslie. And there, in 1994, a single great white launched its attack on a pair of humans, Andrew Carter and Bruce Corby—an attack that may well be the most violent in South African history.

With all of these risks and dangers, it should come as no surprise that some control is needed in popular surfing venues.

18
THE LAW OF THE BREAK

We've alluded to one aspect of surfing that seems out of place given the mellow vibe exuded by surfers...that of localism. As laid back as surfers seem to be, a majority of them are testosterone-driven males who work hard, train hard, and take unusual risks. When surfers have free time and the waves are cranking, they are notoriously unwelcoming to strangers on their break, especially rude ones. Localism is a particularly strong feature of major surfing venues like Supertubes, and according to Shannon, the problem becomes especially acute when visitors arrive in large numbers and try to snake waves from locals:

> Locals, especially in places like Hawaii and Jeffreys Bay, are very aggressive in protecting their break mainly because there are always hundreds and thousands of out-of-towners and foreigners who come to surf there. Most of the time they don't show any respect towards the locals, especially the young kids. This causes a lot of problems as well as fights. Sometimes we have to chase people out of the water as well as out of town!
>
> Disrespectful foreigners might take verbal abuse in the line-ups. If that doesn't solve the problem, they might get punched while riding their boards or find Sex Wax smeared on their windscreens back in the car park. Some get beaten up when they return to the beach.
>
> The main reason why we do it is to ensure safety and order in the water. The locals who work and pay to live nearby will always have priority over the sets. There is always a pecking order, and even the younger locals know it and let the older guys get the first choice.

World-class breaks are often controlled by clubs of locals, usually young, aggressive surfers who tire of having hundreds of foreigners flock to their venues showing no respect for the surfers who live and work there. The term "foreigners," in surf-speak, has nothing to do with nationality. It refers to anyone who doesn't live near the beach. At major surfing venues, foreigners can arrive every winter when the waves are firing and take over entire lineups.

In years past, locals sometimes took steps to control the lineup, even to the extent of sorting people out when they needed to. Such sorting often included dunking, broken boards, slashed tires, waxed windscreens, and in extreme cases, fighting…though none of this is common today. It is important to understand, though, that these clubs do very important work.

Their primary job is to control the line-up. Put another way, they establish the law of the break and assure that locals have a fair chance to surf their home waters. To the untrained eye, a surfing break looks like a vast array of long waves rolling toward shore. In reality, though, there is only one ideal spot—on the furthest wave that will fully form and at a discrete point along that wave—where a surfer can drop in and catch the longest and best possible ride. This point is where the wave goes vertical and starts to break. If two surfers drop in at this spot at the same time, there is a high risk of collision, so the rule is one surfer per wave. The second surfer in line must wait for the next wave to form. Given the limited number of days when big waves are firing, locals refuse to play second fiddle to hordes of visitors who clog the line-ups and snake waves from them. And who can blame local surfers for imposing order on the chaos and putting a finger on the scale in their favor? This control also promotes safety in the water.

Even today, such clubs serve their communities by cleaning and maintaining beaches and surf parks, organizing fun beach days, and keeping surf parks safe. They repair boardwalks, maintain and protect dunes and natural plantation, and place benches at surf spots for spectators. They also approve organizational requests to hold amateur and professional surf competitions. Too many competitions, after all, would have the same effect as too many foreigners.

Shannon's most memorable brush with localism came in the winter of 2004. He was a teen at the time and, by his own admission, a bit cheeky. At the time, he didn't agree that locals should have the right-of-way in the line-ups and be able to take any wave they wanted, especially if he had a priority position ahead of them. When a local would paddle past him, he would drop in on the local, putting two surfers on the wave together. This didn't go well:

My first bump with a local occurred when I was nineteen. This local guy kept paddling past me and taking all of the waves, so, the third time he did this, I paddled back in front of him. When I took the wave, though, he dropped in on me. I yelled at him to get off the wave, but he kept on riding it. At the end of the ride, we both pulled out at the same time, and he paddled over to me, grabbed my board, pushed me off, flipped my board over, and threatened to break my fins out. He kept saying I should never paddle past him or call him off a wave again or he would hurt me and break my board. Later, I dropped in on another local, and he ended up dunking me and telling me never to drop in on him again. Both times, I told them that they didn't own the ocean and could not take all the waves. Of course, this just gave me a bad reputation in the lineup and further reduced my chances of getting decent waves there.

Shannon once had a very strong desire to surf a world-class "left"—a wave that breaks from left to right as seen from shore. This wave was very popular with locals and was special...so special that the locals refused to name it for fear it would be discovered. And heaven help surfers who ventured onto this wave if they weren't in the club or weren't long-time residents. Of course, cheeky nineteen-year-old Shannon didn't care about any of this:

> I wanted to surf this secret break so badly, but I was afraid of getting my face smashed or my car ruined, so I would just drive by it and check it out longingly. But one Saturday, it looked too good to pass up. The left-handed waves were running three to four meters high, and the off-shore breeze was holding up the face of the waves and letting beautiful barrels form.
>
> I thought, "Stuff this, I'm going to surf it." So, I collected Darren Whittaker and another friend, Kawika, and we went back there to surf. We planned to hide my car far away from the surf park, paddle out at different times, and act like we didn't know each other. We didn't want to look like an invasion.
>
> So, the three of us ended up in the water with two locals (I'll

call them Wade and Wesley). Fortunately, I knew both of them, and Wesley was actually a friend, so I didn't expect too much trouble.

Wade was very cool and had no problem with me surfing there. But Wesley, who I was friends with, threw his toys out the cot and tried to chase me out of the water!! I refused to leave, and he kept saying I shouldn't be there. Then he asked me if I knew the other two guys who paddled out before me. I denied knowing them. Then Wesley paddled to shore. I remember thinking that he was going to slash the tires on my car if he could find it. He was gone about fifteen minutes and then returned and continued surfing. During this time, my friends and I caught plenty of good waves. We wanted to cheer each other's rides, but we kept up our act, pretending to be strangers. We wouldn't even look at each other.

Then I caught one of the biggest barrels of my life. It was hollow and amazing, and after a couple of seconds of trying to come out of it—difficult to do on a steep wall of water—the lip of the wave clipped my head, knocked me off my board, and pushed me under the water. The wave tossed me around and held me on the bottom of the ocean. I found myself pinned between big rocks and felt like I was trapped in a cave. The power of the wave kept me there for a long time, and I thought I was going to be stuck there for good! Then, the turbulence weakened, and I was able to get to the surface. Darren got caught in the impact zone with me and got it even worse than I did. He got raked over a reef and had to go ashore.

A few moments later, I saw it—a jet ski coming right at me. I knew what was happening. Wesley had called a guy I'll call Storm, and Storm was coming to sort us out. Storm was driving and a second guy (I'll call him Kobus) was riding on the back.

They flew right at me so hard, I thought the ski might knock me out, but they turned at the last second and used the ski's wash to knock me off my board. All the while, Kobus was yelling at me and calling me names. Then they came at me with the ski again. Finally, they circled me and told me that I should never surf there again, and if they ever saw me there, I'd be in big trouble. I didn't need any more persuading. I got out.

Kawika recalls the jet ski coming for him too. By then, he was alone in the water. The locals circled him and yelled at him before a set came in, came back after the set passed, and came back yet again between waves. He describes the experience as "super gnarly."

When a visitor shows up on someone else's break, you see, it is exactly like walking into an amateur boxing club for the first time. You can do it, but don't brag about how tough you are and hog all of the time on the heavy bag. If you do, remember that cold water works best on bloodstains.

Localism in surfing, you see, is all about paying your dues. In the years since his encounter, Shannon has been part of local clubs that protect breaks and nearby beaches, and he holds no grudges whatsoever. At age nineteen, Shannon just didn't understand how or why locals protect their breaks.

Now, he does.

19
NAHOON'S DARKEST HOUR

In the entire world, only four high-population nations can claim vast shorelines, astounding surf, and a national sports culture significantly disposed to aquatics—Australia, the United States, Brazil, and South Africa. A national surfing title brings the same joy to a South African that a downhill skiing gold medal brings to an Austrian.

Andrew Carter won the South African Surfing Championship as a teen, the best under-18 surfer in a surfing kingdom. His win was not improbable. He had been challenging the waves of the Wild Coast since age six. After high school and two years in the military, he spent his next six years living a life ripped straight from the script of *Endless Summer*:

> My mission was to surf as many of the best left-handed breaks in the world. I surfed Uluwatu, Desert Point, Padang, G-land, Scar Reef, and Lakey Peak in Indonesia, Pipeline in Hawaii, Black Rock and a few secret lefts in Australia, Tamarin Bay in Mauritius, St. Lue in Reunion, Mexican Pipe and Rio Nexpa in Mexico, The Maldives, and a few good spots down south of Costa Rica. I chased down a few good lefts in England and the Canary islands as well. I eked out a living sanding boards and lifesaving. When I ran out of cash, I just slept on the beach. As long as we were in pursuit of perfect waves, it did not matter.

In the mid-1980s, the 5-foot 9-inch 165-pound athlete began surfing professionally, winning two major European events. Such extensive surfing, of course, brings regular—perhaps daily—proximity to sharks, and Andrew was no stranger to them:

> A shark followed me while ocean paddling about two kilometers out to sea once, and I have been followed by sharks on my surf ski. That was pretty scary. While surfing in 1982, my mate got hit

from the side right in front of me, and the shark lifted him completely out of the water, board and all. The shark only got his board, and we paddled like crazy for shore. I have had many wild paddles to shore when rather big fins have been sighted close by. Sometimes, I'm sure they are mistaken identities...quite often a nervous surfer can mix up a stray dolphin with a shark, so at times we just sit our ground after someone yells "Shark!" I have been chased out of the water by sharks about five times that I remember, and possibly five more times that I don't.

In 1994, Andrew, then thirty-one, opened a surf shop, Screaming Blue, in East London. A master shaper, he sold his own line of boards under the Screaming Blue label. He was destined to sell Shannon a custom-shaped board to replace the one he would lose in his dual shark attack at Nahoon in 2000. For Andrew, life was good, and surfing was life.

Among Andrew's surfing mates at the time were twenty-two-year-old Bruce Corby and Bruce's younger brother, Brett Corby, twenty. The Corbys lived just down the road, and both rode Andrew's boards. Bruce was a friendly, outgoing guy whom everybody seemed to love. He was a slim 5-feet 10-inch dude with long sun-bleached hair. He started surfing at thirteen and was a fine athlete. At sixteen, he finished second at the Rip Curl Junior Pro, a major junior competition.

At about 1 p.m. on July 9, 1994, Andrew drove down to Nahoon Reef to catch some waves. Fifteen surfers were in the water that afternoon. Bruce Corby was there too, but younger brother Brett had gone to Durban to attend a Night Pro, a surfing event under the lights. Another of Andrew's good friends, Shaun Ridgard, had been in the water for forty-five minutes when Andrew arrived.

Shaun, twenty-three, was eight years younger than Andrew and had idolized Andrew since his grommet days. "Andrew started handing his personal boards down to me, and that was pretty special to me as a young kid not really being able to afford the best," Shaun recalled. "He basically looked after me and always showed interest in my surfing. Andrew is godfather to my son." Shaun knew the Corby brothers too. By 1994, they had been surfing acquaintances for about five years.

Tragically, Shaun passed away on December 13, 2018, after a brave battle with a rare and aggressive form of cancer. He was a man of faith who helped others in their faith. He left behind his beloved wife, Nia, and his three children, daughters Erin and Mali and son Cian. He also left behind a riveting account of the tragedy that befell Andrew Carter and Bruce Corby at Nahoon Reef in 1994.

"Bruce Corby was a well-liked, happy person with a great sense of humor," Shaun remembered. "He always had time for a chat and wore a permanent smile." Shaun, though, was a reluctant surfer on that July afternoon in 1994. With grim hindsight, he recalled being uneasy from the moment he dropped his board into the water:

> There was definitely a fish smell or something of that sort. I remember sensing that something just didn't feel right when I was jumping off the rocks at the back of the reef, which I think had something to do with the smell. I remember saying to myself, "Geez, it feels sharky today."

The Global Shark Attack File provides a list of recommendations to help people reduce their risk of shark attack. "If you suddenly become uneasy," one recommendation warns, "leave the water immediately."[55] Even a subconscious feeling, you see, can be a good reason to go ashore. You may be sensing something just below the level of conscious cognition.

The waves were breaking at a respectable four to six feet despite a low tide that had exposed most of the reef's rocky extent. After several runs, Andrew, Bruce, and Shaun paddled out along the reef and waited for waves about 60 meters from the reef's tip—the exact spot where Shannon would be struck six years later.[56] Shaun was twenty meters closer to the reef. The time was 1:25 p.m.

When a fresh set of waves rounded the reef, Shaun's proximity to the rocks gave him the first choice. He grabbed the first offering and rode it on a long diagonal trajectory that took him past Andrew and then past a quintet of surfers further in. He didn't remember seeing Bruce who was to his right and a bit further out to sea.

Andrew watched as Shaun sped by. The quintet of surfers, however, paid no attention to Shaun. They were preoccupied. They had just experienced something frightening—a sudden, alarming surge from beneath. It was more of a lifting sensation than a wave. Like a passing submarine, a giant dark shape had rushed through the murk just beneath their boards. The shape had vanished, last seen moving toward the reef...toward Bruce and Andrew who were lying on their boards and looking out to sea. Too stunned to react, none of the five surfers could muster a vocal warning. Barely two seconds later, the beast passed just shoreward of Bruce and accelerated toward its target. Andrew never saw it coming:

> The shark hit me from my left side. I was hit incredibly hard and lifted completely out of the water. The shark clamped its lower jaw under my board and its top jaw over my left thigh. He shook me like a rag doll, as a dog might shake meat off a bone. The force of the bite was tremendous, and I remember thinking the bones in my leg were going to snap. Despite all the teeth lacerating my flesh, there was no sensation of being cut...merely this feeling that I was being crushed in a vice. I will never forget that tremendous power.
>
> The shark then seemed to open its mouth to get a better grip, and possibly due to me pulling away so hard, the board got wedged in the shark's mouth, and I flew off of the board and into the water. Then the shark lunged forward again and grabbed my board and shook it as I watched while lying in the water just a few feet away.
>
> I recall thinking that I could swim away and leave the shark with my board, but in that second I realized that the water was red all around me, and the safety of the beach was a long way away. I decided that the safest thing was to try to get back on top of the board to protect myself. Finally, the shark let go of the board and sank under the water, and I swam for my board. I literally swam right over the top of the shark. I could feel it under me.
>
> I grabbed my board, and luckily, it was still in one piece. As I dragged myself onto the board, a wave broke, and I managed to swing it around and catch it. I was looking left and right expecting to be grabbed again. The second time I looked to my right, I saw the fin break the surface and turn toward me at

speed. I looked away and just started weaving to and fro hoping to make a hard target. Then the wave faded, and I had to paddle across about fifty meters of deep water. I felt I would be attacked again at any second. It was absolutely terrifying.

It took me about three or four minutes to reach the shore, but it felt more like ten. Finally, my board hit the rocks and I crawled over the front of my board and dragged myself into a rocky pool. It was then that I looked back and realized that I had gotten away, but, at the same time, I saw this massive trail of blood in the water behind me. I realized the extent of the bite, and I knew I was in big trouble.

I tried to stop the bleeding by squeezing my upper leg, but my hand just sank into this warm gaping wound. I had not realized how big the bite was—all the way from my knee to my buttocks and hip. Then I laid back and started screaming for help.

Oblivious to the terror unfolding behind him, Shaun Ridgard had finished riding his wave and was traversing along the shoreline toward the slipway, preparing to paddle back out along the reef. As he glanced left, toward the sea, he saw that something was very wrong:

I saw a lot of surfers catching broken waves and heading to shore. I wondered what was going on, and as I looked further out to sea, I saw what I can only describe as a live horror movie. I could see the upper half of a huge shark thrashing about at the side of a surfer's board. The surfer was facing shore and the shark was at a 90-degree angle to him, which gave me a side view of the shark. The surfer was lying on his board and had his body raised with his arms straight, holding the sides of his surfboard and looking back behind him. He was approximately fifty meters away, and I could only catch glimpses of the attack between swells and breaking waves.

At this point, I was in total disbelief, and my first thoughts were, do I keep paddling out to help him or do I head back to shore. I noticed two other surfers quite close to the attack, and given the distance between me and the point of attack, I decided to head for shore in the hope that they would be able to assist him if anyone could.

I arrived on the rocks at the bottom of the concrete pathway. Standing on the end of the pathway looking toward shore, I heard screams to my left. I saw my girlfriend at the time shouting for help and saw someone lying in the shallows at the edge of the rocks. My girlfriend had been suntanning on a small sandy patch at the back of the reef when she saw someone coming in over the rocks and shouting for help. I remember wondering how the guy I saw getting attacked could have gotten to shore so quickly!

I ran over as quickly as possible and, to my horror, found Andrew lying in a rock pool filled with red water. He was quite calm and asked me to tie his leash around the top of his leg which I had already started doing. I lay Andrew's board out on the rocks at an angle as I needed to get him on it to elevate his legs for treatment of shock.

Andrew, who was bleeding out his precious lifeblood in those shallows, recalls his trauma of those moments:

Shaun Ridgard and two girls arrived and one went into overdrive as I shouted for someone to get a tourniquet around my leg and hold up my legs and arms to keep blood in my chest. I had learned this from training I received in shark attack procedure during my lifeguard days.

I saw that my hands had gone completely white. There was no blood in them. Then I started to struggle to breathe and asked the girls to help by pumping my chest. I was certain I was dying at that point. I started losing consciousness, and I was going in and out of darkness as I struggled for breath.

Finally, more help arrived, and they carried me to the car park using my board as a stretcher. The board had a huge bite out of it. Someone had already called the ambulance.

The level of effort and responsibility required of healthy friends in such moments is nothing less than heroic. Shaun Ridgard recalled his efforts to get his injured surfing mentor to the car park:

By this time, two more surfers had arrived, and we lifted Andrew onto his board. I remember my hand slipping inside the back of his leg in the process. His blood was all over me. Some spectators had appeared by this time, and we got a t-shirt off one of them to stuff into the wound and apply pressure...to try and lessen the blood flow. Andrew was not in a very comfortable position, and I knew we had to get him to the car park as soon as possible.

With two people on each side of the surfboard, we awkwardly carried him approximately 100 meters back to the car park, constantly reassuring him as we did. He was still quite calm at this stage. While we were carrying him, I remember him saying to me, "My leg is falling off." I tried to reassure him that it wasn't. I said, "Don't worry, your leg is fine." But then he replied, "No, I mean my other leg is falling off the surfboard." As tragic as the day was, we have a bit of a laugh about that to this day.

By the time Andrew reached the car park, he had lost nearly half of his blood volume. In the grip of a normally-fatal Class IV hemorrhage, Andrew's brain ordered his heart to beat faster to increase supply. His rapid pulse demanded more oxygen, making breathing difficult. Loss of blood pressure brought vasoconstriction, a shutting down of blood flow to the arms and legs to redirect the scarce blood supply to critical areas like the brain and central core. These are the body's last ditch efforts to survive before cardiac arrest. Throughout his terrible ordeal, Andrew was able to maintain a state of semi-consciousness, enough to realize that his plight was neither the only nightmare unfolding at the reef that day nor the worst:

As we neared the top of the concrete pathway, I heard a commotion behind me and looked back to the water's edge. Just on the right-hand side of the pathway where it meets the water, I saw three people. One of them fell over. Then I noticed...all in a bit of a blur...that he only had one leg.

Just thirty seconds after inflicting grievous wounds on Andrew, the shark had turned on Bruce Corby and had bitten off the youth's right leg above the knee. It was Bruce's attack that Shaun had witnessed from close to shore. And the news, Andrew recalls, was grim:

> While I was lying there on my board in the car park waiting for the ambulance, I saw other surfers carry Bruce Corby into the car park on his board. They laid him down about twenty meters from me. I was fading in and out of consciousness, but I have vague memories of people pumping his heart and someone, probably Shaun, telling me that things were not good for him.

The car park had become a MASH unit, and Shaun Ridgard was one of several people agonizing over the fates of two young friends:

> I remember a guy who was helping carry Bruce ask if anybody knew CPR. Someone said he did. I asked if anyone had phoned for an ambulance. Someone commented that we may need a vicar as well. Bruce was in a very serious condition, had lost a lot of blood, and had lost consciousness.
>
> We laid them down on the tarmac, for some reason about twenty meters apart. I was still at Andrew's side and did not know what treatment was being given to Bruce. I was told afterward that he had been given external heart massage. There must have been about forty people gathered around, and I remember people gasping and crying and remember someone yelling, "I don't believe this is happening." I remember seeing Bruce's girlfriend, Samantha, just walking away, sitting down, and crying with her head in her hands.
>
> I was still with Andrew keeping the leash tight around the top of his leg and keeping his legs elevated. At one stage, he mentioned something about dying, and I told him to stay with me, that the ambulance was on its way, and everything was going to be fine. His eyes started rolling back in his head—I could just see the whites—and I shook him and raised my voice saying, "C'mon Andrew, stay awake, buddy!" which made him snap out of it. He regained his wits about him. His survival instinct kicked in, and he was fighting for his life. He had lost a hell of a lot of blood.

I remember at one point going over to Bruce. His leg had been severed just above the knee and someone was elevating that leg to try to stop the blood flow. Bruce's eyes were rolled back, and he was motionless...not a nice thing to witness. Bruce was receiving CPR at this stage. Finally, I went back over to Andrew.

There was not a lot more we could do except wait for the ambulance...and that seemed to take an absolute lifetime. Only one ambulance arrived. I think they had been told that there had been only one shark attack, not a double attack, but another ambulance was summoned and arrived shortly after. They attended to Bruce straight away as he was critical but still breathing. After the ambulances left, I remember feeling empty and helpless. I was definitely in a state of shock at what I had just witnessed.

For Andrew, the ambulance ride was excruciating. As the adrenaline abated, his pain reached torturous levels:

About fifteen or twenty minutes later, two ambulances arrived. Bruce and I went in separate ambulances to Frère Hospital in East London. While I was in the ambulance, they hooked me up to a saline drip that probably saved my life by maintaining volume in my circulatory system. I had lost a huge amount of blood. I remember one medic telling me that I could not have afforded to lose one more drop.

It was during the ride to the hospital that the first pains started breaking through the adrenaline. I remember screaming every time we went over a bump or around a corner. It felt like my leg was being torn off. When I got to the hospital, I was begging for painkillers, but they told me I had already had the limit they could give before taking me to the operating theater.

The bite was down to the bone and extended from my left knee to my left thigh, buttock, and hip. All of the major muscles in my leg had been severed.

Bruce was not so lucky. The shark had attacked him thirty seconds after my attack and had bitten off his right leg above the knee. The femoral artery had been severed and he had lost nearly all of his blood volume.

I had to wait about an hour before going into surgery. There were not enough doctors around, and I had to wait for them to operate on Bruce because his situation was worse than mine. Finally, thankfully, I was given anesthesia.

Fortunately for Andrew, being sandwiched with his surfboard in the shark's mouth had saved him from massive flesh loss and probable amputation and death. The surgical repair involved several hundred stitches and staples and the reattachment of most of his major leg muscles. Miraculously, he was able to regain 100 percent use of the limb. He would surf again.

Tragically, Bruce was not as fortunate. The youth suffered near-total blood loss before receiving plasma and transfusions. In the hours following surgery, his kidneys and other organs began to fail. About 48 hours after the attack, the blond-haired twenty-two-year-old lost his fight for life.

Aftermath

Brett Corby was in a surf shop in Durban when a friend informed him about his brother's attack and told him to call his aunt. "Bruce has been bitten by a shark, and he's in the hospital," his aunt told him. She didn't mention that the shark had taken a leg.

When Brett arrived in East London, other surfers told him what they had seen. The shark had attacked Andrew first. Bruce had paddled toward Andrew to help, and the shark had turned on Bruce.

Brett was able to see his brother, but they were never able to speak. Bruce never regained consciousness.

Andrew, still in horrible pain from his surgical repairs, was not informed of Bruce's death right away. "Andrew looked bad with huge bandages on his leg and butt," Brett recalls. "He was still really shaken."

Shaun also visited Andrew in the hospital. "I was so happy that he had survived," he remembered. Despite the unimaginable horror that he witnessed that day, though, Shaun did not give up his sport:

I didn't surf for about a month. The first time I paddled back out at Nahoon Reef, I only managed to stay in the water for about fifteen minutes, constantly looking over the side of my board. It was terrifying. I have surfed the reef many times since then, but I still feel edgy when I'm out there. But life must go on. As long as there are waves, we will be surfing them. I know that Bruce wouldn't have it any other way.

The horrific double attack made international news overnight and became the dominant news story in South Africa for weeks. Public debate erupted over the future of the shark that had exacted such a horrific human toll, but, in the end, it was not hunted. The animal had bitten each young man exactly once, undoubtedly hoping for a seal. Disappointed, the animal had discontinued each attack. Why punish a fish for doing exactly what it is designed to do? Nahoon Beach and Reef were closed for a week, but surfing continued despite the shark flags. "This is East London," Brett points out. "The guys were back out there before the beach reopened."

Bruce's funeral services were held in the largest church in East London, but the building could not accommodate the mourners. They packed the aisles and formed long lines along the streets outside—hundreds of friends, surfers, and townspeople wanting to pay their respects to a young man who would grow no older. Tears flowed freely among normally carefree youths as a pall settled over the town. Bruce Corby had become Nahoon's first shark fatality in thirty-three years. He had very nearly become Nahoon's second shark fatality in thirty-three seconds.

For Brett Corby, the joy that he always found on his surfboard vanished with his brother:

> I surf with friends on the high tide closer to the beach. I don't surf the reef and have tried to get over my fear, but I don't want to put my family and loved ones through that again. Unfortunately, all of the trials are held at the reef, so it has become difficult to win my Provincial colours.

The damage to Brett's confidence in the water, however, is the least significant of his burdens. He carries a far heavier weight—the loss of his older brother, a brother who had given him so much grief as older brothers do, but a brother whom he loved very deeply. Brett walks hand-in-hand with the emotional pain every day of his life:

> In 1994, Bruce was unemployed. He had previously fallen off a two-story building onto some railway tracks and was collecting disability benefits. Doctors said he would never surf again, but I had never seen him surf better.
>
> Bruce spoke to me the night before I left for Durban. He told me he was going to stop all of the crap he was doing...drinking, smoking, and so on. He told me he had found God, and he was so in love with his girlfriend. He made peace with me and apologized for all the hard times he had given me. When I left for Durban, I was so stoked that my boet (brother) was finally getting his life in order.[57]
>
> Bruce is a legend. He was an awesome brother, too...one who would beat the crap out of anyone who messed with me. My mind was so gone during the funeral. Not a day goes by that I don't think of him.

20
BAD DAY AT BONZA BAY

Three months passed before Andrew Carter mustered the courage to return to the world-class waves of Nahoon Reef. Like Shannon, who would be attacked at the same spot six years later, Andrew felt he had to go back as soon as possible. He had to put his fear, and Bruce's death, behind him. He had to reclaim his life, and his life was surfing. Andrew's return to the cold, dark rocks of the reef, however, took grit:

> It was pretty hairy. I felt as if I was going to be attacked at any moment, so I did not want to be too far from the other surfers.
>
> Since my attack, I have been pretty close to a few sharks, but normally on my surf ski. I just relaxed and paddled away slowly. I paddled over a 2.5 meter great white just three months ago. Sharks are certainly on our minds in the water, and there were four fatal attacks in South Africa during the last year. The Wild Coast is always a little scary. The fear is constantly there, but mostly the waves are good enough to keep it in the back of your mind. But some days, I feel really scared, and I believe a sixth sense is telling me there's a problem. When the birds are diving and the sardines are around, it's just plain scary though.
>
> I know a good many surfers who have been attacked, probably five or six guys who live within a five kilometer radius of my home.

The attacks of Andrew's acquaintances are well-recorded. One thirteen-year-old was knocked from his board and into the air while surfing at Queensberry Bay in 1973.[58] The boy's aggressive action in punching the shark, something seals never do, confused the shark long enough to spare the boy from injury. A twenty-two-year-old was bodyboarding near East London on October 24, 1985, when a 2.5 meter great white nearly severed his left foot.[59] A forty-six-year-old was attacked at Cape St. Francis on April 8, 2001, receiving grievous wounds nearly identical to Andrew's—deep punctures to his thigh, hip, and buttocks, all courtesy of a 2.7 meter great white.[60] A thirty-two-year-old was struck on March 28, 2005, while surfing at Noordhoek. He suffered deep lacerations to his calf and punctures to his right foot.[61]

One attack among Andrew's acquaintances involved a thirty-seven-year-old father of two, Lee Mellin, who was severely bitten in the left thigh while surfing at Bonza Bay in late 2007. Like Andrew, Lee was attacked within sight of Nahoon Reef, but he and Andrew are linked by more than the site of their attacks.

Lee was twenty-four years old when the Corby-Carter attacks took place, and the tragedy affected him deeply. Lee had grown up with the Corby brothers in the Quigney suburb of East London, and the three youths had spent many days together at Orient Beach where the Ainslie brothers were introduced to surfing. Lee knew Andrew Carter well. He surfed with Andrew and made many visits to Andrew's surf shop. Lee rode Andrew's boards, and his wife, Nicola, had worked in Andrew's shop.

Lee was studying engineering in Port Elizabeth when Andrew and Bruce were attacked, but the manner of Bruce's death—his leg amputated in a brutal posterior attack—haunted Lee for years. Indeed, Andrew's attack and Bruce's death were very much on Lee's mind as he struggled to survive his own great white attack thirteen years later.

Hier Kom Kak!

At the eastern end of the Nahoon Reef car park—the end furthest from the reef—a staircase rises to the top of a rocky promontory called Nahoon Corner. At the top, a spectacular northern vista awaits. The graceful arc of Bonza Bay sweeps left and then right, its eastern extent kissing the very horizon. Immediately below the Corner, popular Nahoon Beach extends for one kilometer to the Nahoon River which washes over the sand in wide, occasionally fordable sheets. Further north, at the apex of the curved bay, the Quinera River shallows up as it flows across Bonza Beach. All along the bay, breathtaking lines of white surf roll shoreward in broad parallel bands.

At 6:30 a.m. on November 3, 2007, Lee Mellin drove his silver Nissan double-cab pick-up truck to the Bonza Bay car park to join his friend, Leigh Stolworthy, for a day of surfing. The car park is tucked along the Quinera River where it deepens just behind the beach.

On that Saturday morning, conditions were marginal at best. The sky was overcast, and the water was unusually cold for late spring—a face-numbing 17°C or 62°F. An offshore breeze in the night had given way to a south-westerly crosswind that was chopping the waves at a displeasing two feet.

The two men had Bonza Bay to themselves—no line-ups, no pecking order, no localism issues. A third surfer, Dean Gierke, stopped by and spoke with them briefly, but he left in search of better waves at Yellow Sands.

At 8:45 a.m., the two friends finished a wave and were paddling back out. As they sat on their partially submerged thrusters 100 meters from the shore, Leigh turned to speak to Lee—"to say something funny to me," Lee surmises. Just as Leigh returned his gaze to the sea, however, he sensed movement in his right peripheral vision:

> Lee was about 10 meters to my left, and suddenly I noticed a shark approaching from my right. It passed within two meters of the front of my board and just below the surface. I knew straight away what it was and that we were in serious trouble. I shouted a warning to Lee. Lee saw the shark when it was already between us and moving toward him. It was moving relatively slowly. We both turned towards the beach and paddled slowly but purposefully. We knew instinctively not to make any thrashing movements. Then we lost sight of the shark. It must have turned out to sea in a clockwise direction and then come back.
>
> I looked to my right to see where Lee was. He was lying on his board and paddling. Suddenly, the shark surfaced between us, also heading toward shore, and then it turned toward Lee. The shark seemed slow and almost tentative. I got a good look at its face, mouth, and eyes and knew it was a great white. Then the shark bit into Lee's left thigh. Lee shouted, and then the shark seemed to release pressure and tried to get a better grip on him. At that moment, Lee rolled off his board, and the shark bit down on his surfboard.[62]

149

From Lee's perspective, he knew he was the target the instant the animal resurfaced between the two men:

> I remember thinking in Afrikaans, *hier kom kak!*[63] Sure enough, the shark turned and came straight at me. The shark rolled and bit my left thigh. It felt like stabs from a knife, though the shark didn't rip at my leg or try to shake me. I can barely remember the bite, to be honest—maybe it was the adrenaline. I called out to Leigh, "Help me!" in what Leigh later described as a deep guttural voice that he had never heard before.
>
> The shark let go of my leg, and I managed to climb off of my board just as the shark attacked a second time, this time sinking its teeth into my board. I was hanging onto the front end of the board as the shark wrestled with the back end. It was facing me, and I could see its partially submerged back and its dorsal fin. Its tail fin was thrashing side-to-side, sometimes coming within a meter of me. I hung onto the top half of the board as the shark munched on the lower half. Finally, the board snapped in half.
>
> The shark pulled away with the tail of my board in its mouth. That tailpiece was still attached to my right leg by my leash, though, and I thought I might get pulled under the water.

Leigh could only watch the drama unfold:

> Lee was still attached by his leash to the piece of board that the shark had in its mouth, and it dragged him for about five meters before the leash snapped. The shark was still visible, but it seemed to be struggling with that piece of the surfboard...like it was stuck in its mouth. Then it dived again with that piece of the board still in its mouth. Lee was holding the rest of his board and was spinning around looking for the shark, expecting it to attack again. I shouted at him that it was gone, even though I wasn't sure, and told him to get on his board and start paddling.[64]

Fleeing the vicinity of a great white is as instinctive as running out of a burning building, but Leigh Stolworthy stood fast by his friend. He lingered mere meters from Lee as the attack progressed, knowing full well that the shark could turn on him at any moment. There was nothing Leigh could do except be there to help when the attack ended. No one can fight a one-ton animal in its element, especially when that animal is an apex predator in a realm covering three-fifths of the earth's surface. In reality, Leigh faced the same mortal risk that Bruce Corby faced as he remained at Andrew Carter's side. But remain he did.

Lee will never forget Leigh's aid and encouragement. Nor will he forget the images of Bruce Corby that raced through his mind as he paddled, bleeding, toward a seemingly unreachable shore:

> I kept asking Leigh to watch out behind me. I remembered that Bruce Corby had been taken from behind, so I was conscious of trying to keep my legs out of the water as I paddled on my shortened piece of board. Leigh reassured me that the shark was nowhere to be seen, though he later told me that he had seen it one more time just behind us.
>
> When we got to walking depth, Leigh had a look at my leg. I had a 15-inch-long line of deep puncture wounds on the back of my thigh. The wounds extended from the back of my knee to just under my left butt cheek, but they were not bleeding too badly. Leigh assured me the wounds were not life-threatening. I never felt much pain. I guess the adrenaline was still pumping.

When the men reached the safety of land, Leigh gathered up two large pieces of his friend's surfboard. A third, smaller piece—the one that had jammed in the shark's mouth—washed up a moment later. Leigh remembers thinking that the missing piece could not have drifted in so quickly...not unless the shark had carried it to shore right behind them. But the pursuit was over. Lee recalls his first moments on dry land:

> There was no one in close proximity to us when we reached the beach, and I was able to limp on my own from the beach to Leigh's car. We walked past the lifesaver's shack and advised the guard on duty that there was a shark, and suggested that he should close the beach. He had been oblivious to the attack.

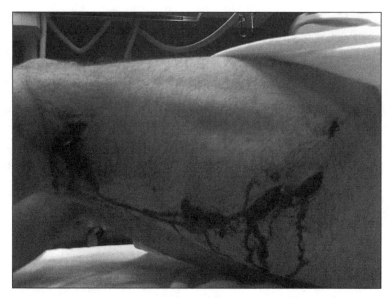

Lee Mellin's shark attack injury (Courtesy of Leigh Stolworthy)

Lee Mellin's surfboard following Bonza Bay attack (Courtesy of Lee Mellin)

When we got to Leigh's Nissan pick-up, I phoned my wife, Nicola, and asked her to meet us at the hospital. I sat next to Leigh in the passenger seat as he drove to the hospital. I had a towel wrapped around my leg and sat on a board bag to try to limit the amount of blood landing on the seats.

I don't remember much pain as we drove to the hospital. There couldn't have been too much pain, because I was only worried about one thing. Leigh and I were having a good laugh because this was the first time that I had not worn underpants under my wetsuit. I knew the nurses were going to strip off my wetsuit, and I was going to be butt naked on the bed!

I was released from the hospital on the Monday after the attack but was back in there the same day with some kidney stones I didn't know I had. They were probably released somehow from all of the fluids they pumped into me after the attack.

I was booked off from work for three weeks but was able to start walking on crutches after two days. The wound on the back of my knee was a problem. It split open, and I had to have it re-stitched by the surgeon. After the stitches were removed, it split open again, but it did manage to heal up fine.

On November 6, Lee's parents, Rob and Carol Mellin, wrote a letter to the editor of the *Daily Dispatch* thanking Leigh Stolworthy for saving their son's life. Here is part of what they had to say:[65]

Stolworthy, who could have swum away when the shark attacked, stayed with Lee throughout the frightening ordeal, guiding him back to shore on the broken surfboard, helping him to get to shore and subsequently getting him to hospital.

When we phoned Leigh Stolworthy to commend him for the courageous part he played in seeing Lee to safety and taking him to hospital, his reply was simply: "You never leave a friend behind."

Lee's attacker was large. All three segments of Lee's board were recovered and when pieced together betrayed a full impression of the shark's

153

massive upper jaw. Shortly after the attack, experts at the Natal Sharks Board examined the bite radius on Lee's board and estimated that Lee had been attacked by a great white in the 4 to 4.5-meter range—14 feet long and considerably longer and heavier than two large refrigerators laid end to end. Both of the sharks involved in Shannon's attack had been of that size.

A single factor may account for Lee's survival at Bonza Bay. The shark may have seen the men while patrolling the surface. Great whites tend to take seals with devastating attacks from depth, and surfers look like seals from below. Seeing surfers on the surface may have been more confusing, resulting in a gentler exploratory bite.

Lee hasn't surfed at Bonza Bay since his attack, but he did resume surfing. On December 27, less than eight weeks after his attack, he drove 120 kilometers southeast to Port Alfred to surf with a friend. Like Shannon's shift to Yellow Sands and Michal du Plessis's shift to Nahoon, Lee's move to Port Alfred was little more than a psychological security blanket. Port Alfred had been the site of eleven prior shark attacks, one of which had claimed the life of seventeen-year-old swimmer, Lorenzo Kroutz, just twenty-one months before Lee's visit. Lee was unaware of the attacks.

To assist Lee in his return to the waves, a local supplier of Shark Shield[66] donated a demo model to him. Shark Shield is an electronic device developed in Australia. The device affixes to the tail of a surfboard and repels sharks with an electric field that emanates from a heavy hose-like tail that drags in the water. Lee had forgotten to charge the unit before arriving in Port Alfred, so he gave it only a ten-minute zap in his car before hitting the waves. Insufficiently charged, the device quickly lost power, but it did give him the initial surge of confidence that he needed to enter the water.

Not surprisingly, Lee Mellin's perspective on sharks changed after his attack. Before his encounter, he had formed a mental strategy about how he would handle a shark attack. After his encounter, though, he better appreciated the adage, "No battle plan survives first contact with the enemy":

> In my mind's eye, I always thought I would fight and try to get the better of the shark. Now, I realize that these are super powerful animals with lightning-quick reactions. They cannot be taken lightly. This was only the second shark I had ever seen since

learning to surf at age sixteen, and I used to be a bit blasé about them being in the surf. Now, I am a lot more conscious of their presence in differing water conditions.

Leigh Stolworthy is more conscious of sharks as well, but he still surfs near his home in Cape Town, a notoriously shark-infested region. "Once a surfer, always a surfer," he will tell you, noting that Cape Town area surfers and swimmers now enjoy a unique warning system:

The ocean has always been my happy place and my soul food, both before and after shark experiences. I live in Cape Town now, and we are fortunate here to have an amazing organization called The Shark Spotters. The Cape Town Peninsula is split by a mountain range, the Table Mountain Range, that runs all the way to Cape Point. The Shark Spotters have lookout points along the mountains overlooking surf spots on both sides. The people who man these lookout points monitor the seas for shark activity and radio down to the beach if there is a sighting. There is a flag system and sirens to warn surfers and swimmers if there is a shark present. I have only heard the siren once. Luckily, I had just finished surfing at the time! My absolute favorite thing currently is surfing with my teenage daughters, sharing waves and ocean knowledge, awareness and appreciation with them.

Lee and his wife, Nicola, are blessed with three children of their own. Lee still surfs but is more careful in all respects. He uses his Shark Shield at Nahoon Reef. He's more watchful and avoids the water when the gulls are diving for sardines. He avoids Bonza Bay and generally surfs in the company of friends. Lee's cautiousness is not the product of fear. It is the product of wisdom. The Wild Coast is a serious place. Only fools challenge it thoughtlessly.

21

TRANSFORMATION

Shannon was raised a Christian. He even received awards for Sunday school attendance as a child. But he only went to church because he was told to. The family attended a Methodist church in East London, and like most pre-teens, Shannon found the services in his words, "slow and lame." Sometimes, he told his family he was going to church and would walk around the city instead. He'd use the money that was given for tithes and offerings to go play on retro arcade machines or buy cold drinks and candy.

The kid was in no mood to praise God for anything. God had let his father lose his business to a cheating business partner. God had let them lose their home. God had let his parents fight and ultimately divorce. God had made him grow up on rural farms without electricity for months at a time. Shannon never lacked health, love, and support, but he was still angry as a kid, and he took it out on everyone. He beat up his friends. He beat up his sister. He fought with his brother. Slowly, though, a light came into his life.

Shannon's discovery of surfing over Easter weekend in April 1998, had introduced him to a new circle of friends, many with a strong spiritual side. In May, Shannon began tagging along with Travis Naude to Friday night youth group meetings at St. Albans's Anglican Church. Some 200 pre-teens, teens, and 20-somethings gathered there to eat, play music, pray, watch surfing movies, play games, and talk about Jesus. When a thirteen-year-old boy in East London mingles with sixteen, eighteen, and twenty-year-old surfing prodigies, he might just as well mingle with rock stars. He wants to dress like they dress, speak as they speak, use the gear they use, and play the music they play.

One of the youth meetings took place on a cool winter night in 1998. According to Shannon, it was a meeting that changed his life forever:

> I remember being in the auditorium with about 200 other youth. All the surfers went to that youth group, and most of the

surfers I looked up to loved Jesus. They were cool, happy people and good athletes. I wanted to be like them and have what they had.

Philip Schonken was the leader of the group. He was about thirty and was a super cool guy. He always had powerful messages for us, and he made a huge impression on me. One Friday night in August, Philip gave an especially poignant talk to us, and he seemed to be speaking directly to me.

I remember Phil speaking of how Jesus came to rescue us from despair, depression, anger, and poverty. He also said that Jesus came to give us life and life in abundance—a life filled with freedom, adventure, and prosperity. And he didn't mean just financial prosperity, but social, emotional, and relational prosperity—a life overflowing so that you can share it with others. I never had this life, and it seemed like everyone around me at the youth group did have it. I wanted that.

Phil then asked people who wanted to accept Jesus to come forward. I remember feeling blood rush to my face. I wasn't used to standing up in front of people. It was an insane mix of emotions. But I stood up and went to the front with about ten other teenagers. Phil asked us to say to Jesus that we will give our lives to Him and that we will try to be good persons and seek His help in life.

I thought that this altar call would change my life, so I was very excited about responding to it. I thought that I would be a new person...that I'd wake up the next morning as a new and changed person...that all my problems would disappear. I never knew much about committing to Jesus, so I didn't understand the whole decision that I had made and how to follow through with it. But I felt happy and stoked to see what would happen in the days to come.

"Immediately, I had more self-control," he says of the weeks and months that followed. "All of my depression and hatred vanished. I never hit Candice again. I even stopped swearing."

Shannon's family had some issues with his decision. They were traditional Christians and didn't understand evangelism. Candice and Brandon thought he was going through a phase. Shane worried that his son had fallen in with a cult that might lead him astray. Quickly, though, the family's doubts abated. They were moved by the changes they saw in the kid.

"All of a sudden, he stopped hanging with bad friends," Candice remembers. "He realized he didn't have to be mean. He was more playful and helpful." The change was so profound that the entire family's faith soared. Shannon, however, had not yet completed his journey:

> For a long time, I didn't feel as angry and depressed as I had before. God definitely heard my prayers and helped me out. But my life and family situations were still the same, and still being a young kid and not knowing much about God and Christianity, I kind of got fed up with things. I tried hard to be a good person and to do good things, I forgot, or perhaps I never knew, that Christianity was more about a relationship with your heavenly Father than being a good person and doing good things. While I still prayed and tried to be a better person, I grew lukewarm in my faith in Jesus. If faith was about doing good things, I didn't understand why nothing was changing. I had stopped smoking, swearing, and cursing. I had stopped beating up my sister and my friends. I was practicing self-control and tried not to lie or steal. Still, though, I felt empty on the inside.

Two years later, Shannon overcame his doubts in a single dramatic moment when he survived his attack at Nahoon Reef. Since that fateful day, Shannon's faith has been painted in black and white—the black eye that stared at him under the waves and the white wave that carried him to shore. The change in Shannon was evident to everyone who knew him, including Alistair Cokayne:

> Shannon would often tell me how God had helped him, and he seemed to enjoy life a bit more after his close call. He is an extremely kind person. He goes out of his way to help people, and even if he can't help someone, he'll find a way to help anyway. If I needed a ride, he'd find a way to pick me up. If I fought with

my parents, he'd let me sleep at his house. I always felt I was home at his place. In fact, we lived with each other, the three of us—Shannon, Travis, and I. He's funny and laughs a lot. He's not cross very often anymore...he's very forgiving and open.

According to Brad Coetzee, humor seemed to replace all of Shannon's earlier anger:

He's a great practical joker. His favorite trick for the ages is talking to you from a distance but not actually saying anything, and you just going, 'What? What??' It was like he was saying, 'Hey, brah, wa fra wa, huh?' It catches some people off guard and they respond like they know what he's saying. It sounds lame, but it's classic. I still do it now and again. He would also do it on the phone.

And talking about phones, he would almost never say 'good-bye.' Whenever the phone call was coming to an end, he would say, 'Hey, Brad!...'' as if he remembered something and then hang up. Annoying!!

As Shannon grew older, he began mentoring younger kids and taking them under his broad wings. He taught them to surf and invested in them his Christian values, but he always did so as an equal and never in a preachy or proselytizing manner. Trent Weyer was one of those younger kids.

Seven years younger than Shannon, Trent later served in the South African Navy and Special Forces and was detailed to protect the President of South Africa. A striking and muscular youth, Trent is expertly trained in diving, swimming, and aquatic operations. Oddly, he came to know Shannon before they even met:

I lived in Britain for six years and remember seeing replays of Shannon's shark attack on television. I had no idea that one day he would be my mate! After I moved to Jeffreys Bay, I was introduced to Shannon at a surf competition. Shannon was always giving surf lessons or coaching people, and I remember hooking up with him for surf lessons. As I got better, he started taking me

Shannon with Trent Weyer of South African Special Forces (Courtesy of Ashley Botes)

to his favorite surf spots, and we became really good mates. Every single day after school, I'd ride my bike to his house, and we would find something to do. We'd go surfing, drive out to J-Bay looking for waves, watch a movie, play games on his computer, or wrestle.

We wrestled all the time and most of the time, he would take me down. He had a bit more skill than me and always used to say that wrestling is not about size but about skill. He did say that I was stronger than him, though! We loved socializing and hanging out with different people together. That's one thing he taught me...to be friends with anybody, no matter who they are.

He is the least shy person you will ever meet. He loves to meet new people and always makes jokes and creates laughter but never to offend anyone. At stores, we would pass some people, and he would call out to them from behind and then walk away, so they thought I had called out to them. I would be standing there feeling like a fool. In the car, he would hit the brakes and bang the side of the car pretending that he had hit some-

160

thing, or he would act like he had gotten something in his eye and swerve the car like he couldn't see. On the phone, he would get to the end of a call and say, "Just remember..." and then hang up, and I'd be sitting there thinking "Remember what!?"

Shannon was always there for me, helping me through things I was battling with, teaching me, and adding values to my life. He told me to hold my values high wherever I am and never to compromise them. When Shannon left for Norway, I realized how important his friendship is to me and how he is a true brother. We both know we would gladly die for each other.

During his last two years of high school, the kinder, gentler Shannon had found Jesus. Unfortunately, he had not yet found himself. Like so many youths reaching adulthood, Shannon had become increasingly troubled by a lack of direction in his life. He needed goals. He needed a mission and purpose:

Coming from a poorer background, divorced parents, and so on, I often felt lost and wondered why I was alive...why nothing ever went well for me. When I survived the shark attack after praying and asking God to keep me safe, I realized that there must be more to life than what we see...that God must have saved me for a purpose. So, I decided to find out more about God, draw closer to Him, as well as find out what I should do in life and how to add purpose to my life. Because I almost died, I thought a lot about life after death, and after having an experience with Jesus, I felt compassion grow inside of me to see other surfers come to know and experience Jesus the way I did. That was and still is my main purpose.

Occasionally, God even nudged the youth a little to keep him on the right path.

22

BUMPED

For a surfer, the day seemed too drab, too average, to be memorable. It was a gloomy afternoon in October 2002. A low overcast hung in the sky over East London like a thick gray blanket, and rain seemed imminent. An on-shore breeze was pushing waves against the receding tide, churning the water to a dingy brown and chopping off the few good breakers at a meter or less. The sea still carried the icy chill of winter, though spring was upon the country.

Shannon, then a strapping seventeen-year-old, and his friend Damon van Mierlo, eighteen, had been in the water for about forty-five minutes. They were floating about 100 meters off of Nahoon Corner, the rocky promontory that separates Nahoon Reef from Nahoon Beach. Conditions at the reef were poor, the Corner holding the greatest promise for decent rides.

The two friends were separated from Shannon's well-chronicled dual shark attack by two years and 360 meters. They scanned the sea for scarce sets, both sitting on their submerged thrusters and floating chest-deep in the sea as they waited. The water was dirty, a fact that sorely tested Shannon's sense of well-being:

> The water was super brown, and that made it feel eerie and dodgy because sharks can't see what they're attacking in such water. Only Damon and I were surfing the Corner, so every time he caught a wave, I was all alone at sea. I kept glancing around and trying to watch for trouble, but I couldn't see through the surface. I had mostly overcome my fear of sharks, but the dirty water made it feel weird out there, especially with Nahoon Reef so close by.
>
> When Damon paddled back out, we sat on our boards and chatted a while. I was facing out to sea. Damon was a bit further out and facing me, just to my right. As we sat there, I decided to

162

pull my feet up onto my submerged board to keep them from dangling in the murky water.

Suddenly, I got slammed really hard from behind by something large. The impact knocked the board right out from under me and dumped me in the water. I couldn't see what had hit me because of the dirty water.

Damon was stunned by the sight:

Shannon was on my inside no more than five meters from me. I was looking at him with my back to the waves having a convo. I didn't see anything or any sign of what was about to happen. All of a sudden he lifted out of the water up to his waistline with a shocked look on his face. His board shot from between his legs and toward me, and he pulled on his leash to retrieve his board. During that time, he was looking at me with these huge eyes! He asked, 'Did you see that? I just got bumped!' I asked him if he was alright, and he said, "Yes!"

For Shannon, the impact brought a flood of bad memories. He wondered if it could all be happening again:

I got a big fright. I felt so naked and vulnerable in the water. To me, my board was my safety and rescue craft to get me to shore and to get me out of any situation. I felt helpless, like a target for the shark to bite. I frantically scratched for my surfboard, jumped on it, and lay down with my arms and legs in the air. Damon did the same. At least if the shark came at me while on my board, I had a chance of surviving. Without it, I was a shark biscuit!

My heart was beating really fast and thoughts of being attacked again were racing through my head. I didn't want my life to end. I was only really beginning to enjoy life now, and I wanted to keep living and experience many things, travel, and lead an adventurous life. I thought maybe if I got attacked again, I would not be as lucky as the previous attack and might lose an arm or leg or worse. It all happened so quickly, I'm not sure Damon even realized what had happened until a few seconds after I got back on my board. We both just lay quietly on our boards hoping for a wave to approach. We were really scared, glancing all over the place and expecting the shark to come back for us. I knew that if this shark was serious about attacking and eating one of us that it would happen at any second. We were helpless and had no idea what to do. We kept looking at each other in disbelief that this was happening.

I decided to pray to God to keep us safe again. After I prayed, I felt more relaxed and that helped. The worst thing to do in any situation is to panic or freak out because that doesn't help at all. I tried to get Damon to relax too. Then I started laughing out loud, but quietly! Damon thought I was crazy! But I knew that God had heard me and wanted to rescue us both. He just wanted us to turn to Him and ask for help.

Damon doesn't specifically remember Shannon praying out loud that day but believes he almost certainly did. "I was in too much shock to focus on anything," he says.

The secret to their safety may have resided in Shannon's calming advice. A seal, the great white's preferred target, will flee from a shark in panic. Sharks expect that. By not thrashing or fleeing in panic, a surfer distinguishes himself from the shark's usual prey.

"As scared as we were," Damon recounts, "we just stayed calm to avoid action on the water's surface, and I'm thankful to Shannon for teaching me this."

After about one minute of waiting, a wave arrived and both men caught it but not without a moment of humor. About ten seconds into their escape, Damon fell. Shannon turned and watched as Damon scrambled back onto his board.

"It was scary but also funny," Shannon recalls. "That shark could have attacked him at any time, and to see how quickly he got back to his board and caught that wave was hysterical. He wasn't in the water five seconds!"

Predictably, Damon saw less humor in it:

My leash came undone on that wave, and I lost my board for a bit. I swam to my board splashing like a petrified dog trying to get out of a pool. It was really scary, but it was pretty shallow there, and I got to shore just after Shannon. *Then* I laughed about it."

Damon's fear is revealing, though. He's an avowed adrenaline junkie who is nearly impossible to intimidate. He's been known to set himself on fire and jump into pools, do face plants on motocross jumps, leap from tall cliffs into boulder-strewn pools, and make midnight leaps from the fifteen-meter-high Batting Road Bridge into the bull shark-infested Nahoon River. In 2013, he took up skydiving and began training for his ultimate goal—a BASE jump.

As for Shannon, he may have gotten lucky the same way twice. During his 2000 attack, the attacking shark got a mouthful of fiberglass fins and called it a day. During his 2002 episode at the Corner, the shark hit the back underside of Shannon's board, again getting a snout-full of fins. In both cases, the feel of sharp fiberglass may have sent the fish in search of seals bearing less armor.

After learning of the incident, a lifeguard closed Nahoon Beach for the day. Experts suggest that sharks tend to hang around for a few days when they find prey in an area, so closing beaches is prudent. You wonder, though, what a beach closure accomplishes. Sharks are in the water all the time. Beach closings foster the impression that, when the beach reopens, the danger has passed. In reality, the danger never passes…not on the Wild Coast. That's why surfers take to the water even when shark flags are flying.

Bumping incidents like this are common. In 2009, Brad Coetzee was surfing Nahoon early in the morning when a friend was knocked off of his surfboard by a large shark of unknown type. "The water was murky, so we didn't see anything before or after, but again we scrambled for the beach," Brad recalls. "My friend subsequently quit surfing because he has a young family at home and feels his life is in danger whenever he surfs."

If you live in the Nahoon area and want to surf, though, you have to accept a certain degree of risk. Sometimes, as Brad notes, that means swimming with apex predators:

We East London surfers have been called out of the water many, many times. It's not uncommon to go to Nahoon Beach and see the shark flag up. I have remained in the water after seeing a dorsal fin in the distance, depending on how the waves are and how many other guys are in the water. Otherwise, I get out. Unless it's a monster shark, we don't tell anyone either. We just get ridiculed for being wussies, especially by the older guys. Weird, hey?

Yes, it is weird. But the rules of engagement in man's battle for dominion over the sea are ambiguous at best.

Shannon has no idea what kind of animal slammed into his surfboard that October afternoon. He never saw it. But the impact was big enough to knock a seated and fully grown man off a surfboard, and that limits the field.

Bumping is not common behavior for great whites. Whites tend to go deep and come up hard, biting their prey viciously on first contact. Like legendary heavyweight fighter George Foreman, they like first-round knockouts.

Bumping is not common behavior for tiger sharks either. Tigers like to fiddle around and circle for a while. Like Muhammad Ali, they float like a butterfly for six or seven rounds and then move in for the kill.

Bumping behavior is, however, routinely employed by another dangerous predator, the bull shark or Zambezi. Bull sharks are relentless. Like Sonny Liston, they get you in a corner and never let you out. Bulls are regarded by most experts as the most dangerous sharks to humans, yet they have not attacked or killed as many humans as great whites. Why is this so?

Well, whites bite you, discover you're not a seal, and often move on. Unfortunately, that one bite can remove a leg or an arm, tear away thirty pounds of flesh, or sever a femoral artery. In the 125 years between 1876 and 2001, 67 of 254 of great white victims perished—about 26 percent.[67]

Bull sharks, though, bite and hold on whether you turn out to be a seal or not. Their tenacity has earned them the nickname, "pit bulls of the sea." Indeed, a bull shark is thought to be responsible for the infamous New Jersey shore attacks in 1916—a twelve-day, five-attack rampage that took the lives of four young males and critically injured a fifth. The attacks inspired Peter Benchley's best-selling novel, *Jaws*, and the 1975 blockbuster movie of the same name (though the movie featured a great white). Remarkably, three of the five New Jersey attacks occurred in freshwater more than two miles from the sea, in New Jersey's Matawan Creek![68] Capable of existing in freshwater, bulls have attacked horses ninety miles up the Brisbane River in Australia, have wandered most of the length of the Amazon River, and have been found in the Mississippi River as far north as St. Louis.

Both qualities of the bull—tenacity and river presence—were evident in three particularly nightmarish encounters in Mozambique on January 23, 1973. A bull shark attacked two young boys who were swimming in the Limpopo River fully 150 kilometers from the ocean. One boy lost a leg and the other lost an arm. That same day, another young boy lost an arm to a bull shark 3.5 kilometers up the Limpopo. Miraculously, the three boys survived.[69] Seven years earlier, a bull shark attacked a canoe on the Limpopo a whopping 545 kilometers from the sea.[70]

The Eastern Cape region of South Africa, however, was believed to be the extreme southern limit of the bull's Indian Ocean range—an unlikely place to find one. At least that was the case until January 24, 2009. On that summer day, a 1,000-pound, four-meter-long bull shark was caught more than five kilometers up the Breede River in the Western Cape, the far southern tip of Africa. Two days after electronic tagging and release, the animal swam another fifteen kilometers upriver passing within meters of fishermen.[71]

Just one day after the huge female bull was tagged in the Breede River, a suspected bull shark ripped twenty-five-year-old lifeguard Sikhanyiso Bangilizwe into three pieces at Port St. John's about 600 miles to the east, part of the horrifying Second Beach saga.[72]

Shannon's bump occurred at East London, halfway between the Breede River and Port St. John's. Could he have been bumped by a bull? There's no way to know, but if anybody could run into a bull shark at the very frontier of its range, who else would it be?

When you read of the shark attacks visited upon Shannon and his countrymen, the frightening vicissitudes of shark encounters become clear. The results are chaotic. Some sharks attack relentlessly and aggressively, inflicting fatal wounds (Zimmerman). Some inflict fatal wounds with single exploratory bites (Corby). Some inflict serious injury with a single bite (Carter, Du Plessis, Mellin, and Ainslie). Some just toss you off your surfboard (Ainslie and Coetzee).

And some sharks, it seems, just scare you half to death. A couple of Shannon's friends can tell you all about that.

23

CLOSE ENCOUNTERS

When Shannon made the first team on Hudson Park High School's water polo team in Standard 8 (Grade 10), he quit his school and club swim teams. He wanted to invest himself fully in water polo and surfing. The sports had non-conflicting seasons—water polo in summer and surfing in winter—and allowed him to excel at each discipline while providing him ample time for free surfing.

Circling Greg

Hudson Park's surfing team is blessed with a stellar history, and Shannon learned a lot from its past and present stars. One of his best friends on the team, Roseanne ("Rosy") Hodge, and a former team member, Keegan Nel, went on to win multiple national surfing championships. Another team member, Paul Love, earned fourth place honors at the International Surfing Association (ISA) World Championships, Nel finishing an equally impressive fifth.

One of the brightest surfing talents to emerge from Hudson Park is Greg Emslie. Greg, who graduated seven years before Shannon, went on to win three open division South African Surfing Championships and surfed the ASP (now WSL) world championship tour for several years. In the final round of the 2007 Quiksilver Pro in France, he narrowly lost to eventual world surfing champion, Mick Fanning.

On May 30, 2010, Greg won his third national title at St. Mike's on the Kwazulu Natal South Coast. The thirty-three-year-old, known as "Bigfoot" despite his compact 5-foot 7-inch 155-pound frame, also led his Eastern Cape Border Team to a President's Cup victory that day—the national team title—but it was a great day that nearly wasn't.

One week earlier, Greg was involved in a bizarre encounter with one of Shannon's old buddies. The story was reported by Craig Jarvis in ZIG-ZAG News on May 23, 2010,[73] and is shared here with the kind permission of Craig, ZIGZAG, Rosy Hodge, and of course, Greg Emslie.

On Saturday, May 22, Greg went for a training session with Rosy at Queensberry Bay, just thirty minutes up the coast from Nahoon. The two waited at sea for a while, and a nice set finally arrived. Rosy caught a wave first and rode it out. Then, as she turned to paddle back out, she noticed something odd. Greg had not caught a wave at all. Instead, he was still out at sea and yelling at her. She was certain she hadn't snaked his wave and was confused by his agitation. As she paddled nearer, though, she realized that Greg had a serious problem:

> Earlier in the day, we had had some dolphins around and when I saw the two fins I thought there were two dolphins by Greg. As I got close, I saw it was a giant shark, showing its dorsal and tail fin, and I realized that Greg was in serious trouble.[74]

The shark was a great white, about thirteen feet long. For two or three minutes—minutes that seemed like an eternity—the shark circled Greg. The beast cruised right on the surface looking at him and making occasional lunges at him. Greg was consumed by thoughts of home:

> All I could think about was that I hadn't said goodbye to my wife and kids. We had been to a kids' party in the morning so my wife and kids had fallen asleep, exhausted, and I slipped out for a surf. I always say goodbye to them, and this time I didn't.[75]

Rosy continued paddling toward him, but Greg ordered her back. There was absolutely nothing Rosy could do, and Greg feared that a second presence might trigger an attack. "Rosy was so brave," he remembers.[76]

Greg and the great white were in constant eye contact, so there was no question of mistaken identity. The shark knew it wasn't looking at Andre the Harbor Seal; Greg knew he wasn't looking at Flipper. Then Greg saw an approaching wave, a green chariot of salvation. Greg and the shark both weighed their options:

> The shark definitely checked out the wave as well and was waiting to see what I was going to do. The shark was so close and the situation was so tense, and I thought that if I started paddling,

it would simply attack. So, I waited until the last split second. I did like one stroke, caught the wave, and went left and straight over the bricks.[77]

Greg's position atop the wave offered no protection. Shannon had been attacked on the very crest of one. Underwater surfing photos reveal that the back-lit view of a wave is far clearer than most people imagine given the turbulence and froth at the surface. Still, Greg made it to shore without incident, crawling onto the rocks next to an emotionally overwrought Rosy. Despite her courage in the water, the waning of adrenaline brought emotional release. She was in tears and went home to be with her parents. To this day, she feels vulnerable, even on dry land.[78] For his part, Greg was changed by the event much in the same way that Shannon was.

"Well, first things first," Greg reported to Craig Jarvis. "I'm going to church...I'm serious!"[79]

The attack begs a question, though. What was Greg's uninvited guest— more accurately, his undesirable host—up to? The shark had not attacked in the classic manner of a great white. There had been no missile-like assault from depth, no single devastating bite. There had been only an odd surface reconnaissance. For whatever reason, the great white had taken almost three minutes to decide that Greg Emslie was not a seal. Or maybe the shark was merely curious. Or maybe it wasn't hungry. Or may it was just unlucky.

Experts suggest that we err when we attach too much cognitive power to white sharks. In the last analysis, they're just fish. Most of a white shark's brain is devoted to sensory perception—sight, sound, smell, taste, and the astonishing ability to detect electric fields in the water. A great white has small gel-filled capsules around its snout called ampullae of Lorenzini. These incredibly sensitive electro-receptors give the shark the ability to detect electric fields as small as one-billionth of a volt. My electronically inclined friends assure me that it takes more than a trillion times more voltage to spark someone's ear after shuffling your feet on a rug!

A shark's brain is a bit like the computer used by Neil Armstrong and Buzz Aldrin aboard Apollo 11's lunar excursion module, Eagle. The progenitor of the modern PC, Eagle's guidance computer weighed seventy pounds and had a laughable 32K of RAM.[80] It could perform only eight functions at a time and could display its output only in coded numbers. But the computer's limited capability was good enough to get humans to another world. Similarly, a shark's brain is very good at handling a limited number of functions. Greg Emslie's circling visitor may have been evaluating what it thought was disabled prey. Whatever its objective, it was hardly the only great white to stare down a human and move on.

Circling Dylan

Dylan Lightfoot was just five years old when Shannon was attacked. They later became friends, and Shannon even coached him a bit. Dylan went on to become a professional surfer who earned his way to the Qualifying Series for the World Surf League and enjoyed two major victories in 2019.

In 2010, fifteen-year-old Dylan was surfing at Elands Bay, which is noted for its excellent left-handed waves. The teen was surfing the beach break with his younger brother, Ryan, and another friend. The waves were only running about two feet in height…"Nothing hectic," Dylan recalls. As he sat on his board facing out to sea, he saw a dark shape approach from his front right. It was a two-meter shark, almost certainly a juvenile great white but fully capable of killing a human. The shark looped behind him and came around his left side, completing a 360-degree circle. The shark began swimming more and more aggressively, circling the youth four more times, each time moving faster and closer. Fortunately, Dylan was near the shore. As a wave approached, he turned his board suddenly and caught it, immediately fleeing to very shallow water. "The shark didn't react," Dylan recalls. "I still have dreams about it."

Dylan recalls another episode at J-Bay that highlights the shark safety precautions taken during competitions. He was one of several monitors working the J-Bay Open on jet skis. (Jet skis are used to pick up surfers if a shark is sighted or if an injury occurs during the contest.) After radio word came of an approaching shark, one of the other monitors raced toward the reported position of the shark as a drone searched from above. Soon the monitor and the drone turned and began approaching Dylan. Finally, the drone was right above him. Still, he could not see the shark due to the glare. Only those operating the drone could see it. The shark, as it happened, followed a seal right through the competition area.

The Board that Stopped Bobbing

Consider also an incredible case reported in Ralph S. Collier's Shark Research Committee Web page, "Unprovoked White Shark Attacks on Surfers,"[81] and shared here with his permission. On August 15, 1987, a forty-year-old surfer was sitting on his surfboard in waters just south of Half Moon Bay, California, when he sensed that his board was no longer bobbing or drifting. Without moving his head, he glanced down and saw the head of a monstrous great white shark gently clenching the front of his board from the left side. The shark's enormous head was practically in his lap, its huge eye looking at him and its teeth less than an inch from his left hand. The surfer slipped off the back of his board, ripping the fingers of his left hand open on the shark's teeth as he did. He held onto the back right rail and stared at the shark across the length of the board. Finally, the shark disengaged and swam directly beneath the man as he scrambled back onto his board and raced for land. One of the two teeth found embedded in the board was four centemeters across at the base, consistent with a shark that was 5.7 meters, or 18 feet 8 inches, in length![82]

Consider Shannon as well. After his initial attack in 2000, he found himself deep in the water and face-to-face with a 4.5-meter great white. He recalls the shark's "huge eye" looking at him from two-foot range...so close that he reached out and almost touched the shark's mouth. Yet, no attack ensued.

Shannon never forgot how God had spared him that day at Nahoon Reef. What he didn't know is why and for what purpose God had spared him. With high school to finish and water polo matches to win, his search for answers would have to wait.

24

LOST AND FOUND

During the middle of Shannon's matric year, 2002, his father's hard work and constant travel began to pay off. Shane rented a nice house in the comfortable Nahoon district of East London, just four kilometers from the beach. The kids were happy to move back in with their father. For Elaine, the family's departure was likely a bittersweet break.

Shannon graduated from high school in December, and free of classes and team practices, he had time to devote to his first love. The lure of the waves captured him fully in 2003:

> I took full advantage of being out of school and having more time. I started focusing more on my surfing. I got better and better every day...as well as more addicted. I surfed two or three times a day if the waves were firing.
>
> I decided to take correspondence courses in theology through the University of South Africa (UNISA) and studied in the mornings with a youth leader for our local church, David Palos. He was taking theology courses too and lived just 100 meters from me. I would surf with David quite often, or, if not, with my best friend, Travis Naude. If I had no lift to the beach, I would just run to the beach or hitchhike.
>
> I never took more than three courses at once, so I had plenty of time for surfing. I studied about three to five hours a day unless the waves were really good.

Shannon worked two jobs. He spent three weekday afternoons coaching the under-15 girls' water polo team at his former high school and worked evenings as a server:

My girls' water polo team was a little above average. I would then go straight from water polo practice to my job as a server at the Las Vegas Spur Steak Ranch near Hemingway's Hotel Casino and Mall on the north side of town. But I hated waiting tables. I could barely keep up with my orders because people were super interested in the shark attack! I would have to tell the story over and over again every day, and it made waiting tables a bit hectic—for me and my boss. You want to be friendly, but you have a lot of work to do.

Friday nights were reserved for youth group meetings. Afternoons and Saturdays were for surfing. Shannon's surfing improved dramatically in 2003, but his sense of purpose languished. He was calmer, happier, and gentler, but he was unfulfilled. He was not advancing. The correspondence course brought him none of the answers he needed—answers about the meaning and purpose of his life. He had lost several friends too. A number of his old pals from St. Albans had turned away from God, looking instead to drugs and alcohol. He chose not to follow. He wanted something more meaningful.

That a young surfer would need direction is hardly surprising. Society treats them much like it treats skateboarders—as an unmotivated, self-indulgent, and uneducated mob of school-bunking, "dude"-speaking adrenaline junkies. Such generalizations, of course, are hideously unjust, and their effects on young surfers are profound—angry parents, lost jobs, poor grades, and the inevitable embrace of alcohol, Transkei Gold, or blow. A few surfers, gear manufacturers, and surf coaches earn good livings as professionals, but most young people who take up the sport eventually need some direction. Fortunately, some older surfers understand that.

In late 2003, an experiment began to unfold in Jeffreys Bay. Victory Christian Church purchased a three-level, fall-away brick home at 19 Pagoda Crescent. The attractive home needed work but had "surfer's paradise" written all over it. The house was a 100-meter walk from the beach at Point and just a few hundred meters north of Supertubes, easily one of the top five surfing venues in the world.

The church planned to turn the house into a Christian gap year school called Surf Masters, a place where young surfers could take a year off after high school, study the Bible, and gain stability, maturity, and a sense of responsibility through hard work and charitable outreach.

Desmond Sawyer, an expert board shaper with his own line, *Des Sawyer Fine Surfboards*, agreed to live there with his family and run the school. Des (he hates being called Desmond), his wife Cara Bertie-Roberts Sawyer, and their three children, Micaela, sixteen; Daniela, thirteen; and Stephen, nine, moved into the second and third floor of the house in late 2003. Des began fixing up rooms on the first floor for his arriving class of students. The plan was to bring teens in, charge them with responsibilities around the house, engage them in regular Bible study, involve them in outreach efforts, and, of course, let them surf that amazing break just a stone's throw away. The school was looking for five or six kids for its inaugural semester starting in January 2004. Shannon knew nothing about it, but God made sure he got the word.

Roy Harley, International Director of Christian Surfers International and National Director of Son Surf South Africa, knew about the Surf Masters project. More importantly, he knew of Shannon's desire to further his ministry. Roy spoke with the coordinator of Son Surf in East London who, in turn, made inquiries. Within weeks, Shannon excitedly accepted an offer to join Surf Masters. And why not? It was a chance for him to fulfill both of his goals—to grow in his faith and to surf one of the truly great breaks on the planet.

The initial per-student tuition at Surf Masters was R3,000 per month—about $425 at prevailing exchange rates. Shannon didn't have it, but Surf Masters wanted the famous shark victim with the real story of divine intervention. There was something genuine and decent about the youth, and everyone sensed it. So, Des and Roy helped him find sponsors, and Des chipped in some personal support as well.

Yet again, Shane had doubts about his son's decision. "He feared Surf Masters was some sort of cult or something," Shannon remembers. "He wanted me to complete my degree at UNISA, but I told him that Surf Masters was just for three months." Travis Naude was against my move too but for personal reasons. "Travis and I were best friends and always surfed together, so he didn't want me to leave East London."

Still, Shannon was determined to go. What he lacked in understanding, he had always made up for with faith—faith tested during his shark attack at Nahoon Reef. At Surf Masters, he expected to learn more about God and God's purpose for his life. What he didn't expect was that his faith would be tested again, before he even arrived at Surf Masters, and tested in much the same way.

25

A Second Test of Faith

Brandon Ainslie recalls a quiet conversation that he had with his younger brother in 2002, just two years after the attack at Nahoon. "Shannon told me he felt like God was between him and the shark when they were face-to-face," Brandon recalls. "He felt that God would protect him, at least until God called him home. He even commented that God would protect him even if he swam toward an angry great white shark." The comment was prescient. At Jeffreys Bay in 2003, Shannon had a chance to test that precise theory.

Since the sixties, Jeffreys Bay has been on the bucket list of every surfer in the world. Located in the western part of the Eastern Cape, the beautiful resort town is in the same conversation with Bells Beach, Waimea Bay, and Tahiti's monstrous Teahupoo. Well, okay, it's no Teahupoo. You can see Teahupoo's towering waves from Mars, waves requiring precisely six things to ride—a jet-ski, a jet-ski driver, a tow rope, a surfboard, and two brass… well, let's just say that every sand-for-brains in the world has heard of J-Bay.

The winter storm surge pivots around Cape St. Francis and flows north hitting J-Bay's north-south-oriented beaches at acute angles. The long, right-breaking lines produce Odyssean rides that can carry a fit surfer nearly 2 kilometers! The setup there is suitable for World Championship Tour events like the Billabong Pro, now a WSL tour event called the Corona Open J-Bay, that is held there each winter.

Five months before he moved to J-Bay to join Surf Masters, Shannon traveled there to compete in the Under-20 division of the Billabong Polar Ice Junior Championship. At 6 a.m. on Friday, August 8, 2003, he hit the water at Point just north of Supertubes to warm up for the early morning event. He had not yet learned about the Surf Masters project. He had no way of knowing that, in five short months, he would be living in a house barely 100 meters from the competition beach.

Despite the early hour, forty teens were in the water making the line-ups a bit…well…hectic. The weather was depressing—typical mid-winter gloom and overcast. Sand churned by the surf had given the water a murky brown tint. The waves were running at one to two meters and were being chopped by the on-shore winds. But it was early. The swell was building.

For thirty minutes or so, dozens of young surfers jockeyed for practice waves and tried not to snake each other in the process. At 6:30 a.m., Shannon was resting on his board waiting for a wave and looking out to sea. Behind him, about five meters away, was fifteen-year-old Joseph Krone. Small waves were lapping at Shannon's board, and sunlight warmed his face as he rocked gently in the rippling water. Then, in the blink of an eye, the tranquility was shattered:

> Behind me, I heard violent splashing and someone yelling "Shark!" I quickly looked back and saw a huge great white ripping Joseph to pieces. The shark's head and body were shaking violently. There was crazy splashing, and I couldn't see Joseph. I remember thinking, "Oh, no, it's happening all over again." My heart rate soared. My first thought was, "He's dead!" There was just no way to survive that. Then I thought of the Carter-Corby attack and how the shark had attacked two surfers. I thought the shark would let go of Joseph and come for me, especially given my reputation with sharks! I wanted to get out!!
>
> I raced toward shore. Everybody did. The shark was between me and the shore, so I paddled around the left side of it and tried to reach a rocky point nearby. I passed within a few meters of the tail of the shark and kept my eye on the shark the whole time. I continued about five meters past it, but when I looked back to my right, I saw Joseph pop up right next to the shark. They were less than a meter apart. I saw no blood, and the shark was still thrashing violently right next to him, tearing up his surfboard.

Needless to say, the tranquility of Joseph Krone's morning fared no better:

> I was paddling back toward the south and was resting on my board. The shark hit from my left side and behind me. At first, I

thought it was a joke, that someone was pushing me, but then the board lifted sharply and flipped me into the water. The next thing I remember, the shark yanked sharply on my leash and pulled me under, and then my leash snapped very fast. And leashes are tough to break.

When I came to the surface, the shark was right next to me, splashing and shaking my board violently in its mouth. Other surfers began paddling away from me very quickly, my brother among them, but he didn't know it was me who was attacked.

When Shannon saw the boy surface amid the tumultuous thrashing, he realized that his destiny lay at sea, not onshore. He had played this scene before. He knew he had to help:

I knew that if God rescued me before and promised to do it again, I had to go back and help Joseph. I knew I had to be the Good Samaritan regardless of my feelings, emotions, fears, weakness, and inability to fight off a shark. I had to trust God for help and protection. I also knew what it was like to have been left alone in the water after my attack and have no help at all. Joseph's board was gone, so he needed help. But it was hard. It was very hard.

One part of me felt sorry for him and wanted to help. Another part of me thought I was stupid and wanted to consider me and my safety first. I knew the latter was a selfish motive and that I needed to go back out and help Joseph. I prayed and asked God to help give me strength.

Shannon swung his board back out to sea and paddled toward the embattled teen. "God, please keep me safe," he gurgled as water splashed off the front of his board and into his mouth. Smoothly, but deliberately, he glided away from the safety of the rocky point and toward Joseph, circling wide-right around the great white's flailing tail. He approached the shark from the seaward side where Joseph was treading water. The boy's back was almost touching the animal's wrenching torso.

"I was dazed," Joseph remembers. "I noticed Shannon paddling steadily but calmly back out to me from twenty or thirty meters away. When he got to me, he spoke to me in very comforting tones, asking if I was bitten. I told him, 'I'm okay, no bite.'"

Shannon was unconvinced. Shock had masked the pain of his attack at Nahoon Reef in 2000, so he inquired twice more about possible injury. The dark-haired youth insisted he was unharmed. Finally assured, Shannon asked a purely astonishing question.

"Do you want to jump on my board?"

Thrusters submerge under the weight of one seated surfer. They sink under the weight of two. Shannon was offering to give his board to the boy and, faith notwithstanding, the last thing Shannon wanted to do just then was go swimming.

Shannon could not get Bruce Corby out of his mind. On that fateful day in 1994, a shark had inflicted grievous wounds on Andrew Carter, and just thirty seconds later, had inflicted a mortal leg amputation on Corby. By paddling out to Joseph, Shannon had put himself in Corby's position. Worse, he was offering to give the boy his only, if inadequate, means of protection. Joseph, though, declined the offer.

"I was in shock and just didn't think about it," Joseph remembers.

Shannon thought the boy was crazy. "If that had been me, I wouldn't have hesitated to take the board!" he insists, but there was no time to debate the issue. Shannon began ushering the boy away from the shark and tried to reassure him:

> I told Joseph that I had just prayed and that we would get out of the water safely. Just then, the shark broke off its attack and submerged beneath us. Remnants of Joseph's surfboard—three large pieces and assorted chunks of rubble—bobbed up to the surface nearby. I still feared for both of us. I wanted people to see God come through for both of us, but, after the shark disappeared, I thought that it might attack again at any second... maybe Joseph, maybe me. It was petrifying.

Joseph swam alongside the board, occasionally grabbing it as they glided down the faces of waves. Ten meters from the shore, Joseph, who is a powerful swimmer, broke away from the board and sprinted hard for the rocks, Shannon in close pursuit. A throng of alarmed surfers had gathered there after fleeing the sea, none of them more stunned than Joseph's younger brother, Daniel, who had seen it all unfold from close range:

> I was probably about fifteen meters away from my bro when it happened. I was busy paddling back up the point after a wave when a girl that was next to me started screaming "Shark!" That's when I looked behind me to see the shark with the board in its mouth. It was thrashing it around the same as a dog would do. I went into a bit of shock for sure, but I didn't know it was my brother who was being attacked because he was under the water. I remember wondering who it was and where he was. Then, as I was escaping to shore, my brother's head popped up from under the water right next to the shark. I was completely stunned and in shock at the sight of that.
>
> I was quite amazed at what Shannon did. He seemed so calm and did exactly what needed to be done. He didn't look like he was scared at all.

He may not have looked scared, but his heart would have been visible just behind his teeth! They say that the definition of courage is being scared to death and saddling up anyway.

Mere minutes after Joseph pulled himself onto the rocks, three major fragments of his surfboard washed ashore—two large and one small. The smaller piece, the chunk removed by the bite, was a foot wide. Later, a local professor determined that the bite marks were consistent with a 3.5-meter great white—a twelve-footer.

Daniel recalls that his brother, after arriving onshore, was too dazed to function and was suffering from the same dramatic mood shift that Shannon had experienced at Nahoon in 2000:

> I asked my brother if he was okay, and he wasn't very responsive. I could see that he was in major shock. I think he told me that he felt he was in shock, but he didn't say anything else to me. I could see that he wanted to be left alone. People were asking him questions, and I could see how much he hated it. I didn't

see it happen, but apparently he did end up getting angry with some people.

After Joseph gathered up the scraps of his obliterated board, the quiet youth left the beach in a sullen, blank state. He was so bewildered that he even forgot to speak to Shannon, though he thanked him the next day.

Like so many other surfers, though, Joseph refused to be put off of his passion by a shark. He had come within inches of a hideous death. He was certainly entitled to some shore leave. The crazy thing is, he didn't put in for any.

Officials canceled Friday's heats and announced that the competition would resume on Saturday at St. Francis Bay, sixteen kilometers to the south. Hearing this, Joseph made the half-hour drive to St. Francis Bay on Friday afternoon, borrowed a surfboard, and took to the sea mere hours after his attack. Later that day, officials decided to roll the dice and move the event back to Point. There, shortly after 8 a.m. on Saturday, fifteen-year-old Joseph Krone paddled back out to the very spot where he had been so viciously attacked just twenty-six hours earlier. Other surfers, many of whom had abandoned the event because of Joseph's attack, were shocked by his mettle and his power of concentration. Joseph surfed beautifully. He came in second in his first two four-man heats and advanced to the semi-finals of his highly competitive division.

Daniel came away from his brother's traumatic weekend with a lingering regret, one he need not have harbored:

> The part that I don't feel very good about is that I paddled straight out along with everyone else instead of trying to help my brother, but I was far away before I realized it was Joseph, and Shannon was quite quick on the scene to help my brother out. So that kind of encouraged me also just to get out, because my brother was being helped and was not alone. I talked to Joseph about it later. He told me that he understood my actions fully, knew that I acted in complete terror and shock, and didn't want me to feel bad about it.
>
> If it were to happen today, I might act differently, I think, especially if the person who has been attacked is alone. It wouldn't

have to be a family member either. I think if it were to happen today, I would definitely try to help the person.

Those are not idle words. Like soldiers terrorized by their first battle, we learn a lot from our life-and-death experiences. Having witnessed his brother's attack, Daniel gained the same level of maturity and understanding that Shannon gained from his attack three years earlier. He discovered that you can stand tall in the face of death—a tough lesson to learn when you are young, but a lesson learned by untold millions of soldiers throughout history.

Shannon is convinced that he too would have fled the water in a panic if someone else had been attacked by those two sharks at Nahoon Reef. Indeed, when Shannon was asked about the surfers who had abandoned him at sea that day, he admitted, "I wouldn't have had the guts to help me!"

That may have been true of fifteen-year-old Shannon in July 2000. But like a veteran of prior battles, eighteen-year-old Shannon, steeled by his faith and his prior experience at Nahoon, was able to summon the courage to help Joseph Krone in his time of need.

Faith, more than anything, drives that courage. "Before my attack, I would only surf if there were at least four or five other surfers in the water," Shannon confesses. "I was afraid of sharks. I had a big-time fear of them. After my attack, though, I surfed at Nahoon alone. My Christian faith gave me strength. I felt God would keep me safe."

That inner strength was evident to his friends. Brad Coetzee remembers the intrepid spirit that Shannon exhibited at Nahoon Reef in 2001, just one year after his attack:

I can describe Shannon as very much alive if that makes sense. It's like there's a fire in his spirit...a lot of inner strength. I was watching a local surf contest one day at Nahoon Beach. The waves weren't great. The swell direction was all wrong, but Nahoon Reef was giant with nobody out. Shannon surfed his heat, won it, then ran up the beach, handed in his singlet, ran down the beach to Nahoon Reef, and paddled out on his own. This was after his shark attack. I was amazed.

Looking back at the Krone attack, it may not be immediately obvious that Shannon assisted the fifteen-year-old in any meaningful way that morning. Joseph is a strong swimmer and might have made it to shore just as fast without the surfboard escort. And if the shark had come back for seconds, Shannon couldn't have stopped it. Two men cannot fight a one-ton great white in its element. Ten men cannot. But Shannon did assist Joseph in one extremely significant, if less obvious, way.

By paddling out to Joseph, Shannon placed a second human target in the vicinity of the shark. That target reduced Joseph's risk of dying that morning—whatever you believe that risk to have been—by about 50 percent. As soon as you appreciate the accuracy of this math, you'll appreciate the magnitude of Shannon's gesture. Joseph's father, Nicolas, certainly appreciated it. He rewarded Shannon with a gift in which, according to Nick, "Shannon partook with typical enthusiasm." He gave the kid a shark cage dive.

26

SURF MASTERS

Five months after the Krone attack, Shannon returned to Jeffreys Bay for good. He arrived at Surf Masters in January 2004—a bit late as it turns out. He missed his class's two-week orientation in the backcountry.

The orientations were joint affairs with thirty or forty students from other Christian gap year programs. Some of the programs focused on surfing. Others focused on music or leadership. The orientation involved camping, five-kilometer runs, treehouse construction, all-night rafting trips, and orienteering tests. Winning teams were awarded extra sleep and food. Losing teams were rousted early, given limited food rations, and made to do push-ups. "I attended the second orientation, and the team-building exercises were intense," Shannon recalls. "Some of the guys wanted to quit!"

Back at the house in J-Bay, Des prepared two bunk rooms for his students—four male students in one room and one female in the other—but the house was still a work in progress, and the students provided the labor. "The house had just been purchased and needed a lot of work," Shannon notes. "The garden was a disaster, and the room where Des did his board shaping was a total mess; polystyrene debris was everywhere."

Shannon's peers at the school ran the gamut of personal description—a long-haired dude with a beard, a tall thirty-something male, a fellow South African surfer, a Dutch boy, and the only girl in the class, also Dutch. Of course, when you cram unfamiliar males together in a bunk room or bring males and females into the same living quarters, problems are inevitable. Shannon recalls some of them:

> There was ample testosterone. In my second semester, we had one rather aggressive student named Tom. He and a cheeky friend of mine named Dustin got into it once. Tom punched him in the chest and a few fists were thrown. I had to break them up. The next month, Tom got into a fight with another young guy named Jono. As Surf Masters grew, we had up to sixteen stu-

dents living there, about 40 percent of them girls, so we had boy-girl issues all the time. The problem was so common that we made a rule that you couldn't start a relationship while at school. Anyway, many students took gap years at Surf Masters because of problems in their lives like family conflicts, drugs, and boy-girl issues, so it is only natural that some of those problems carried over.

A typical weekday started with breakfast at 7 a.m. The cooking, cleaning, and table setups were performed by the students. Morning prayers were held three days a week. From 9 a.m. to noon on weekdays except Fridays, students had Bible lectures and studies. They spent their afternoons cleaning the house, upgrading the deck, landscaping, washing cars, or engaging in community outreach. The students often worked at local surf parks and helped the Supertubes Surfing Foundation maintain local beaches. Their outreach efforts brought them in contact with other surfers who were looking for meaning in their lives—not to proselytize them but to help them. On Sundays, the students helped their sponsor, Victory Christian Church, by setting up and tearing down chairs, parking cars, and cleaning the sanctuary and bathrooms.

Of course, you can't billet young surfers in a house a hundred meters from one of the world's premier breaks and not give them time to surf. Well, you could try, but your students wouldn't be around long. So, Shannon had ample opportunities to ply his trade:

We had loads of time to surf, and the beach was just a three-minute walk away. We could surf on weekday afternoons, especially while doing beach outreach, and we had time off from Friday afternoon through Saturday evening. I broke many boards during my years at Surf Masters and had no money, so I had to borrow friends' boards and I broke most of them too! One of Des's frustrations with me was that I was so slack, living off of sponsors and not being driven by the need for money.

During his very first semester at Surf Masters, Shannon took Des's son, Steven, to the shore and taught him how to surf.

"Shannon would push me onto the waves," the slightly built, tow-headed youth remembers, "because I was only nine years old and not strong enough to catch them."

Shannon was completely in love with Surf Masters. "I learned more in my first two weeks there than I did in a year of theology courses through UNISA," he tells friends. Part of the reason he liked Surf Masters was that some of its programs gave him a better perspective on life and himself:

> We did this study course in which we discussed our past experiences and how our identity and self-esteem were shaped by them. During the course, we learned how our experiences, our upbringing, misunderstandings, and the words spoken to us all play a major role in how we see, perceive, and understand ourselves, God, and life in general. Traumatic experiences early in life create filters in our minds and hearts. These filters warp our views of ourselves and God's will towards us. These filters shape the way we respond and react to situations and people, whether aggressively or passively, whether with confidence or lack of it, whether with hatred or compassion.
>
> The course was very intense for me because I had to go back and re-live a lot of the experiences that I had gone through as a child—things my parents said to each other, my parents' divorce, our family's financial difficulties, and my feelings of worthlessness. The course forced me to revisit certain lies that I had told myself at the time—that things were my fault, that I wasn't good enough, that I was to blame for my parents' divorce, that I would never amount to anything. Most of my issues dealt with my low self-esteem and how that warped my perception of God and life.
>
> There is a scripture in *The Holy Bible*, John 10:10 (OXP), in which Jesus says, "The thief has come only to steal and kill and destroy; I came that they may have life and have it abundantly."[83] To understand that, I had to speak openly of my innermost thoughts, fears, and experiences and of all the hurt and pain I had felt as a young kid. I had to allow God to heal and restore me from the lies that had eaten at me and had brought me to the

brink of suicide. The course allowed me to start believing in God's plan for my life and taught me that God wants to bless me and give me hope, a future, and a purpose. It allowed me to see the truth about myself...to see that life is a wonderful adventure...that I am valuable, worthy, and important to God...that true worth comes in doing God's work and in helping others.

Shannon liked Surf Masters so much, he spent four years there. He needed R30,000—nearly $4,000—for this second year at the school (they had switched to full-year terms by 2005). Deon du Toit, a surfer and a member of the Surf Masters Committee, came to the rescue. Roy Harley helped as well. They could sense the lad's passion and spirit and felt they had to help.

In the second year, Shannon conducted Bible studies, organized student activities, and started a Son Surf chapter in J-Bay. He began working with young surfers at local contests and offering free, but highly effective, coaching instruction. He catered the contests and invited surfers to attend evening events at Surf Masters after the competitions. Shannon brought in professionals to mingle with the kids at these evening events—national surfing champions and major equipment reps like Clinton Theron, Marketing Manager for Element Skateboards. The kids talked with their surfing idols, socialized, enjoyed games, and played guitars. Fifty kids showed up for a party at Surf Masters after the Billabong Pro, and six of them later became students at the school.

The school's outreach efforts paid dividends in the lives of some troubled teens, and Shannon, in particular, was adept at identifying with their problems. He had suffered through his dark days of depression, fighting, and family disruption. He knew things would get better. The kids didn't.

Shannon spent many hours with kids who were experiencing what he had experienced—poor grades, parental divorce, anger, depression, and suicidal thoughts. His example and his counsel helped turn them around, some going on to earn college degrees and experience professional success. Such is Christian outreach.

Shannon's relational and coaching skills were so effective, Des Sawyer had an idea. He thought Shannon should organize a for-profit surf school for Surf Masters. So, in 2005, the two men developed a business plan. Des and another investor, Deon du Toit, gave Shannon money to purchase wetties and accessories. Des had plenty of surfboards to loan the students.

In his third year at Surf Masters, 2006, Shannon needed no sponsors. After renovations, there were extra rooms, so Margreet Wibbelink and Shannon were able to have separate rooms while the Sawyers still lived upstairs. When the Sawyers moved out, Margreet and Shannon were in charge, so his tuition, outreach expenses, food, and surf trips were covered. But he had to work for it. "We were house leaders and had to make sure that all of the students did their duties, went to their lectures and worship sessions, performed their community service, took their tests and exams, and resolved their differences," he recalls. "There were twelve students when I helped run the school."

That same year, Shannon opened the entry-level surf school that he and Des had discussed. The school began meeting at Dolphin Beach three kilometers south of the house but struggled financially. Shannon found it difficult to compete with surf schools that had well-established relationships with local backpackers (hostels). Worse, he didn't work hard enough to market his business because he was, in his words, "still trapped in a poverty mindset." He was happy to earn just enough money to surf. Still worse, his heart lay in coaching advanced surfers, not in teaching beginners.

He did enjoy leading the school, though, and he thrived in the school's outreach programs:

> We organized two outreaches during my third year—one in Cape Town and one in Transkei. The one in Cape Town was an outreach to surfers. I would go to schools, surf clubs, surf schools, and churches to share my testimony about the shark attack and get a few of the other students to share their testimonies. The outreach in Transkei, however, was focused on helping the poor.

Transkei

Ninety percent of South Africa's people are black, and most are miserably poor. Entire regions of South Africa are still quite primitive. One of those regions is Transkei (tran-SKY). Formerly known as Bantustan, the region is home to natives who speak Xhosa, a language that features unusual "click" sounds. It is also the homeland of Nelson Mandela. Occupying nearly 1,500 square miles, Transkei subsumes most of the Wild Coast and extends inland to South Africa's border with Lesotho (leh-SOO-too). As Shannon can attest, Transkei is as wild and dangerous as advertised:

> Surfers venturing onto the Transkei coast have disappeared, some murdered for their possessions and cars. And Transkei has the most dangerous driving in the world. Corrupt cops sell driver's licenses there, and people pass trucks on hilltops. I nearly have an accident every time I go there. The people there are a law unto themselves. There are dead animals all along the roads. On one trip to the capital of Mthatha, I counted thirty dogs, three cows, and three horses dead along the road. In Mthatha, most of the robots [traffic lights] don't work. And corrupt cops sell gun permits to anyone who can afford the bribe.
>
> On one outreach to Mdumbi, we helped the owner of a run-down backpacker [hostel]. We painted his rooms, fixed his fences, and planted vegetables for him. On other trips, we taught local African men life skills like hygiene and vegetable gardening. We even provided them with seeds. We also went to hospitals to paint walls, do maintenance work, perform skits for the sick, and pray for the dying. Most of the people in hospitals there are dying of AIDS. It's so horrible. Nearly a quarter of the people in Transkei are infected with HIV.

Advanced Surf Camps

In 2007, Des Sawyer and his family returned to Pagoda Circle to run Surf Masters with the help of a British surfer, Steve Bollon. Shannon rented a guest house across the street with his friends, Clinton Theron, Jan-Lo-dewyk ("Ludi") du Toit, Lindi Meyer, and in 2008, Cornel Viljoen. Free of his school responsibilities, Shannon got serious about developing his advanced surfing school.

He began by organizing three-day high-performance camps. For each camp, he rented a guest house for up to eleven students. On the beach, he videoed students and offered video analysis with the help of South Africa's National Surfing Team coach, the legendary Graham Hynes. Generally re-

Shannon and future world longboarding champion, Steven Sawyer (Courtesy of Cara Sawyer)

Steven Sawyer with father Des at Surf Masters (Courtesy of Cara Sawyer)

garded as the greatest surfing coach in South African history, Hynes was inducted into the Surfers Circle Walk of Fame in 2017.

Shannon hired other experts as well. Michael Ginsberg, an international surfing judge and head judge, talked to campers about scoring strategies. Len Kok, a sports psychologist, spoke about the proper mental approach to competitions. Des Sawyer lectured on board hydrodynamics and board shaping. After the surfing instruction, the campers enjoyed dinners and social events.

In early 2009, Shannon and Steve Bollon moved to an apartment closer to J-Bay's premier break, Supertubes. Bollon, a soccer coach, performed outreach in Transkei as well and helped build TransCape, an outreach program that uses soccer camps to increase AIDS awareness.

During his years at Surf Masters, Shannon honed his surfing skills with valuable coaching assistance from Des Sawyer and Coach Hynes. Shannon surfed for the Border team during his first year on Pagoda Circle, winning about 90 percent of his contests in J-Bay. He then made the Eastern Province team for four straight years (2004-2007), winning an impressive 40 percent of contests wearing his provincial colors. His school and coaching duties prevented him from competing often at the national level, but he did finish fifth at the prestigious Volcom, a national event held at Port Alfred.

His real goal, though, was not standing on podiums; his goal was seeing his students standing on podiums.

27

THE SURF COACH

The value of a surf coach cannot be overstated. I learned this the hard way long before I met Shannon Ainslie.

After my last senior exams at Duke University in 1970, I took off for Myrtle Beach, South Carolina, with three underclassmen. I had a free week before graduation, clearing the way for some beach time. We had a beach house all to ourselves in the then sparsely populated Dunes Section of North Myrtle Beach, just outside the entrance to the Dunes Golf Course. From the front door, the ocean was just a 100-meter romp over a sandy lane, some dunes, and a wide beach.

My blond hair was bleached almost yellow from sunlight. I had an amazing tan, and at age twenty-two, was in the best shape of my life. I had lifted weights and run at least three miles for ninety consecutive days.

We spent each day body surfing, catching rays, and wandering the shops and arcades downtown, though there were no video arcades. Video games hadn't been invented yet. At night, we went to clubs and looked for girls. We invited new friends back to the house and often brought home huge buckets of shrimp. We didn't rent movies, though. VCRs hadn't been invented yet.

At 2 a.m. one night, we noticed a storm far out on the Atlantic. The sky above was clear, but a rising last quarter moon was looming over the top of a dense and fearsome cloud deck a good fifty miles offshore. Lightning flashes danced in the storm with intriguing constancy. So, we decided to go swimming.

In the dark of night, helpful for reasons of modesty, we streaked across the secluded roadway, over the dunes, and into the warm water. The gradient of the ocean bottom was so gentle that we were able to wade eighty meters out and still touch bottom. The storm was driving in moderate waves, and we lost visual contact with shore when the surf broke behind us. We could only see three things—the ocean, the storm, and the moon. It was quite surreal.

Of course, we were Darwin-class idiots. Even the mildest rip current could have spelled doom, and it was prime feeding time for sharks. As noted in the Global Shark Attack File, "There is strong evidence to suggest that sharks move in closer to a landmass (island or shore) following sunset."[84]

When we were furthest from shore, one of my friends punched me in the leg under the water. When I glanced around, though, no one was there. All three of them were treading water a good ten meters away. Not one of them could have hit me. But what had? I get chills just thinking about it.

If I had seen the movie *Jaws*, I wouldn't have gone near the water that night. Fortunately, *Jaws* hadn't been invented yet. When the movie did come out five years later, I almost threw up as I watched the opening scene in which a girl swims to a buoy at night and meets a horrible fate.

One day, we went to the boardwalk and rented surfboards. What we didn't rent was surf instruction. We were clueless. The boards beat us black and blue for the better part of the afternoon. I cannot think of any part of my body that didn't get battered, and yes, I mean that part too.

We didn't think to practice standing on the boards in white water. We didn't know where to locate ourselves relative to the break. We didn't know how or when to paddle shoreward to catch a wave. We were just popping up on our knees in the middle of the tumult and eating sand. We could have used Shannon Ainslie that day, but Shannon hadn't been invented yet either.

Champions

One of Shannon's prize pupils was Steven Sawyer, a surfing prodigy for whom Shannon was a role model. Shannon taught him to surf, after all.

Recall that Shannon eschews working with newbies, but Steven was Des's son and lived with Shannon at Surf Masters. Besides, Steven was a newbie for only a week or two, if that.

"At first, I had to push him into the waves because he was so small, but Stevie learned super quickly," Shannon says admiringly. "Some people take years to read waves, but Stevie did it in a few weeks, so I could coach him from the beach early on. He has fantastic style, a good stance, and wonderful coordination."

By age sixteen, Steven Luke Sawyer had become a national junior surfing phenomenon, amassing eleven event titles and thirty-one top three finishes, and five podiums at South African Junior Surfing Championships (including national runner-up honors in 2011 and a national longboarding title in 2009). He earned multiple recognitions as provincial and national Junior Surfer of the Year, membership on South Africa's national surfing team, a first-place finish in the 2010 South Africa-New Zealand Challenge, and advancement to the quarter-final round of the 2010 ISA World Junior Championship in New Zealand.

In 2010, Steven had an open division national title squarely in his sights. Competing in the final round of the South African Surfing Championship, he was leading with just five minutes to go when he lost a fin and with it, valuable points on his last two waves. He finished second to three-time national champion and former ASP world tour professional, Greg Emslie. Greg was twice Steven's age.

But a national open title awaited Steven. As he developed a successful career as a singer, he didn't lose his touch on the waves. In 2016, he won the South African national longboarding championship and with it, a trip to China to compete in the world championships. Two years later, a lifetime of surfing—one that started with Shannon pushing the little kid into a wave fourteen years earlier—came to full fruition. Steven, twenty-four years of age and riding boards shaped by his dad, won the WSL World Longboarding Championship in Taiwan, defeating longboarding legend Kai Sallas 16.10 to 15.10 in a dramatic twenty-five-minute final.

Shannon seems destined to play a positive role in the lives of young people—a gift partially crafted by those two great white sharks at Nahoon. "Shannon loves kids," Cara Sawyer says of her son's coach and role model. "They trust him completely. Everything he does is relationship-based. It's his passion that the kids love. He understands how kids think."

Despite his coach's history, Steven doesn't worry much about sharks, though his mom certainly does. "I pray constantly when he's in the water," Cara admits. "I'm really nervous when he's out there, but I trust in the Lord. Some locations worry me more than others, though, especially Nahoon Reef, Mossel Bay, and Ding-Dangs."

Nahoon you know about, but Mossel Bay has a prodigious set of shark problems of its own. Just 650 meters off the city beach is Seal Island. Raise your hand if you know what lives on the island. Raise both hands if you know what lurks in the water around the island. Major surf spots at Mossel Bay are Ding-Dangs and the Inner and Outer Pools, and they lie just two and four kilometers, respectively, from Seal Island's nearly constant patrol of great whites. Indeed, Seal Island is so rife with great whites that commercial shark cage diving companies operate within sight of the surfing beaches!

To hear Shannon tell it, Steven's success as a surfer doesn't mean that he was an atypical teenager:

> Steven hates paddle skiers. He calls them "goat-boaters" and "egg beaters." Paddle skiers tend to be older and slower, and they often snake waves from surfers. It's a lot like the reaction that snow skiers had when snowboarders came along, only with the coolness factor reversed.
>
> Once, the South African Paddle Ski Championships were set to be held at Magnitudes, just south of Supertubes. Normally, the J-Bay Underground, the local surf club, doesn't allow paddle skis on their break, but they allowed them to use one area for their competition.
>
> Well, Steven got mad at this forty-year-old paddle skier and decided to burn him, forcing the paddle skier to turn off of the wave. Then Steven surfed away and did an aerial. The man got very angry and approached Steven, so I paddled over to them. Steven was laughing at this man and telling him, "Don't paddle ski on my home break." By then, three other paddle skiers had moved in and were cursing at both of us, and the forty-year-old looked like he wanted to get physical. I warned him, "You aren't touching Steven."
>
> Steven is extremely confident, and he's not afraid of anything—not older surfers, not girls, not big waves, not sharks. He will quite often paddle past older non-local surfers in the line-up, but you have to do that when you're younger or you'll never get a wave. Many have threatened him, but most locals like Steven feel they should be ahead of non-locals on their home break.
>
> Steven once got into it with a Peruvian guy who is fifty but looks thirty-three. He came to J-Bay in 2009 and constantly

snaked waves from younger guys. Steven called him on it, and
the Peruvian guy told him, "We're all part of the ocean...in Peru,
we take any wave we want." Steven wasn't convinced. "This is
not Peru," he shot back, "and this is how we like it here!"

Impatience used to hold Steven back on occasion. After a bad heat, he
would sometimes exit the water, throw down his board, and sulk. Shannon
speaks of one occasion when Steven's temper nearly cost him a legitimate
shot at his first open (non-age-restricted) national championship:

Before the 2010 Mr. Price South African Open at Nahoon Reef,
Steven and another champion (and now professional) surfer and
friend, Dylan Lightfoot, hit the water to warm up before the
contest. About twenty minutes before the contest started, Dylan
went out about one minute ahead of Steven, and the announcer
called Steven back but let Dylan go catch a wave. [Dylan knew
nothing of this.] Steven stormed ashore, threw his board, said he
hated the contest, and told me that he was going home. I took
him to get some coffee and calm him down. Steven competed
and made it all the way to the men's open division final, finishing
second. He was actually leading the reigning South African surfing champion, Greg Emslie, thirty-three, with two or three minutes to go in the event final.

That Shannon could calm someone down using caffeine tells you something about his abilities as a coach. Shannon regularly pulls the "Hey,
Steven!" gag on the youth before hanging up the phone. The prank became
such a source of humor around Surf Masters that Des Sawyer started doing
it to his son.

Steven also bears some scars from Shannon's physical lifestyle. "Shannon used to beat up Steven all the time," Cara laughs. They constantly
punched, wrestled, and tackled each other. (During my joint interview with
both of them, they spent most of the time snapping each other with rubber
bands.) One time, Shannon tried to get Steven in a headlock from behind,
and Shannon's thumb took a nice gouge out of Steven's cheek. Steven
pranked back, of course. He once tossed a fishnet over Shannon in a local

grocery store. Shannon went right to the checkout line with the thing on his head. Shannon's humor even takes to the waves. Shannon tells the story of a game called "shotgun" that he and Steven occasionally played in the line-up:

> We were surfing at Secrets, a nice break that we keep to ourselves. Steven yelled "Shotgun!" which means no duck diving under waves. You just have to lie there and take it. Well, we were in some pretty big waves, and Steven yelled "Shotgun." I just got destroyed! The wave held me under for like fifteen seconds, and I tried for about five seconds to reach the surface. When I finally got back to the top, Steven was laughing so hard he was crying.

Shannon has coached other highly successful surfers. Emma Smith finished third in the South African Championships under-17 division in 2010 and made the South African national team the next year. Gina Smith won the under-15 title in 2010 ("comboing" everybody, meaning that each of her opponents would have had to replace both of their best scores to beat her). Gina also won the under-17 title in 2012 and made the South African national team twice. Dylan Lightfoot went on to earn a spot in the WSL Qualifying Series and won major events including the 2019 Royal St. Andres Hotel Port Alfred Classic and 2019 Vans Surf Pro Classic at Lambert Bay.

Soon, though, Shannon began looking for surf coaching opportunities abroad. He wanted to travel and earn money for future travel. Such an opportunity arose in 2009 in the last place you might expect.

Dylan Lightfoot, Gina Smith, Tobias Schroeder, Remi Peterson, Emma Smith, Jerry Van Wyk, Steven Sawyer, and Daniel Jeggels receiving surfing awards (Courtesy of Cara Sawyer)

Shannon with future pro stars, Matthew McGillivray and Dylan Lightfoot (Courtesy of Emma and Gina Smith)

28

NORWAY

Imagine the buzz of an alarm clock as it arouses you from a deep and dreamless slumber. You feel a sharp chill on your face as you cast a half-open eye at the digital display flashing "6:00 a.m." You close your eyes tightly, refusing to abandon the warm embrace of the billowy down comforter piled high atop you, but you bolt upright and roll out of bed, your feet hitting the cold floor of fine Brazilian teak. You wrap your arms tightly around your bare torso to ward off the cold. Stumbling in the darkness, you peer through the louvers at the bleak nightscape outside—a broad field of snow and ice arrayed beneath a looming overcast. You hear the crash of breakers along the North Sea coast just beyond. It's a typical December night in Norway, eighteen long hours of darkness with three hours of remaining life.

You throw on a sweater and jeans, not bothering with boxers or socks because you need warmth too quickly. Groggy and shivering, you plod down the hall to the kitchen where you hear a stiff north wind pelting the house. The thermometer on the sill outside is pinned on -17°C...just 1°F. You're alone, the guest of three hosts who are all away at work. You're thankful you're not working with one of them on a North Sea oil rig.

The coffeemaker mocks your shivering with a ponderous drip, but you crave its warm promise. You sip from the steaming cup as you wander back to the bedroom. You waste no time shaving for no one will care how you look today. You throw on thermal underwear and don boots, thick gloves, a ski hat, and a full parka. You take one last hit of caffeine, suck in a deep breath, and step out into the Stygian cold.

You don't walk to your car for you have none here. Instead, you walk toward the bleak shore, your feet snapping through plates of ice. The moisture in your nose freezes as you breathe, and you cough dryly as the brittle cold stabs at the tender tissues of your lungs. You scramble down a frozen dirt embankment to a narrow band of icy hardpan at the water's edge. You turn right and begin your four kilometer trek up the coast, the north wind

Surfing Norway style! (Courtesy of Hallvard Kolltveit)

Shannon on face of wave, Norway (Courtesy of Hallvard Kolltveit)

Shannon in the barrel, Norway (Credit: Hallvard Kolltveit)

clawing at your face. For forty-five minutes, you slog through the snow, sand, and darkness... through frozen, forlorn blackness that only an Inuit could love. Emanations from your nose freeze in icy lines across your face. Your lips stiffen, unable to form the bad words you feel like uttering.

Finally, your trek brings you to the broad, light sands of Bore (BORE-ay) Beach, a long gentle arc stretching three kilometers northward. For twenty minutes you troop through patches of snow-encrusted sand until you spy a familiar gap in the dunes to your right. Hiking up the sandy passage, you follow a sand-blown road to a green-painted building with a steep corrugated roof, one of several shacks near a sparsely occupied campground. You unlock the door, grateful for the shelter, for the chance to make more coffee, for the whirring of the electric heater. You remove your parka and set about your work sanding and repairing dinged or creased surfboards. It's dirty work...dusty work...work requiring a facemask and elbow grease. But it's part of your job. Soon, the vigorous labor, the thermal underwear, and the room heater conspire against you, and you strip shirtless as beads of sweat lay tracks down your chest and back.

At 8:30 a.m., the first hint of twilight casts its deep blue hues on the snow outside. You're tired of the work and have free time before your hard-core students arrive. You walk to the clothes rack, strip, and step naked into a neoprene wet suit, pulling the snug-fitting garment to your waist with intense effort. The suit is six mm thick in the torso and five mm thick in the legs and arms, far more robust than the four and three mm suits you wear in your native land. It won't be thick enough today. You pull the sleeves over your arms and struggle to grasp the zipper in the back—placed there to protect your surfboard from abrasion. You grab a neoprene hood from the shelf and stretch it over your head, leaving only your face exposed. You add neoprene gloves and booties and grab your favorite thruster. Then you step out into the windswept gloaming, lock the surf shack behind you, and hide the key near the door. You can hide it in plain sight. No one is watching.

You walk along the road, plod down through the dunes, and arrive at the sea. In the dim, gray light, you see two and three-meter waves rolling ashore—big waves, fun waves. Then you do something completely unnatural. You do something crazy. You step into the zero-degree water...the kind of water that killed 1,517 *Titanic* passengers in less than twenty minutes.

Even with the thick wetsuit, you are rocked by the cold, so you paddle furiously to generate tiny flickers of warmth. The waves are big, so you must duck dive under them to reach the takeoff zone. With each immersion, the cold sea slashes at your face like a panther's claws. Ice water seeps into your hood and races in electric sheets down your neck, back, and ribs. After one good ride, you duck dive again, but the water begins to hammer icy nails into your skull. You suffer brain freeze—a blinding headache that comes as cold blood enters the cranium. Your head is about to explode, so you paddle ashore and sprint for the warm shelter of the surf shop. But the pain endures. Your headache lasts for two long days.

You're Shannon Ainslie. You're a surf coach working in Norway. Nothing will deter you from the pursuit of your passion—not man-eating sharks, not jellyfish, not building-sized waves, not bone-breaking cold. And you're in Norway to teach others to share your passion.

Of course, "surfing" and "Norway" are words that you seldom hear in the same story, much less in the same sentence. Then again, they say there are only two seasons in Norway—July and winter, and winter is the most beloved of all seasons for a true surfer.

Route to the Best Rights

Shannon arrived in Norway on June 17, 2009, to take a job with the Triplehead Surf Shop in the coastal city of Stavanger (pronounced sta-VAHN-gair, with a rolled "r" at the end). His primary duty was to give surf lessons and to run an agreed-upon five surf camps at Triplehead's surf outlet at Bore Beach, a beautiful North Sea surf and swim Mecca about a thirty-minute drive southwest of the city.

It might be more than a thirty-minute drive, for Norway isn't exactly speeder friendly. Radar traps are ubiquitous, and 80 kph (48 mph) speed limits govern open country roads. Go ahead, put the hammer down. Try it. The fines for even moderate speeding run 10 percent of your annual income, and if you decide to blow out the carburetor, you can expect eighteen days in jail, community service, suspended driving privileges for three years, and monstrous fees to get your license back. Oh, and the blood alcohol limit in Norway is an ectoplasmic 0.2 percent, so, if you use mouthwash in the morning, you should probably ski to work.

Shannon landed the Triplehead job through a connection in South Africa. The job was an opportunity, the twenty-four-year-old thought, to make enough money to travel the best right-handed breaks of Hawaii or maybe Australia and Indonesia.

Triplehead's owners—an Aussie, Stephen Harris, and a Norwegian, Thomas Olsen—needed a skilled and ideally prominent surfer to promote their business and teach customers to surf. Word of their need filtered back to Kristian and Line Breivik, Norwegians who were running a backpacker in South Africa when Shannon met them. Shannon had taught their kids to surf, and they had sent their backpacker customers to him for surf lessons. He was perfect for the Norway job. His athletic prowess and good looks would attract Norwegian females, and his shark-attack fame would lure the males.

Shannon flew to Oslo and then to Stavanger, but he only worked the downtown shop for a few days, mostly to attract customers. Like all Scandinavians, Norwegians study English from grades 1 to 12, but a language barrier still arose. Younger kids—the most likely surfers—had only a few years of English and were embarrassed to attempt it. Harris and Olsen, however, had a greater need for Shannon at their surf outlet on Bore Beach. They wanted him to teach surfing, run camps, and represent Triplehead at surfing competitions during the summer and fall. Shannon even organized a surf contest, the Triplehead Open, and won it. A cynic might yell "Fix!" but he'd be wrong. Shannon won virtually every Norwegian surfing contest he entered, all except a competition in Stadlandet, Norway. There, the hefty first prize included a paid trip to Portugal and an expensive wetsuit. An Aussie won the event, but even the winner confessed that Shannon had been the superior performer that day.

Shannon planned to teach surfing during the summer and work on a salmon boat in the fall and early winter, until his visa expired in December. Watch *The Perfect Storm* or a few episodes of *Deadliest Catch* if you want to know more about the joys of commercial fishing. The work is cold, hard, and ridiculously dangerous. The job is rated by the American insurance industry as the most dangerous profession, four times more lethal than commercial truck driving.[85] Still, it's the kind of work where you can haul in big kroner in a few weeks. In the end, though, Shannon never went down to the sea in boats. His surf coaching worked out too well. He was popular with clients and attracted new students well into the winter when the big waves arrived.

While Shannon was in Norway, he was a guest in the home of three of Harris's friends, Per Arne Zahl (Perry was a surfer representing Triplehead), Asle Stenvaagnes, and Torger Svindland. The three men shared a nice house in the deep country along the two-lane Nordsjøvegen Highway. The house was one of two homes tucked alongside the Hodne Galleri Og Rammeverksted, a framework gallery that strongly resembles an upscale red barn in Vermont. The house sits just behind a stone wall that runs along the windswept country road. You wouldn't expect that two houses and a frame gallery would warrant a speed limit change, but the limit near the homes drops to just 60 kph or 37 mph. The sea laps against a rocky shore 200 meters west of the house, and the nearest town, Kleppe, home to 14,000 residents, is 7.5 kilometers inland.

Unfortunately, long cold walks were a reality for the South African. He didn't always have a car. His three hosts were frequently away at work or with their girlfriends, and Perry's car was buggered a good deal of the time. Occasionally, Shannon's friends Stephen Harris or Keala Kekaulike Naluai would collect him and drop him off at Bore Beach, and in the summer,

Shannon would often bicycle there. But when winter raised its hoary breath and his three hosts were away, he faced those brutal pre-dawn hikes with only auroras to keep him company on the few clear nights. When alone at the house for prolonged periods, he walked to Kleppe to buy food—usually loaves of bread, sandwich spreads, peanut butter, cheese, salami, cereal, and pasta. The round trip walks to Kleppe took two to three hours, especially in the ice, snow, and wind. Walking on the narrow roads was safe, of course. Given Norway's speed limits, a motorist could hit you and not break your Oakleys.

Scandinavian winter was new to Shannon. Any winter was new to him. At twenty-five years of age, he had never seen snow before. In his sub-tropical homeland, finding snow is rare and always a cause for celebration. In June 2010, for example, Michal and Jean du Plessis happened upon several inches of the white stuff while driving in the Eastern Cape highlands near Cathcart. Overjoyed by their frozen discovery, seventeen-year-old Jean couldn't get naked fast enough. Of course, the Border surfing star is hardly shy. In late 2012, he jumped naked into a stinging nettle bush in his successful bid to win Linkin Park tickets in a public video contest. Then, on November 28, 2012, he announced in a Facebook status that he had not worn underpants in more than two years—a record that he proudly pursues to this day, doctor's visits excepted.

Quiksilver sponsored Shannon during his stay and provided him with a nice parka, a surf jacket, a high-grade wetsuit, accessories, and thermal underwear. SrfSnoSk8 gave him wetsuits, boots, and gloves. Frost Surfboards, Kristian Breivik's label, provided him with top-performance surfboards. Shannon rode for Kristian and wore the company's logo during his Norwegian competitions.

The Shark Week star with the South African accent—the coolest accent in the world to this ear—was an immediate hit with Norwegian girls. At times, though, he was too big a hit.

"The girls don't see good surfers much in Norway, so they were hitting on me and an American surfing buddy of mine all the time. And Norwegian girls' values are...well...a little different."

The youth with a solid Christian upbringing was unaccustomed to the simultaneous affections of multiple gorgeous women. After the surf contest at Stadlandet, he found himself being pawed over by six or seven blondes in tight quarters, several of them touching him and trying to kiss him at the same time. "It was hectic," he laughs. (You expected a different word?) So, he excused himself to the bathroom and never returned but not for lack of appreciation of the feminine beauty around him. Later in his Norwegian stay, he enjoyed the constant company of a spectacularly beautiful girlfriend.

At parties, the muscular surfer was popular with females and males alike. He was always standing at the center of huddles fielding questions about those two crazy fish at Nahoon. Now and then, however, he attracted one fan too many.

After winning the Triplehead Open, Shannon went to an after-party at the Gnu Bar in Stavanger. As he chatted with a group of Swedish friends, a young man approached. The stranger was a well-built, 5-foot 11-inch Aussie skinhead in his mid to late twenties, and fully *gesuip*—Afrikaans for drunk. He was a self-avowed "Bra Boy," a member of the notorious Australian surf gang from Sydney, and he wasted no time living up to his gang's reputation. Approaching aggressively, he invaded Shannon's personal space, dropped his pants and boxers, and bellowed, "What the f—k is your name and where the f—k are you from?"

Back in the day, such a menacing run-up would have un-caged the wolverine in Shannon. But this was the new Shannon—the calmer, more tolerant one. Still, the level of offense was high, and there were women nearby.

"Back away and pull your pants up," Shannon laughed derisively. Shannon and his friends moved away from him, but Bra Boy followed, his privates still on display, and his mouth still in overdrive.

"I said, 'Who the f—k are you, and where the f—k are you from??'" he insisted, this time grabbing Shannon's arm.

No longer amused, Shannon brushed off the intruder's hand and told him to "bugger off." Then Bra Boy grabbed Shannon with both hands.

"I'm not going to answer you. Step back!!" Shannon yelled, shoving him away.

The offender was lucky. Shannon-the-teen would have had Bra Boy on the floor already, and Shannon-the-adult was far bigger and stronger than the teen version.

Suddenly, perhaps inevitably, Bra Boy threw a punch. Of course, he had no idea what he was doing. His punch was directed at a winner of twenty schoolyard fights...at a kid deemed too violent for karate competitions...at a water polo player ejected for slugging a much larger opponent six times under the water...at a veteran of brotherly brick wars. Still, Shannon withheld his fists. Ducking the punch, he shoved his indecent aggressor into a wall. Eight or nine other males sought to restrain the crazy Aussie, but he managed to break free and come at Shannon one last time. Tired of it all, Shannon grabbed surfing's answer to a soccer hooligan and ran him full force into the wall. Bouncers dealt with the remains.

Shannon's restraint was admirable. He had the desire and the power to reduce the troglodyte to a pile of cinders, or at least light him up, but he kept his cool. Had he not done so, he might have been a guest of the Norwegian people beyond the expiration of his visa. Norway is a country where you can be fined 10% of your annual income for speeding. Imagine the penalty for deliberately draining government-provided health care funds by rearranging someone's face, even a face in rich need of rearrangement.

29

THE KILLER WHALES

Several months before the December 17, 2009 expiration date of his visa, Shannon applied for an extension and was permitted to stay in Norway beyond December with the caveat that he could not work. He specifically asked whether he needed to leave Norway to apply for the extension and was told that he did not.

During the interim, he continued living with his three hosts, and, unable to work, drained most of his Triplehead savings. He did some private work repairing surfboard dings, but, in the end, he merely depleted his funds for nothing. In March 2010, Shannon inquired about his extension request and learned that immigration had no record of it. Worse, he was told that his application would be invalid unless made from outside the country. Finally, he gave up in frustration and went home. By contrast, the United States issued him a ten-year visa, allowing three-month stays, for his American visits in 2013 and 2017. Americans love sports heroes!

As with all youthful travel, Shannon's nine-month sojourn in Norway proved to be a worthwhile adventure unto itself—a new language, new friends, new customs, new surf breaks, new experiences, and new food.

Well, maybe the food wasn't all that new. Many Norwegians joke that their national dish is frozen pizza. Shannon, during his many years in Norway, noticed that Grandiosa brand frozen pizzas have seemingly cornered the market. Anyway, it's not unusual for the entire frozen food section of a store to be filled with frozen pizza boxes. Perhaps locals identify with the frozen pizzas since Norwegians, too, stay frozen most of the time...frozen of body, that is, but never of heart!

Amazingly, frigid Bore Beach and frozen pizza weren't enough to satisfy Shannon's Boreal surfing goals. In the summer of 2012 (northern summer), he returned to Norway and went to work as a surf instructor with Unstad Arctic Surf at Unstad Beach on northern Norway's spectacular Lofoten Islands. He was teaching people to surf 193 km (120 miles) north of the Arctic Circle. That's considerably further north than Nome, Alaska!

Shannon posing in Lofoten Islands (Courtesy of Andreas Wolden)

Several years later, Kristian and Line Breivik, the Norwegian friends who had arranged Shannon's initial work in Norway in 2009, moved from J-Bay to Lofoten Islands. In 2015, they asked Shannon to join them in a new business venture there—the Lofoten Surfsenter. The business consists of a surf shop and surfing school located at Unstad Beach and holds the distinction of being the northernmost surf school and shop in the world. Shannon couldn't join the Breiviks there until 2016, but he worked with the Surfsenter for the next five years...so successfully that Shannon was named National Surf Coach for Norway in 2018 and will be taking Norway's national team to the European championships, the world championships, and perhaps someday, to the Olympics.

In November 2021, Shannon passed all of his language and citizenship tests and was granted permanent residency in Norway. One month later, he moved south to Stavanger, Norway's third largest city, to start his own surf coaching business. He is available for surf coaching and surf camps worldwide and can be found at www.surfcoach.no.

Sea Hunt

The absence of dangerous sharks above the Arctic Circle is welcome compensation for the cold surfing conditions. One can only imagine the relaxation that the arctic water brings to a young surfer from South Africa whose home waters abound in great whites, whose friends have been attacked and killed by great whites, and whose own body has felt the raw power of an attack by not one, but two, of the world's most perfect eating machines.

Shannon displaying surfboard with bite mark in Norway, 2021 (Courtesy of Kristin Folsland)

Sharks are always on Shannon's mind at home. They have to be. You cannot paddle out into the waters where you were attacked, where Andrew Carter was brutally mauled, and where Bruce Corby lost his life, without tendrils of fear creeping like vines into the dark crevices of your mind.

During the 2017 Lofoten Masters surfing competition, though, Shannon surfed with no fear of that which lay beneath. He was in the Land of the Midnight Sun, freeing his mind to focus on the next wave and the next chance for points. It was Saturday, September 23, 2017, and Shannon had worked his way to the event semifinal with three other surfers. The air was a crisp 45°F and the water a bone-chilling 53°F. The waves were fairly small and breaking close to shore. A large crowd was watching from the beach, and a few onlookers were perched atop a dune. Several were taking videos, and at least one was live-streaming the event online.

The heat was about four minutes old and Shannon had just come off an excellent ride, probably leading the heat. About ten yards from shore, he turned and began to paddle back out. Just as he reached the first breaking wave, in about six feet of water, he noticed something to his left, down the wave. Like his friend, Alistair Cokayne nineteen years before, Shannon was suddenly confronted with a shocking sight:

> An enormous black thing was coming straight at me! There were no warnings or signs, so it got me by surprise and was coming at me at great speed. Nahoon flashed through my mind, but I thought, no, it couldn't be...not here...not in Norway. In a second, it was under the nose of my board. I quickly sat up on my board and tried to get my feet out of the water as well. As I did, I saw this huge black animal directly under me. It rolled and looked up at me and I could see its white belly. After it passed under my board, it slowed down and turned seaward. I thought maybe it was coming back!

What he didn't see right away was something that everyone on the shore already knew—the huge animal was not working alone. Trailing it was a second animal. Incredible as it may seem, Shannon Ainslie was under yet another dual attack while being videoed.

> I looked back and saw a second giant animal coming straight at me, also at great speed. But this one slowed down about two meters short of me and veered seaward. Then they both surfaced very close to me, moving very slowly with their tall dorsal fins towering above me. They were so big, maybe around five or six meters in length! Then they submerged and disappeared.

The "attackers," of course, were orcas...killer whales. They shared a quality with Shannon that those two great whites back at Nahoon did not. They were fellow mammals. The aborted attack was a form of professional courtesy. Video of the event was shown to the Norwegian Orca Survey which confirmed that Shannon had been the subject of an orchestrated attack. Orcas are known for coordinated approaches to prey (ideally seals or sea lions), one orca diverting the attention of the prey while the second orca moves in for the kill. They're good at it too, often playing with seals before a kill, and still succeeding. And they are known to make attacks near the shore as the seals flee.

Several spectators had spotted the orcas earlier. They were seen 100 meters away before submerging and did not appear again until they commenced their attack run. What is remarkable, though, is how fast the two beasts managed to communicate with one another. The first orca raced toward Shannon, checked him out, slowed quickly, turned, and surfaced. Almost instantly, the second orca cut off its run before even reaching Shannon, seemingly waved off by the first.

Orcas are apex predators, at the very top of the oceanic food chain. No other animal preys on them, not even great whites which orcas can kill with ease. Sharks give them a wide berth. But orcas are friendly to humans. They are in the dolphin family, after all, and smart. There is not a single recorded case of an orca in the wild killing a human being. They are also notoriously picky eaters, eating only that which their parents teach them is safe.

Shannon is far too young to have ever seen an episode of *Sea Hunt*, a popular U.S. television series starring Lloyd Bridges that aired from 1958 to 1961. The show always featured orcas as terrifying maneaters. The show needed a villain in the deep, and sharks did not take stage direction very well. Orcas, on the other hand, are eminently trainable which has led to their controversial use at Sea World and similar aquatic exhibition parks. Fortunately, public protest has led to a phasing out of orca exhibitions. You'll find no louder voice calling for their freedom than that of Shannon Ainslie who witnessed, firsthand, their skill, their intelligence, and most of all, their amicable oneness with humankind.

As the orcas slowly submerged for the last time, everyone headed for shore, but not before Shannon, relieved, stoked, and still sitting on his surfboard, raised his fists in grinning exultation.

We were all freaking out and weren't sure if we should stay out of the water or get back in again and continue with the heat. I wasn't that scared. I got a fright when it happened, but I know that they are friendly animals and too intelligent to attack a human in the ocean. I have always wanted that experience, so I was so happy and stoked. My adrenaline was rushing and pumping like crazy.

Shannon waited a minute or two and was first to reenter the water, his three competitors following. Ultimately, he won the semifinal heat and advanced to the final where he lost. The day, however, was not lost. Yet again, Shannon had spent a harrowing moment with the raw power of nature, and yet again, that power had come to him in twos. Given his survival of a Victoria Bay storm, his dual shark attack, his brazen assist of a boy under a great white attack, and his dual orca attack, you can hardly blame the sea for needing a two-to-one advantage.

30
THE MESSAGE

Norway has not been Shannon's only destination. Surfing and surf coaching have taken him to twenty-six countries spanning the globe—countries as far as the United States, Brazil, Indonesia, Iceland, Norway, Israel, Costa Rica, Mexico, Malaysia, Qatar, Portugal, and Morocco, to name just a few. He has also visited most of the breaks in his native land and nearby Namibia and Mozambique. Understandably, people draw close to him at every stop. Some know of his relationship with God; others do not. But everyone is moved by his incredible story.

The more you know about Shannon's shark experiences and what he has done with them, the less you believe that the video recording of his dual shark attack happened by chance. What are the odds of being captured on video while surviving an attack by not one, but two, great whites?

Professor Jeffrey S. Rosenthal of the University of Toronto calculates that a random person's chance of being attacked by a shark each year is approximately one in 9 million.[86] This statistic, of course, depends heavily on individual habits. For example, Shannon has spent 23,000 lifetime hours in the water, easily a hundred times more than most people. So, we'll say that his odds were one in 90,000 each year and over twenty-five years of surfing and swimming, about one in 3,600. Shannon gets videoed while surfing for about two hours every month—about one hour for every 200 hours that he's in the water. So, the odds that Shannon would be videoed being attacked by a shark during his surfing career thus far are on the order of one in 720,000. (Even this figure may be generous given that so few shark attack videos exist. Then you must factor in the odds against Shannon being videoed during an attack by two sharks, beasts notorious for their solitary hunting style. And we won't even talk about the video of him being charged by two orcas.)

Shannon finds no serendipity in these events. He finds purpose in them. When audiences hear his story, they too begin to see purpose in them. And he has many audiences.

Shannon is asked to speak constantly. He is invited to address church congregations, youth groups, surf competitions, Christian surfers' organizations, and surfing camps including his own. Some of his audiences have exceeded a thousand people. Twenty years after his attack, he is still being interviewed by television producers. *Discovery Channel*, for one, invited him to do a televised interview in Johannesburg in March 2013. The interview took place just five days before Shannon traveled to do some surfing in the United States and Mexico. The *Discovery Channel* interview touched Shannon in an unusual way:

> The *Discovery Channel* crew picked me up at the airport and took me to their studio where we recorded a few hours of the interview. There were three camera operators, a soundman, and a director. No one in the room knew that I was a Christian, so they had no idea what to expect. The director asked me all of the usual questions, and when I described the day of my attack and how I escaped, the guys seemed blown away. I told them how the two sharks attacked me and how I was left bleeding and helpless 100 meters out to sea with little hope of escape and no waves to carry me in. I told them how afraid I was and how, as a fifteen-year-old kid, I did not want to die like that.
>
> Then I told them how I asked God to help me out and how, after I prayed, all of my fear disappeared and that odd white wave came out of nowhere to carry me to shore. They seemed surprised by that, and the director questioned me even more about my fears and emotions that day, and about my faith. I told him that I had never experienced God before that day and that the encounter had changed my entire life.
>
> The director then asked me about my surf coaching and why I choose to do that. I told him that I teach surfers about more than just surfing. I use surfing as a tool to share God's love. I gave the director a few examples of how God had changed the lives of some of my students, and he seemed fascinated. He was especially interested in hearing how God had "worked" in my life and how very real God was to me.
>
> After the interview, I had a few hours to kill before I flew home, so the director took me out for lunch and surprised me by sharing some deeply personal issues that he had been facing.

He told me how hopeless he had felt before our meeting. He told me that my story had inspired him so much that he wanted to share his struggles with me because he needed help and hope.

Now, this guy is way more intelligent, smarter, and wealthier than me. He is a successful guy in the world's eyes. Yet he said he felt emotionally and relationally unsuccessful. I felt surprised and privileged that he confided in me and asked me for advice on family and personal issues—issues that I cannot reveal, of course. He didn't have a relationship with Jesus yet, but he was very open to what I was saying. I told him how I truly believe that God is with us all the time and is the only One who always cares and who can help us cope with our problems and fears. I ended up praying with him for a few minutes. He said he felt encouraged and motivated. Later, he sent me a message thanking me for sharing my story and for spending that time with him.

On February 24, 2014, nearly a year after his *Discovery Channel* interview, Shannon went to dinner with a group of Norwegian surfing students who were attending one of his ten-day surfing camps in South Africa. He took some heat for his faith that night, but he remembers how it became a valuable teaching opportunity:

On the second night of the camp, we all had dinner at Nina's Real Food in Jeffrey's Bay. Suddenly, one of my students, a guy in his mid-20s, I'll call him Erik, asked me about my faith in a somewhat skeptical tone. "So I heard that you're a Christian??" he laughed. "Why are you a Christian? I thought only lame people were Christians."

His comments grabbed everyone's attention. A few others laughed along with him, but then they all got quiet and stopped eating. I think they were interested in how I would handle it.

I never intended to talk about my faith that night, but, since it came up, I knew I couldn't get preachy with them or try to beat them over the head with a Bible. I knew I couldn't tell them they had to believe the way I did or that they would go to hell if they didn't. I don't think that approach works with young people.

Instead, I just talked about my attack. I told them how hopeless my situation seemed when I was attacked by the sharks. I told them about being under the water, bleeding, and seeing that dark cold eye staring at me from two feet away. I told them how, after I prayed, my panic vanished and the resulting calm allowed me to make good decisions. I told them how that crazy wave appeared in a flat sea and took me straight to shore—a wave that even my brother thought was strange.

Much more importantly, I told them how God had continued to rescue me after my attack. I told them how God had saved me from severe depression, loneliness, anger, a sense of failure, and the brink of suicide.

I could see changes in their expressions as I spoke. Some of them were hanging on my words. Many seemed moved by my answer because it was couched in terms they could relate to. Some of them suffered from family problems, fears, shortcomings, lack of purpose, and depression. Hearing from another young person who had found a way to overcome such problems meant a lot to them.

I noticed that no one was laughing anymore. Even Erik was quiet and thoughtful. The whole crew was quiet. I remember hearing two or three people mutter something like "wow" under their breath as I spoke about my experiences. I could tell that some of them were wondering if God could help them too. All I wanted to do that evening was just make them think.

Most of them had never experienced God in their lives. I knew that many of them had gone to church but had not been moved by traditional services. I told them that I too had been forced to go to church as a kid, and it had not changed my life because I had been too young. But during my attack and in the years that followed, God had touched my life in astonishing ways. It was like God had been with me all along, just waiting for me to ask for help.

My answer stirred conversation in the group, and I noticed that we all seemed to connect much better during the rest of the week. There was a friendlier, kinder vibe. A few of them asked me questions about God later in the camp. I tried to tell them that God is not some guy out there who counts our sins to punish us. I told them that God wants to be in our lives 24/7 regardless of how good or bad we are. I told them that God is with us whether we want Him there or not and that when we discover God, He becomes an irresistibly attractive force in our lives.

In another camp I ran, an eighteen-year-old told me that he was having problems with drugs and alcohol and had never gotten any support from his family. Like me, he had considered suicide many times. He said he was particularly excited to hear my story. He told me, "As you described your childhood, I thought you were describing me!" He needed to find a route to a happier, more fulfilling life, and he could see that I had found one. I was so excited to connect with him that way.

I truly believe that God created us to have a relationship with Him and to carry that love into our relations with other people. I believe that God created us to appreciate His creation and to make His creation even greater through our kindness to others. That was my message to the crew at the camp—that God is the source of everything we truly need, if only we ask Him.

Shannon is often challenged with tough questions about God. He might be asked, for example, why God didn't save Geoffrey Zimmerman and Bruce Corby when they were attacked. Geoffrey, after all, had been an innocent church-going fourteen-year-old when he was taken. Bruce had been killed mere days after telling his brother, Brett, how God had made positive changes in his life. Both young men had been faithful, yet they died.

This is a troubling question that has tested man's understanding of God throughout human history, and this very question came up during one of Shannon's advanced surf camps in J-Bay in 2013. Shannon tackled the question head-on:

I told them that I look to two passages in the Bible for help with this question. In The *Holy Bible*, Jeremiah 29:11, God says, "For I know the plans I have for you, says the Lord, plans for welfare and not for evil, to give you a future and a hope."[87] And in

John 10:10, which is very meaningful to me, Jesus says, "The thief comes only to steal and kill and destroy; I came that they may have life, and have it abundantly."[88]

When I read those passages together, I begin to understand God's heart toward us. He has come to give us life in abundance. His plan is never to kill us, harm us, or take from us. There is evil on earth that comes to do all of that.

God doesn't promise a life without storms or that we will survive those storms, but He does promise comfort, strength, and support through the storms. The comfort, strength, and support come from the knowledge that we will enjoy life with Him after our time on earth—our time on earth being little more than the blink of an eye in all of eternity. I think that is the true future that God promises us.

God's plan is not one that we are permitted to understand, but we can see it at work. While we might be devastated by the death of loved ones, and especially the young, we must realize that every human, no matter how short his or her days, can gain the kingdom of heaven and affect the rest of us in profound ways. The value of life is not measured by its span. Rather, the value of life is measured by the purpose that life fulfills in God's plan. The value might lie in great works, in raising a family, or in doing God's work. The value of a life cut short may lie in its effect on those who survive...on those who can make a difference in the lives of others. Perhaps the deaths of the young and the innocent open our hearts to each other and to God, giving those short lives the fullest measure of meaning.

God's plan, then, is the key for Shannon. Perhaps the hundreds of kids who mourned Geoffrey Zimmerman in 1961 came to understand the transience of their mortal lives and moved closer to God. Perhaps Bruce Corby was given just enough time on earth to let God into his life. Perhaps Shannon was given extra time to take God's message to thousands of others. Whatever God's plan may be, Shannon is certain of one thing. He is certain that life, no matter how long, is best and most abundant when lived in a relationship with the Creator who gives us life and promises us eternal life.

31
WAVE OF A LIFETIME

In the final scene of the popular movie, *Point Break*, Bodhi begs FBI Agent Johnny Utah to remove his handcuffs and let him surf to certain doom in the lethal waves of a "50-year storm" at Bell's Beach, Australia. Intrepid surfers all long for their 50-year storm, a chance to test themselves against the biggest water that Nature can throw at them.

Brandon Ainslie has seen that quality in his younger bru—in their fights, their brick-throwing wars, their karate, their one-mile river swims, their water polo matches, and their surfing. "It wasn't that he didn't want to be underestimated, but rather that he was not scared of anything," Brandon surmises. "I think these two aspects are different from one another. He was just not afraid. If someone caused trouble, he would not back down, even if the other guy was bigger."

It was the same with Shannon and waves. "Three meters makes me nervous, and five meters is just nasty," Alistair Cokayne attests, "but Shannon loves big wave surfing and gets very excited." Steven Sawyer agrees. "He always has a 'go for it, head-on' attitude with no shortcuts and no backing away," he says of his first surf instructor. "He always goes for the nastiest waves, even if he ends up coughing up blood." Steven has a specific episode in mind.

Shannon's 50-year storm came in late September 2007 at Supertubes in Jeffreys Bay. He had been in the water for nearly three hours that morning, sharing the line-up with forty other surfers. The day was warm and sunny. The wind was calm, but unseen winter storms were driving a mounting swell. Soon, Supertubes was singing at full throat. Huge five-meter walls were carrying the boldest surfers on long diagonal trajectories toward the north. These were quad-burning rides for which Supertubes is famous.

At noon, the ocean started to erupt. Just sixty meters beyond the rocky shoreline, the waves began reaching staggering heights. One by one, surfers were getting caught inside on massive six- and seven-meter-high hydraulics and being carried all the way to Point, some 500 meters to the north. There, the violent surge was bouncing exhausted surfers across the shoreline rocks, snapping their leg ropes, and shredding their boards. Most of them didn't have the extra equipment, much less the genetic brass, to stay in the water. Within an hour, the towering sea had driven all but eight indomitable souls to the safety of land.

But even two-story water wasn't going to send Shannon Ainslie scrambling for shore, not when three-story waves were breaking just a little further out. The problem was getting to them. To catch waves, you have to get past the break to the place where the swells begin to grow—the so-called backline.

Paddling through six- and seven-meter waves, however, is a violent undertaking. In the impact zone where the waves collapse, you get driven into seabed rocks and tossed in relentless rolls, pitches, and yaws hoping you have a surfboard and a pulse when you surface. Your only chance of getting through such huge waves is to duck dive under them—an exhausting, breath-robbing, and terrifying experience even for veterans.

Duck diving is a lot like playing chicken. You wait until the wave looms over you like an attacking T-Rex and then, at the last second, you dive for safety between its front legs. You jam the nose of your board into the base of the wave and plunge deeply into it, almost as if sledding. Deep underneath, you prop a foot or knee on the back of the board to bring it level. As the wave passes, your eardrums scream from a near doubling of atmospheric pressure. Once through the turbulence, the rising backside of the wave cycle lifts you back to the surface where you gasp for air and prepare for the next onslaught.

To say that duck diving a giant wave is difficult would be an epic understatement, as Shannon can attest:

> Duck diving or swimming under a huge wave is very challenging both mentally and physically. You have to dive deep underwater, hold your breath for a long time, and stay strong mentally, especially when you get tossed around so much and so hard by the waves. It is disturbing sometimes when you feel the wave shake you all around. You have absolutely no control. So, if the water is clear enough, which it was that day, as you dive under the water you try to find air pockets to swim through and try to avoid

the explosions caused by the wave. It's difficult to do, but if you can avoid even one explosion under the water, it helps a tremendous amount.

In the fifteen years since he had learned to surf, Shannon had transformed from a skinny 3-foot 4-inch boy to a 5-foot 9-inch man of linebacker strength and proportions—the product of those remarkable hours atop his board…the equivalent of over ten years of full-time employment. He wanted those huge waves sixty meters out…out where no one else was going…out where no one else could go.

Diving, gasping, and diving again, Shannon plowed head-on into waves the size of houses. And they came his way relentlessly. Finally, he made it past the watery foothills and reached the Himalayas beyond. As he did, the sea exploded. Waves rose to staggering eight-meter height, and Shannon committed himself body and spirit to his lifetime dream of catching just one of them. This was his moment. This was why he had spent so much time swimming, surfing, and learning to hold his breath as a hedge against panic. He was alone in the land of giants—a David wandering an aquatic Valley of Elah in search of Goliath:

After a lot of fighting, paddling, and beatings, I made it to the back. There were only about five of us left at this stage. I sat the furthest out because I wanted to catch the biggest waves. The other guys looked a bit nervous and scared, but I was nervous and scared too. I knew that my six-foot three-inch thruster was too small for these monster waves. I needed at least an eight-footer. So, I knew that I needed to relax, catch my breath again, prepare myself mentally, and position myself perfectly for the wave I wanted to catch. I knew I could not afford to make any mistakes.

Then, glancing over his shoulder, he saw it—his Goliath. A titanic blue mound began to rise behind him, an ominous mass destined to break fully three stories high. A rogue wave of this size can drop ten tons of water on a surfer who gets caught inside—roughly the weight of two unloaded dump trucks.

If perspective is needed, imagine treading water in the deep end of an Olympic swimming pool. You cast your gaze upwards, past the one-meter springboard, past the three-meter high dive, and all the way up to the ten-meter platform. Now, imagine that the platform is the top of a growing mound of water that will soon lift you skyward, steepen, and form a sheer wall beneath you.

For Shannon, it was the wave of his dreams. It was his wave of a lifetime. It was his 50-year storm:

> I knew that my board was too small, but I had to try to catch this wave because it would be the biggest wave that I had ever caught. I put my head down and committed to the takeoff, taking long, deep, and hard strokes toward shore. There was no fear at this stage. I was too focused on what I had to do. All the violence around me just switched off. When I felt the wave starting to lift me, I paddled with everything I had and popped up onto my feet. I felt as if I had caught the wave and started gaining a lot of extra speed and momentum. It felt really good, and I thought I had it all under control. But just then, the wave went completely vertical and started to break.
>
> Suddenly, there was no more water under my board—just three stories of air. Time just stopped. Thoughts raced through my mind about all the crazy wipeouts I had seen in surfing movies and how fatal they can be. I thought of jumping off my board so I wouldn't land on it and break my leg, but I refused. I wanted to try to drop in. Instead, I fell freely for ten meters—nearly thirty-three feet. When I hit the flat water at the bottom, my legs gave way and my chest slammed into the water. My breath was knocked completely out of me—like getting sucker-punched hard—and I had no air at all. Then this massive wall of water crashed right on top of me and slammed me into the sea bed. I don't know what it feels like to have a building fall on top of you, but that's what it seemed like. There was so much force and energy. I felt like a giant hand was gripping me and shaking me like a rag doll.
>
> I was held under for an eternity, tumbling like I was in a wash-

ing machine. I must have done seven flips under the water. It's so scary having no control. You can't swim out of it. You can't fight it. It felt like forever, and what made it worse was having no air in my lungs at all because of the impact. My chest was screaming for oxygen, and I started panicking and struggling not to inhale a huge breath of water. I remembered all the times I had trained to hold my breath and tried to relax and wait for the wave to let go of me.

Finally, the back of the wave shot me to the surface, and I took a huge gasp of air. It was like a drink of water to someone crawling across a desert. Instantly, I was super stoked that I had been able to take on a wave of that size. I threw my hands up and screamed and shouted at the top of my lungs. A couple of surfers closer to shore looked at me like I was crazy.

Almost immediately, I felt a pain in my chest and started coughing up blood. But there was no time. Other waves were coming in fast behind me, and my board had three major creases in it. I still had work to do.

I got to my feet on another wave—a beautiful five-meter tube—and just rode it and rode it and rode it. When I measured the ride on Google Earth, it turned out to be over two kilometers long, the longest distance I have ever surfed on a single wave. For the next three days, though, I continued to cough up blood, I guess from the impact I took falling off the wave, and maybe from getting water in my lungs too. *But it was worth it!*

If you're struck by the fact that going over the falls, nearly drowning, and coughing up blood for three days were, for Shannon, small prices to pay for a failed attempt on a monster wave, you're well on your way to understanding surfers. They are not the goofy blonds you envision—the ones who use words like "gnarly," call each other "bru," and regard even the slightest impatience as hostility. They have phenomenal athletic skills and are seriously courageous...and I very much include in that assessment the many women who challenge big water as well! Surfers ply their sport in violent waves far from shore, and they wear no life jackets. They spend hours being cold, tired, and awash in their own urine. They ply their sport with the most dangerous predators on the planet. They are smashed into seabed boulders and tumbled in airless desperation. If they live, it's all worth it. If they don't live, well, heck, maybe it's still all worth it. No surfer enters such water with absolute assurance of seeing another sunrise. Still, they enter the water.

I'm in no position to argue with this adventurous philosophy. In June 2000, I fell in a small crevasse at 19,000 feet on the east ridge of Chimborazo in Ecuador. At one point, I stopped, sucked for air in the 45 percent sea level pressure, and took amused stock of my situation—2,700 miles from home, 100 minutes past midnight, fifteen feet of empty fluff beneath my dangling boots, four miles above sea level, two miles above the cloud deck, and one very bright full moon casting an eerie glare on a mile-long sliding board of ice in front of me. I remember having an out-of-body experience and thinking, "What am I doing here?"

Some activities are worth the risks, but only if you prepare yourself for them. Chris McCandless's fatal trek into the wilderness of Alaska, chronicled so ably by Jon Krakauer in his book *Into the Wild*, was bold, yet unwise. He was unprepared. Possession of a simple elevation map might have saved him.

But Shannon had prepared. He had developed swimming skills on his water polo and swim teams. He had developed endurance in his mile swims and self-imposed anaerobic workouts. He had spent over 3,000 days on a surfboard preparing for his wave of a lifetime. He had learned not to panic.

Coming home alive is always the best way to end the day, even if you're coughing up a little blood or shaking blood from fingers laid bare by a fourteen-foot great white. And yet again, Shannon Ainslie had come home.

Brandon had often noticed this fearless quality in his brother. Oh, sure, Shannon gets scared. He sometimes gets the shakes when talking about his shark attack. But he is one of those extraordinary people who can overcome even the most fundamental of fears—of drowning in stormy seas or of being eaten alive—and perform with dead calm in the face of those fears. He can test ten-meter waves when others have fled to the beach. He can swim without flotation toward the ocean's abyss to avoid death on pounding rocks. He can paddle toward friends while they are under violent attack by giant sharks.

The more you know about Shannon Ainslie, the more you realize that his confidence is neither feigned nor false. It is a confidence rooted in his faith. After allowing Jesus Christ into his life, the anger and depression of his early teens vanished, thoughts of suicide disappeared, a great white stared at him and did nothing, and a billow arrived on a calm sea to deliver the injured boy to shore.

He now accepts fear as the cost of sharing the shark's domain, and his homeland has prepared him for just such acceptance. In South Africa, blacks and whites have each taken their turn accepting the same fear—the fear that comes with sharing another's realm. Shannon believes he was born for this time in South Africa's history. He believes he was born to assist in the healing that his country seeks and needs, healing that must ultimately come through faith in God. He will become a Norwegian citizen, but he will remain a South African citizen and return often. He does not run from South Africa.

Similarly, he does not run from the sea. He takes his faith to the beasts for which the sea exists. He rides the waves, appreciating that he is only a visitor upon their frothy crests...just as he is a visitor upon this earth. He rides the waves with the knowledge that God rides with him and protects him, if not in this life, in the next.

AFTERWORD

More people drown in a single year in the United
States than have been killed by sharks throughout
the entire world in the last two centuries.
—Global Shark Attack File

By the time Shannon Ainslie had turned eighteen, he had encountered sharks four times. Only one of his encounters resulted in injury—a broken wrist and lacerations requiring thirty stitches. After that bite, the attacking shark, a one-ton great white, disappeared. A second great white, also present at the scene, stared at him under the water from two foot range. It too disappeared.

Admittedly, a different story unfolded at Second Beach where eight people died from shark attacks in a span of seven years. But Second Beach is an anomaly. In the last analysis, the death toll at Second Beach, in the heart of the Transkei district, may have more to do with human shortcomings—our failure to address questions of safety, sewage disposal, and access to quality emergency health care—than it does sharks.

Sharks are vital to the health of our oceans, and they cause us surprisingly little trouble. In a very real way, they are like trees growing along the edge of a ski slope. Slam into a tree while skiing, and there's a good chance you'll be seriously injured or killed. In fact, skiers are killed by trees far more often than surfers are killed by sharks, yet no one suggests that we cut down trees at ski areas. Trees are part of the natural beauty around us. We enjoy seeing them. We need them as habitats and oxygen producers. But we shouldn't ski too close to them. Similarly, we need to adapt our behavior to the small risk that sharks pose and lessen the chance that these magnificent creatures will become confused about our identity.

Sharks have inhabited earth's oceans for 420 million years. If that time span were represented by one calendar year, human beings wouldn't arrive on the scene until 7:49 p.m. on New Year's Eve. They've been around 2,100 times longer than we have. They deserve our respect and admiration. We are the foreigners on their break and the late-comers to their planet. Sharks are God's creatures, after all. They do only that which God gives them the light to do. If only the same could be said of us.

ENDNOTES

[1] Candice and her father, Shane, changed the spelling of their last names from Ainslie to Annesley following genealogical research performed by Shane. Shannon and Brandon kept their original last names.

[2] Hanke, S. H. (2009, February 5). R.I.P. Zimbabwe dollar. The Cato Institute. Retrieved on May 4, 2014, from http://www.cato.org/zimbabwe

[3] Ibid.

[4] World Bank Group. (n.d.). Life expectancy at birth, total (years)–Zimbabwe. https://data.worldbank.org/indicator /SP.DYN.LE00.IN?locations=ZW. Licensed under Creative Commons Attribution 4.0 international license (CC by 4.0): https://creativecommons.org/licenses/by/4.0/.

[5] United Nations Development Programme. (2010). Human development report 2010. Cited under Creative Commons Attribution License 3.0 IGO found at https://creativecommons.org/licenses/by/3.0/igo/legalcode. Retrieved on May 4, 2014, from http://hdr.undp.org/sites/default/files/reports/270/hdr2010_en_complete_reprint. pdf.

[6] The term "coloured" refers to people of mixed race who do not qualify as black as defined in South African law.

[7] Statistics South Africa. (2010, July 20). Statistical release P0302. Retrieved on May 4, 2014, from http://www.statssa.gov.za/publications/P0302/P03022010.pdf. In mid-year 2010, the estimated racial constituency of the South African population was 79.4% black, 9.2% white, 8.8% coloured, and 2.6% Indian/Asian.

[8] Wild Coast, Eastern Cape. (n.d.). SA-Venues.com. Retrieved on May 4, 2014, from http://www.sa-venues.com/ attractionsec/eastern_cape_wild_coast.htm

[9] International Swimming Hall of Fame. (n.d.). Matt Biondi (USA). Retrieved on August 19, 2015, from http:// www.ishof.org/matt-biondi.html

[10] Shark Research Institute, Inc. (n.d.). Incident Log. Global shark attack file (GSAF). Retrieved on multiple dates in 2011-2015, from http://www.sharkattackfile.net/incidentlog.htm.

[11] International Professional Surfing (ISP) was the world governing body for professional surfing until 1982. Each year, the ISP hosted 10 world championship tour events in surfing and longboarding. A surfer's top eight results were accumulated to determine world championship standings.

[12] The AMS Group. (2013). Nahoon Reef surf forecast and surf reports (South Africa-East London). Surf-forecast.com. Retrieved on May 5, 2014, from http://www.surf-forecast.com/breaks/Nahoon-Reef

[13] Shark Research Institute, Incident Log, op. cit. Global Shark Attack File records show 23 shark fatalities in South Africa during the 25-year period from January 15, 1986 to January 15, 2011.

[14] Brittan, I. (n.d.) Bali living blog. Retrieved on May 5, 2014, from http://baliliving.wordpress.com/comming-soon/scottburgh-1/

[15] Shark Research Institute, Incident Log, op. cit.

[16] East London's daily newspaper, *Daily Dispatch*, was founded in 1872 and played a significant role in opposing South Africa's apartheid government. Its editor from 1965 to 1977, Donald Woods, befriended banned non-violent anti-apartheid activist Steve Biko in 1977 and courageously published articles opposing apartheid practices. Later that year, Biko was arrested and died in captivity, reportedly of a hunger strike. Woods, who possessed evidence that Biko had been beaten to death in prison, was banned shortly thereafter and made a dramatic escape to Lesotho with his family on New Year's Day 1978. He moved to England where he published his book, *Biko (1978)*, outlining the atrocities of the government regime. Nine years later, Woods's efforts were chronicled in Richard Attenborough's powerful movie *Cry Freedom* (1987) featuring Denzel Washington as Biko and Kevin Kline as Woods. The movie, which features scenes of police shooting black children indiscriminately and closing credits listing scores of activists killed by the regime, received international acclaim and signaled the death knell of apartheid. Less than three years after the movie's release, negotiations leading to the dismantling of apartheid began.

[17] *Daily Dispatch*. (1961, February 2). Shark kills schoolboy at the Nahoon Beach. Retrieved from microfiche archives.

[18] Ibid.

[19] *Daily Dispatch*. (1961, February 3). Terrifying moments. Retrieved from microfiche archives.

[20] *Daily Dispatch*. (1961, February 2). Shark kills, op. cit.

[21] *Daily Dispatch*. (1961, February 3). Terrifying moments, op. cit.

[22] *Daily Dispatch*. Shark kills, op. cit.

[23] Ibid.

[24] *Daily Dispatch*. (1961, February 4). More than 400 attend funeral of Geoffrey Zimmerman. Retrieved from microfiche archives.

[25] Ibid.

[26] *Daily Dispatch*. (1961, February 3). Killer shark likely a 10-foot blue pointer. Retrieved from microfiche archives.

[27] Khan, M. A. (2015). Mako shark facts: Shortfin mako shark facts. Animals Time. Retrieved on August 19, 2015, from http://animalstime.com/mako-shark-facts-shortfin-mako-shark-facts/

[28] Mako sharks are members of the family *Lamnidae* (mackerel sharks) which includes great white sharks and salmon sharks. Mackerel sharks are endothermic, or "warm-blooded," meaning they can maintain body temperatures higher than the surrounding water. Thresher sharks in the family *Alopiidae* are also endothermic.

[29] *Daily Dispatch*. (1961, February 3). Government action on shark menace? Retrieved from microfiche archives.

[30] University of Florida, Florida Museum of Natural History (2021). International Shark Attack File. https://www.floridamuseum.ufl.edu/shark-attacks/

[31] Nowak, M. and Ricci, L. A., editors (2005). Post-apartheid South Africa: The first ten years. International Monetary Fund. Retrieved on May 5, 2014, from http://www.imf.org/external/pubs/nft/2006/soafrica/eng/pasoafr/pasoafr.pdf. Note: The "extended" unemployment rate includes not only those who are seeking work but also those who have given up trying.

[32] South African and American schools employ different grade-level terminology. In South Africa, "reception year" or "Grade R" is the equivalent of American pre-school. "Sub A" and "Sub B" are American Grades 1 and 2. "Standard 1" is American Grade 3 and so on through "Standard 10" which is Grade 12. Primary school ends with Standard 5 (Grade 7). High school lasts five years, beginning with Standard 6 (Grade 8). The final year of high school, Standard 10, is universally referred to as simply "matric" (muh-TRIK') because, at the end of that year, students sit for exams that may qualify them to matriculate at South African universities. Education is mandatory in South Africa until age 15 or completion of Standard 7 (Grade 9 in the U.S.).

[33] Shark Research Institute, Incident Log. op. cit.

[34] University of Florida, Florida Museum of Natural History (2021). International Shark Attack File. https://www.floridamuseum.ufl.edu/shark-attacks/

[35] Ibid.

[36] The exact Google Earth coordinates of Shannon's attack are: 32 59 46 S 27 57 13 E.

[37] YouTube. (2008, November 23). Surfing shark attack with two great white sharks (4.5 meters). www.2besaved.com. Retrieved on May 5, 2014, from http://www.youtube.com/watch?v=lSsZr1agCyY.

[38] The Internet Movie Database. (n.d.). Shannon Ainslie. Retrieved on May 5, 2014, from http://www.imdb.com/name/nm3292357

[39] Jean du Plessis, at age 21, won the University Sport of South Africa (USSA) Surfing Championship held at Victoria Bay from June 25-27, 2014. His victory helped his school, Nelson Mandela Metropolitan University, secure the men's team title as well.

[40] The exact Google Earth coordinates of Michal du Plessis's attack are: 32 54 36.35 S 28 4 52.00 E

[41] The exact Google Earth coordinates of David Bornman's attack are: 34 7 1.02 S 18 20 59.44 E

[42] Shark Research Institute, Incident Log, op. cit.

[43] The exact Google Earth coordinates of Second Beach are: 31 38 54 S 29 31 11 E

[44] Shark Research Institute, Inc. (n.d.). GSAF 2003.09.12. Global shark attack file (GSAF). Retrieved on September 6, 2006, from https://sharkattackfile.net/spreadsheets/pdf_directory/2003.09.12-Bornman.pdf Marie

[45] Shark Research Institute, Incident Log, op. cit.

[46] Ibid.

[47] United Nations Educational, Scientific, and Cultural Organization

(UNESCO). (n.d.). Underwater Cultural Heritage. Wrecks. Retrieved on April 25, 2022, from http://www.unesco.org/new/en/culture/themes/underwater-cultural-heritage/
underwater-cultural-heritage/wrecks.

[48] The Association of Surfing Professionals (ASP) has conducted world championship tours since 1983 and became the World Surf League (WSL) in 2015.

[49] Shark Research Institute, Incident Log, op. cit.

[50] Drownings and Near Drownings (Residents and Non-Residents), Hawaii State Department of Health (2013, September). Retrieved on September 6, 2021, from https://health.hawaii.gov/injuryprevention/files/2013/09/ drowning_Datachapter2007-11a-1MB.pdf

[51] University of Florida, op. cit.

[52] The "Red Triangle" is a region of the Pacific Ocean off the coast of San Francisco. The vertices of the triangle are Point Reyes, the Farallon Islands, and Monterrey Bay. The area is rich in seals and, hence, great whites.

[53] Shark Research Institute, Incident Log, op. cit.

[54] Ibid.

[55] Shark Research Institute, Inc. (n.d.). Recommendations. Global shark attack file (GSAF). Retrieved on August 4, 2014, from http://www.sharkattackfile.net incidentlog.htm.

[56] The exact Google Earth coordinates of the Carter and Corby attacks, accurate to within 10 meters, are 32 59 47 S 27 57 13.2 E, roughly 30 meters south of the location of Shannon's attack.

[57] "Boet" means "brother" in Afrikaans.

[58] Shark Research Institute, Incident Log, op. cit.

[59] Ibid.

[60] Ibid.

[61] Ibid.

[62] Natal Sharks Board-Shark Attack Information Sheet and attack description provided by Leigh Stolworthy.

[63] Afrikaans to English translation: "Here comes sh-t."

[64] Natal Sharks Board-Shark Attack Information Sheet and attack description provided by Leigh Stolworthy.

[65] Mellin, R. and Mellin, C. (2007, November 6). "You never leave a friend behind," says shark hero. Letters to the Editor. *Daily Dispatch.* Retrieved on May 26, 2011, from http://www.dispatch.co.za/2007/11/06/editorial/letters.html (link deactivated)

[66] The Shark Shield website is http://sharkshield.com/.

[67] Hays, J. (2009). Facts and details: Great white shark attacks. Factsanddetails. Retrieved on May 6, 2014, from http://factsanddetails.com/world/cat53/ sub337/item1273.html; University of Florida, op. cit.

[68] The exact Google Earth coordinates of the Matawan Creek attacks are 40 25 17.22 N 74 13 42.52 W.

[69] Shark Research Institute, Incident Log, op. cit.

[70] Ibid.

[71] McCord, M. and Lamberth, S. (2009, March). Catching and tracking the world's largest Zambezi (bull) shark Carcharhinus leucas in the Breede Estuary, South Africa: the first 43 hours. *African Journal of Marine Science* 2009, 31(1): 107–111.

[72] Port St. John's shark death. (2009, January 27). Wavescape. Retrieved on May 6, 2014, from http://www.wavescape.co.za/environment/sharks/port-st-johns-shark-death.html

[73] Jarvis, C. (2010, May 23). Two top professional SA surfers survive radical shark encounter in East London on Saturday. ZIGZAG News. Retrieved on May 30, 2010, from http://www.zigzag.co.za/news/enviro/5889/Two-top-professional-SA-surfers-survive-radical-shark-encounter-in-East-London-on-Saturday (link deactivated)

[74] Ibid.

[75] Ibid.

[76] Ibid.

[77] Ibid.

[78] Ibid.

[79] Ibid.

[80] Computers in Spaceflight: The NASA Experience, Ch. 2. National Aeronautics and Space Administration. Retrieved on September 6, 2021, from https://history.nasa.gov/computers/Ch2-5.html

[81] Collier, R. (n.d.). Unprovoked white shark attacks on surfers. Shark Research Committee. Retrieved on May 6, 2014, from http://sharkresearchcommittee.com/unprovoked_surfer.htm

[82] Ibid.

[83] *The Holy Bible* (1962). Oxford University Press. (Original work published 1611)

[84] Shark Research Institute, Inc. (n.d.). Global shark attack file (GSAF). Recommendations. Retrieved on August 4, 2014, from http://www.sharkattackfile.net/incidentlog.htm

[85] Toscano, G. (1997). Dangerous jobs. *Compensation and Working Conditions, Summer 1997,* 57-60. Retrieved on May 6, 2014, from http://www.bls.gov/iif/oshwc/cfar0020.pdf

[86] Rosenthal, J. S. (2021, February 8). Personal communication [email].

[87] *The Holy Bible* (1962). Oxford University Press. (Original work published 1611)

[88] Ibid.

ABOUT THE AUTHOR

Chuck Allen

Charles E. Allen III is a native of Louisville, Kentucky, and a graduate of Duke University (B.A. 1970) and the University of Kentucky College of Law (J.D. 1977). He served as a United States Air Force officer from 1970 to 1974 and received the Air Force Commendation Medal for his service as a Squadron Section Commander at Dover Air Force Base in Delaware.

From 1977 to 2003, Chuck practiced law with Kentucky's largest law firm, Frost Brown Todd LLC. He became a member of the firm and vice-chair of the firm's Labor and Employment Law Group in 1982 and concentrated in labor and employment litigation and administrative law. He has tried cases in state and federal courts and has handled appellate cases before the Supreme Court of Kentucky, several circuits of the United States Court of Appeals, and the Supreme Court of the United States.

Chuck served as president of the 22,000 member Astronomical League, a national federation of astronomy organizations, from 1998 to 2002 and has been League vice-president since 2020. He is founder of the League's National Young Astronomer Award and is a prolific public educator with more than 1,200 hours of public astronomy lectures and programs to his credit. He is also a former earth and space science judge and lead-judge for the Intel (now Regeneron) International Science and Engineering Fair. He is recognized in Marquis' *Who's Who in America* and is a 1997 inductee into his high school's hall of fame.

Chuck is an avid skier and also a mountaineer with climbs in the Rockies and Andes.